D1222114

UNIVERSITY OF WINNIPEG, 515 Portage Ave., Winnipeg, MB. R3B 2E9 Canada

Toward a Phenomenological Rhetoric

TOWARD A PHENOMENOLOGICAL RHETORIC

Writing, Profession, and Altruism

Barbara Couture

Southern Illinois University Press

Carbondale and Edwardsville

Library of Congress Cataloging-in-Publication Data

Couture, Barbara.
Toward a phenomenological rhetoric : writing, profession, and
altruism / Barbara Couture.
p. cm.
Includes bibliographical references and index.
1. English language—Rhetoric—Study and teaching—Theory,
etc. 2. Report writing—Study and teaching—Theory, etc.
3. English teachers—Training of. 4. Knowledge, Theory
of. 5. Phenomenology. 6. Truth. I. Title.
PE1404.C65 1998
808'.0427—dc21   97-25211
ISBN 0-8093-2033-9 (cloth : alk. paper)   CIP

In Memory of
Rev. Walter A. Markowicz, Ph.D.
1919–1995
"Priest, Teacher, Pilot"

Contents

Acknowledgments

I WISH TO THANK the editors of the *Journal of Advanced Composition* for permission to reprint in part "Against Relativism: Restoring Truth in Writing," which first appeared in Vol. 13 and forms the basis for my first chapter. I also am in debt to Robert L. Carter, dean, and Edward Sharples, interim dean, both of whom encouraged my work on this project by giving me the time to complete my research while serving as an associate dean in Wayne State University's College of Lifelong Learning. I am grateful, too, for the comments of numerous colleagues in response to various papers I have given at meetings of the Conference on College Composition and Communication, the Modern Language Association, and the Rhetoric Society of America on topics that have been developed further in this book. For assistance in the preparation of this manuscript, I wish to thank my student assistants Jeremy Dunckel and B. Alan Katz in the Division of Metropolitan Programs and Summer Sessions at Wayne State's College of Lifelong Learning.

At Southern Illinois University Press, I wish to thank Carol Burns, copy editor; Angela Reynolds, copy editor; Nancy Riddiough, copy editor; and, especially, Tracey J. Sobol, acquisitions editor, for her faith in my vision for this project and for her continuous encouragement as I developed the book. I also wish to thank Jone Rymer, of the School of Business Administration; and my colleagues Ellen Barton, Gesa Kirsch, Richard Marback, and Ruth Ray in the composition program of the Department of English at Wayne State University for their friendship, collegiality, and encouragement. Special thanks go to Thomas Kent for his reading of my manuscript and for his scholarship, which I studied along with that of many other critics and rhetoricians to whom I am also in debt for inspiring the theory I have articulated here. I must also acknowledge my parents, Angela and Chester Zawacki, for "being there" for me, as always. Finally, I wish to thank my husband, Paul, for his caring patience and endurance as I "talked at him" about this work and even read portions aloud over breakfast, lunch, dinner, and especially when we were "trapped" together in the car for any length of time. He isn't even a rhetorician. But then, he listens.

Toward a Phenomenological Rhetoric

Introduction

WE BELIEVE IN PRINT. We inspect it in the morning, hoping for clues in the news or the horoscope; scan through dozens of e-mail messages at work, deciding which to answer and when; add to the proliferation of the written word with our own letters, memos, reports, articles, and perhaps books; and we escape in others' writing, discovering hidden pleasures in the lines of glossy magazine features, catalog descriptions, and best-selling novels. The written word—for some of us at least—has a centrality that in other times was reserved for the Almighty. It is a god we honor and expect to redeem us in return. We trust that the ceaseless record of crime, war, and politics in the news will keep us mindful of our priorities and responsibilities as a society. Our correspondence at work documents our achievements, agreements, and progress within bureaucracies. Articles and books bespeak our selves and our aspirations, both social and personal. Countless encounters with fiction, history, philosophy, and poetry connect us to other souls who for a moment seem to be on our path. Little else is so encompassing, demanding, engaging, and entrancing as the written word. It is for many of us our visible spirit—even more so for those of us engaged in its study and teaching.

I am in the business of writing. As an English professor, I have taught it, studied both creative and expository writing, trained graduate students in writing theory, designed and implemented university writing requirements, written technical manuals, and produced textbooks and scholarly articles on writing. As a college administrator, I have written policies and procedures to guide others' actions; pushed out countless administrative messages, memos, and reports; and elaborated with sometimes tenuous certainty the language of grants and contracts. In my private life, I have dabbled in short story writing, put my faith in "To Do" lists, and indulged in the pleasures of writing to those I love. I am an addict for the written word and in this addiction have been struck with the fact that writing is indeed essential to my spirit. A belief in the essential good of writing drives my research, my teaching, my deep appreciation of literary art, and my patient tolerance of bureaucratic prose. My faith in writing is linked both to my profession and personal philosophy— a link that leads me to interpret writing as conscious behavior with the potential to bring the one and the many to a common good.

In the midst of my ardor for writing and faith in its beneficence, however, I have felt a growing discomfort about its potential to bring us to truth and

I

promote our collective welfare, one that, ironically, largely has been generated by scholarship in my own profession. We, the academic community that thinks about, teaches, and investigates writing, no longer trust writing—or, at least, our scholarship no longer invests us in such trust. We no longer firmly avow that writing depicts and ennobles us; we suspect rather that it deconstructs and "writes" us. Our thoughts, beliefs, and ways of expressing ourselves to others have always already been written, as Jacques Derrida and his followers might say. The agency we so value in personal expression is an illusion, as is our very ability to discern reliably the people, objects, and events we experience every day as viably present and stable. As social constructionist theorists have claimed, we are both empowered by and subject to the way writing is read and written by communities that share it. The truth we think we discover is subject to a social history that begins to incorporate us as soon as we enter into conversation with others. Should we find "truth" in our writing and that of others, we do so only because we have chosen to believe in what a community of readers and writers together has found to be true. We recognize, at the same time, that this truth is contingent, that is, true for us and perhaps for no others. Within the framework of this textual theory, rhetoric as the art of "persuading someone that a position is true" has become the technology supporting relative truth. To be sure, rhetoric provides the means to compare and contrast ideas so that we may choose to follow the very best. But rhetoric also leads us to dismiss some ideas, urging us to accept those that are more persuasive as the truth—for the moment, at least.

For my part, I am uncomfortable with the relationship between rhetoric and truth as much of current theory constructs it. I am unwilling to think that truth is relative or that we must always contest and dismiss each other's ideas in order to identify, express, and establish the most persuasive truth. Nor do I wish to believe that writing cannot and does not figure centrally in an innate human quest for an enfolding truth, one that accounts for the differences that divide us. Yet my rejection of antifoundationalist approaches to truth and its meaning, in order to be believed, must reflect more than the mere angst of my disappointment about our current state of affairs; it must have some philosophical ground and, further, it must lead to a better construction of the purposes and uses of rhetoric than now lies before us. I cannot ignore, in other words, that the perspectives I hope to counter are deeply grounded in philosophies that dominate current critical theory as well as much of our daily living.

In my view, the exclusion of truth from writing that now marks our textual scholarship reflects a critical turn that has been accomplished in two moves: first, in our acceptance of philosophical relativism as the basis of all truth claims, a stance that validates conflict and persuasion as a foundation for rhetoric; and second, in our acceptance of personal resistance as *the* method of securing a true and valued self-identity, a stance that necessarily excludes some lived experiences from the realm of personal truth. In this book, I attempt to reconcile the aims of writing and truth seeking through providing an alternative to these constraining philosophies. To accomplish this aim, I propose a phenomenological rhetoric of writing, one that interprets writing as an activity integral with our conception of ourselves and others as purposeful beings. In short, I defend and explain writing as a practice that develops truth and value in human experience. This task, as I see it, involves explaining how truth came to be separated from writing, both philosophically and rhetorically, and proposing to restore truth to writing through invoking a new model of how truth gets made and spoken, a model encompassed by what I have defined as a phenomenological rhetoric.

This book is arranged in two parts. In the first half, I establish the need for a phenomenological rhetoric and its grounding in phenomenological philosophy. My purpose here is to articulate the difficulty of validating rhetoric as truth seeking by foregrounding specific critical positions that prevent us from reconciling rhetoric with this goal. I have located within these critical arguments strong figures or controlling metaphors that have placed limitations on how writing and interpretation are perceived to be related to truth and self-identity.

In chapter 1, I invite the reader to examine how the premises of philosophical relativism justify argumentative rhetoric as the preferred means to forward a version of truth. In countering this view, I analyze philosophical relativism as two critics have represented it of recent: Jasper Neel (*Plato, Derrida, and Writing*) and Barbara Herrnstein Smith (*Contingencies of Value*). I suggest that their arguments for relativism are based on three uncontested premises: (1) a deterministic view of history as it influences human action, (2) a belief in the objective nature of truth, and (3) an assumption that human existence reflects a directionless system in stasis. In attempting to counter these assumptions, I explain alternatives that suggest a broader conception of truth, one that rejects relativism and presses beyond the contestual rhetoric that supports it. In doing so, I review perspectives on subjectivity and integrity in communication offered by Ann E. Berthoff, Peter Elbow, Susan Miller, and other rhetoricians and composition theorists.

In chapter 2, I examine how much of contemporary critical theory has excluded truth from our worldly or social experience through associating self-identity with resistance to external forces. Self-representation is associated with resistance regardless of whether human beings are thought to be free agents, on the one hand, or fully socially constructed, on the other. As a demonstration of how resistance defines the self in both individualist and social determinist views of human action, I briefly critique these polar perspectives and their variants as they have been advanced by Karl Popper, V. N. Volosinov, and, more recently, Paul Smith. Resistance as a mode of self-representation puts specific constraints on rhetorical practice and limits the full potential of rhetoric to engage the self with the outside world. In the last half of this chapter, I explore ways in which the desire to defend the self against external assault has encouraged rhetorical practices that explicitly develop narcissism and fetishism as self-protective mechanisms. In explaining and elaborating these psychological defenses as rhetorical practices, I draw insights from psychoanalytic criticism, contemporary rhetorical theory, analytic philosophy, and sociology. My purpose is to show how textual expression is limited by a construction of self that stakes identity on *resistance to* rather than *acceptance of* an integral relationship with the world. This latter definition of subjectivity suggests the need for a new philosophical base for addressing questions of human existence and agency, one that presumes no exclusion of truth from subjective experience.

In chapter 3, I introduce phenomenology as a critical alternative to both relativism and resistance through revisiting the philosophy of Edmund Husserl and Maurice Merleau-Ponty. I realize, of course, that my endorsement of phenomenology follows Derrida's sharp critiques as well as the wide acceptance of rhetorical pragmatism as an ethical response to our loss of faith in foundational truths; hence, my position at first blush may appear out of step. My purpose here is not so much to deny the specific claims made against phenomenology as to reinterpret the grounds upon which phenomenology has been said to advocate the foundation of truth in subjectivity, a reinterpretation that may render these past critiques moot. To this end, I elaborate three central premises of a phenomenological interpretation of truth in human experience: (1) all essences or truths are located in subjective experience; (2) truth is an outcome of intersubjective understanding; and (3) intersubjective understanding progresses toward truth through writing. Through examining Husserl's later work in the light of both favorable readings by Merleau-Ponty and critiques by Derrida and others, I show how phenomenology proposes a method both for attending to the world consciously and for using language to elaborate truth in its intersubjective complexity. If we develop the expressive capacity of our consciousness to acknowledge and determine how diversity expresses a common truth, we have before us the foundation for a new rhetoric—one that abandons the Western sophistic tradition of arriving at truth through conquering and consensus, and grounds it instead in conscious commitment to collaboration with others in truth seeking.

In the second half of this book, I show how rhetorical practices that are guided by phenomenological principles can be validated as conscious, public, and collaborative efforts to know the truth of the world we share. In specific, I interpret and define two rhetorical practices so guided: *profession* and *altruism*. I propose, in chapter 4, that individuals become truthful writers through practicing profession, the activity of interpreting the world through conscious reflection and offering that interpretation to others. To amplify the act of profession, I invoke perspectives on the role of the human subject in knowledge making advanced by Husserl, Pierre Teilhard de Chardin, and other phenomenologists. Contemporary critiques of the phenomenological approach by Derrida, Kathleen Haney, and Paul Ricoeur also are presented here, as well as successor approaches to knowledge and consciousness, represented in the work of Martin Heidegger and Frederick A. Olafson. Three dimensions of rhetorical profession are explored here: first, phenomenological reflection, a perceptual exercise through which one attends to the world with open acceptance; second, reasoned receptivity, a fully open practice through which one reconciles the objective world with one's self assessment of it; and third, regeneration, a process through which one's assessment of the world transforms both the world as seen and the "I" within it. In order for profession to take shape as the means of seeking truth, the writer must seek neither contention nor conflict with others, but rather assimilation and resolution of difference.

In chapter 5, I move from the author's desire to present a view to the object of that view, another human person. I propose here that the act of rhetorical profession, if it is to lead us to shared truth, must be altruistic, ever concerned with serving the interests of others. And so the writer's practice of reflection, as a component of rhetorical profession, must lead to true acknowledgment that others' interests are as valid as his or her own; the writer's reasoned receptivity to diverse ideas must be truly authentic, invested in our common human function as material and spiritual beings; and, finally, the writer's regenerative process of expression must be driven by an ardent quest for knowledge of what is "other," a quest guided by loving care. In proposing this theoretical scheme, I incorporate the perspectives of analytic philosophers and of scholars who have sought to explain our consciousness in terms of personal relations, moving from Thomas Nagel's *The Possibility of Altruism,* an argument for the rationality of selfless action, to Martin Buber's more poetic account of the interpersonal foundation of knowledge, his well-known *I and Thou.* I also give quite detailed attention to the philosophical reflections of Alasdair MacIntyre and Charles Taylor on the relationship between truth and moral consciousness.

In my concluding chapter, I compare my guiding principles for a phenomenological rhetoric with existing criteria for evaluating the truth and rightness of discourse. Here I introduce three evaluative standards, labeling them "congruence," "consensus," and "commensurability," which I show to emerge from contemporary rhetorical theory proposed by Jürgen Habermas, Charles Altieri, and Thomas Kent. My aim is to reinterpret these standards for seeking and presenting knowledge as they might be guided by altruistic profession. In a phenomenological rhetoric, writing does not cancel out writing, one argument does not win over another; rather, writing is evolutionary, dynamic, always in the act of creating meaning in a system of meaning making that is not closed, but rather continually enfolding new experience. The process of enfolding new experiences and building toward truth is not a contestual one of displacement, substitution, or even supplementation, that is, a continual exchange of one relative truth for another, but rather a collaborative process of growth and transformation, a continual communal effort of truth seeking. To explain how writing that is guided by phenomenological principles might also follow standard criteria for valid and effective communication, I refer to a specific communication situation in which writing figured in my work as a university administrator, describing it in some detail. Through this illustration, I suggest how writing functions both to ensure that new activities improve on past action in creative and productive ways and to commit writers and their readers to a collective effort to establish a shared truth. In practicing rhetoric as altruistic profession, writers can enact a phenomenological approach to truth seeking within the tradition of rhetoric as persuasion.

In closing this introduction, I must acknowledge that in some ways what I aim to accomplish here amounts to a sea change in our approach to practicing rhetorical argument. Like any paradigm change, it has not been constructed from whole cloth. Certainly, movements in the hard sciences toward relational descriptions of physical phenomena and arguments in philosophy for an externalist view of meaning have influenced the perspective I offer. Patterns have also been cut by feminist theory, which asks us to abandon domination as a technology to determine meaning for ourselves and others and to foster in its stead nurturance and care as a way of enfolding all in a shared enterprise. The argument I present in this volume is an attempt to talk about rhetoric in ways that are in step with these developments, through urging us to drop the restrictive philosophies of relativism and resistance that have dominated our construction of rhetorical practice, and to trust again in the virtues of truth seeking and acceptance. I am asking, in the end, that we begin to practice rhetoric not as a strategic defense against ignorance and ideology, but rather as an open commitment to knowledge and truth. As with all births, this infant idea joins the contributions of many others; my hope is that others as well will encourage it to grow.

1

Writing and Truth
Beyond the Limits of Relativism

IN THE NOT too distant past, the aim of writing to be truthful was considered neither naive nor politically motivated. It was simply part of what made writing a human activity. Certainly, the practice of writing has long been celebrated as a personal achievement, one that makes us better, truer. And the invocation of truth in writing marks our most precious documents, those that define our mutual purpose and progress as a community or nation.

Yet current textual scholarship calls into serious question the power of writing to secure a common truth, one that transcends differences in gender, race, community, or profession. In fact, the truthlessness of writing has been utterly exposed by critical and rhetorical theory. The consequences of this exposure have been fairly dire, at least as far as the damage done to our traditional aspirations for the printed word. For instance, gone now is our belief in the power of writing to present faultless logical argument. In its place is the deconstructionist suspicion that written argument creates objective presence where there is none, as well as the feminist claim that it discounts intuitive knowledge. Absent is our hope that writing can ensure harmonious and just social relationships. In its stead is the social constructionist view that writing sustains discriminatory social practice and regulates individual behavior. And passé is our respect for the aesthetic power of text to transform individual experience into universal truth. Replacing it is dismay that writing often gets things done in the world through subjugating individual agency to a collective need. Traditional belief in the redeeming potential of print has simply not been sustained by scholarly conceptions about what writing is and how it functions.

Many developments—intellectual, social, and technical—account for the fix we are in. Our specific belief that language creates selves rather than fixes concepts and ideas originating in consciousness, of course, reflects the linguistic turn in philosophy. This externalization of consciousness in language, a social product that changes with culture and time, threatens any universal conceptualization of meaning that might correlate with a unitary theory of consciousness. Our world history denies universalist conceptions of meaning as well. The aftermath of two world wars, the buildup and distribution of nuclear power, and the spread of guerrilla and terrorist warfare have dismantled humanist utopian dreams of world peace under a single, unassailable, and benign reign. And, too, the ever-expanding technical advances that have allowed us to accumulate masses of data on physical phenomena, plant and animal forms, and human cultures and habitats have confirmed our singular inability to grasp this plenitude of written information, let alone evaluate its inconsistencies and confirm, once and for all, its true significance. Yet in the face of all this uncertainty, academics, for the most part, have continued to treat writing (and the information it conveys) as if it can indeed be trusted to reveal truth, maintain peace, and dignify human experience. In short, what we as teachers or scholars want to do with writing fails to match what many of us have been saying about it.

We still wish to treat language and skill in manipulating it as tools to use in the noble enterprise of making conditions better for ourselves and others. My purpose here is not to defend or explain this aim, but rather to explore the dilemma that it poses for us: We are trying to use language as if it can be truthful while believing that it cannot be. This dilemma is exacerbated by the influence of antifoundationalist critical and linguistic theories, to be sure, but more important, it is perpetuated by the philosophical premise behind these approaches, the presumption that meaning and its truth are relative. Philosophical relativism provides the grounding we need in order to proceed as if language can be used to define truths when absolute truth is uncertain; it also explains our overtly manipulative use of language to justify separate, oppositional, and conflicting conceptualizations of the world around us. The argument that validates rhetorical relativism goes something like this: There is no truth that binds us all; therefore, the objective to find such truth through speaking or writing is moot. Given that the truth cannot be found, the best we can do is to believe the most credible or strongest argument *as if it were true* and dismiss our search for the truth.

Rhetorical relativism presumes no reliable standard for judging the value of an action or determining whether it is based on true principles; it merely provides a tool to distinguish the difference between one way of seeing and another, a perception that, if left unguided by some ethical stance could lead either to endless and unresolvable bickering over which position holds greater value or to a *truth* accepted on the sole basis of a rhetorical argument that proved most powerful. This vision of truth seeking categorically rejects any epistemology that suggests a unitary path to knowledge and likewise dismisses the idea that rhetoric and its practice in writing can lead us to a common truth. Consequently, I would argue, it is a view that divests both written argument and literature of their ability to achieve an ethical stance, one that supports a common good.

Despite the damaging consequences of relativism for the rhetorical enterprise, its presumptions have gone largely unchallenged in current theories of textual interpretation; in short, relativism has a stranglehold on textual theory that must be released prior to any foundationalist epistemology such as phenomenology, which I am forwarding in this volume, even can be entertained. Hence, in this chapter I begin my argument for a unitary approach to knowledge and truth by tackling its counterpoint, philosophical relativism. I have chosen to challenge the hold of relativism on textual theory by offering a reading of the main arguments posed in two critical works that strongly support it, one defending relativism in rhetoric, the other in literary valuation. In *Plato, Derrida, and Writing,* a study of Plato's and Derrida's views on writing, rhetoric, and critical theory, Jasper Neel dismisses the relationship of truth to writing. He distinguishes truth from writing by claiming that writing is strong discourse and strong discourse is not truth but a critical strategy; we need not mistake writing for truth and, further, in evaluating writing we should not concern ourselves with it. In *Contingencies of Value,* Barbara Herrnstein Smith tackles the problem from the other end; she dismisses the notion of truth and reifies value in its stead. She claims that truth—as it has been conceived philosophically as an absolute good—is nonexistent; what exists is value, which is a function of exchange (that is, something is gained in giving value to something else). The reason that literary writing or anything else is valued has no relation to truth, but rather to what is secured by declaring it has value. Achieving truth is not possible; rather, it is possible only to determine what is better or worse in a given situation.

I have chosen these two works because they represent the same argument interpreted from the perspectives of rhetorical theory and literary aesthetics and because they make a point of denying the relationship between philosophical truth and writing. These works also represent a culminating stance in rhetoric and criticism. Neel and Herrnstein Smith postulate where we are now—at least some of us—in the wake of the deconstructionist's antifoundationalism and the hermeneut's validation of multiple interpretations of reality. In performing a reading of these works, I examine the consequences of our having accepted relativism as a philosophical ground for textual theory and, in doing so, suggest the need to move beyond it.

My focus is on the premises that underlie Neel and Herrnstein Smith's arguments and lead these authors to interpret truth and writing in ways that make them necessarily incompatible. In presenting a case against their claims, I first offer a brief introduction to the major arguments made by both these theorists and follow with a critique of the positions they share. This analysis reveals that their vision of writing and truth is bolstered by three assumptions about the nature of truth in human experience:

1. a historicist interpretation of human will as it is determined by ideology;
2. an essentialist interpretation of objective truth; and
3. a fundamentalist interpretation of human activity as it progresses over time.

These three assumptions prevent us from describing truth as a function of development, change, and growth and, as a result, prevent us from assessing truth as an essentially human phenomenon. Relativism bolsters these perspectives, I argue, inscribing human experience as a series of moments, each contingent upon the next and none leading to anything. The only way to move beyond a reductionist view of the world as white or black, good or evil, valued or worthless (depending upon one's place in time) is to resist relativism. We must reclaim truth as an essential function of our subjectivity, of our daily interaction with one another, and of our constant effort to reflect on ourselves in order to understand one another. It is the very phenomenon of continuous human interaction that produces truth, and there is where it can be found.

In the closing pages of this chapter, I explore the consequences of defining truth as a human phenomenon that guides rhetoric and of reconstruing writing as the tool that records our past and inscribes our future as truth seekers. If we are to restore truth to writing, I conclude, we must first restore truth to ourselves. Yet, again, current theory poses further difficulties for conceiving our very selves as truthful; these problems are explored in chapter 2.

Neel's Rejection of Truth in Writing

In *Plato, Derrida, and Writing*, Jasper Neel attempts to create a morally defensible role for writing through dignifying the aims of rhetoric while denying that writing seeks truth. This stance shapes his effort to redeem writing as it is accused of displacing truth in Plato's *Phaedrus* and of erasing it in Derrida's critical theory. Neel characterizes the pitfalls of giving in to either Plato's or Derrida's philosophical view of writing, one that measures its relationship to truth, thus:

> Writers who give in to Plato in effect cease to be writers and become philosophers on a quest that . . . requires writers constantly to admit abashedly that they do not know the truth. Writers who give in to Derrida become philosophers who never finish unworking all those discourses that conceal or remain ignorant of their own written rhetoricity; such writers feel obligated always to work backwards in order to show that what would be required to begin a discourse is already gone. (203)

Neel goes on to draw a categorical distinction between the aims of rhetoric and philosophy and reaches the conclusion that to have one is not to have the other. At one point in his argument, he concedes that this distinction is not a necessary or even helpful one, noting that writers who are liberated from philosophy "need the Platonic ideal, the notion of the forever-absent truth toward which discourse moves" and "at the same time, writers need deconstructive strategy to prevent discourse from presenting itself *as* the truth" (Neel 203). But having made this concession, Neel chooses to recognize neither Plato's nor Derrida's work as philosophical, work that in itself seeks the truth. In order to discuss Plato's and Derrida's contribution to explaining the role of writing in conducting the quest for truth, Neel elects to interpret their writing as purely rhetorical, a device for persuading someone to accept a position. He thus renders irrelevant the success of their works as attempts to seek truth, and, further, he interprets the search for truth in writing as fruitless.

To counter Plato's argument for an absent but absolute truth, Neel deconstructs *Phaedrus* to reveal its potential for multiplicity of meaning and concludes that "Plato—the most influential writer and sophist of all time—is caught stealing writing from us" (Neel 24), that is, Plato reveals writing to be unreliable in our quest to establish valid knowledge. It is with some delight that Neel catches Plato "stealing writing from us" through deconstructing *Phaedrus,* but the discovery is a fairly hollow victory. Deconstruction as an analytical tool reveals the potential for multiplicity of meaning in Plato's discourse but cannot support Neel's conclusion that Plato steals writing from us. Neel admits, in fact, that he has not proven the latter, yet chooses not to explore the consequences. For example, he notes that Plato's dialogue is structured overtly to set up writing as a "corrupt" replacement for dialectical speech, but at the same time this structure covertly redeems writing as the preferred medium to pursue knowledge: "Structure is what remains behind as the trace of the effort to create a place in which knowledge can come to know itself and present itself to the world" (Neel 38). True to his rhetorical stance, Neel prefers to cast the fact that Plato leaves his writing behind as Plato's mistake rather than probable intention, reminding us that Plato held that "truth as a possibility depends on the impossibility of truth's appearing in writing" (80). Thus, we learn from Plato, Neel claims, that the goal to find truth expressed in writing is fruitless.

Having shown how Plato makes truthful writing an impossibility, Neel proceeds to show how Derrida makes writing truthfully an impossibility. In nine brief passages, each offering an interpretation derived from his extensive reading, Neel defines *presence, transcendental signified, the trace, absence,* and five other terms in the Derridean lexicon. Each term points to the infinite play of meaning in writing, a prospect that Neel finds to be terrifying for writing and specifically for writing teachers. He says, for example, of Derrida's concept of the "transcendental signified" or the idea of "meaning without a signifier" (146):

> If Derrida is right, no such transcendental signified exists or could exist out-side the presence of God. Thus, when we tell our students to pick a thesis or to discover a central idea and treat it fully, we merely exacerbate their fears of writing. They believe fully in self-presence and the transcendental signified. Though perhaps not consciously, they also know all too well that the more they write the less their own presence is self-assured and the fur-ther the transcendental signified that would pin (or pen) down their mean-ing in absolute clarity slips away. (Neel 150)

This lapse into uncertainty in search of the transcendental signified is an un-desirable state, Neel claims, because it leaves writers unable to assert anything in writing; a representation can never produce the transcendental signified, an absolute meaning or truth that classically is realized in the figure of God. The only way out of this situation of never being able to express an absolute truth is to liberate writing from philosophy—that is, from any concern with notions of truth conceived as absolute but unwritten (Plato) or as written but indeterminate (Derrida). The goal that writing should achieve in truth's stead is to produce "strong discourse," that is, discourse that withstands "the scru-tiny of public life" and leads "to a best choice at a given time, in a given place, with a given set of circumstances" (Neel 208).

Herrnstein Smith's Rejection of Truth in Human Experience

In *Contingencies of Value,* a critique of the notions of truth and value in art and life, Barbara Herrnstein Smith attempts to prove not only that truth is contingent on local criteria that we protect from surrender (whether these be criteria for a well-formed argument, political action, or moral behavior) but also that truth without contingency—that illusive unattainable truth of Plato's speculation—does not exist. For Herrnstein Smith, contingent truth is a reality we can and must live with because it is all there is. Unlike Neel, Herrnstein Smith does not deal with how truth seeking remains separate from writing, art, or any other human enterprise. Instead, she tries to explain how we came to believe that what we value is truth, separating this "truth" from "objective truth," which simply doesn't exist. Herrnstein Smith demonstrates that value is radically contingent on criteria that are supported socially, and she argues as well that so must be truth. She claims that since I am different from you and always will be, what you value must be different from what I value and always will be—"value is radically contingent" (30). By extension, truth, which is after all what we believe to be behind value, is radically con-tingent; there is no common—let alone absolute—truth in human experience.

In effect, Herrnstein Smith does not attempt to explain truth or value, but rather illustrates how our diverse claims about what we value in art, writing, politics, or religion ultimately become separate truths that can never be enfolded by one truth.

In the initial stages of her argument, Herrnstein Smith tackles the question of what really happens when a work of art or literature is declared to have aesthetic value, that is, judged to be superior aside from "all other nameable sources of interest or forms of value—hedonic, practical, sentimental, ornamental, historical, ideological, and so forth" (33). She deftly illustrates that aesthetic value is seen to be noncontingent or devoid of any economic utility simply because judgments in value "appear to reduce to differences in the 'properties' or 'qualities' of the objects themselves" (39–40), an illusion that is maintained when members of a community are in strong agreement. Herrnstein Smith explains this occurrence thus: "A co-incidence of contingencies among individual subjects who interact as members of the same community will operate for them as noncontingency and be interpreted by them accordingly" (40, italics removed). Hence, what is a contingent value quickly becomes seen as an objective value. In a chapter on axiologic logic, or the logic of philosophical judgments of value, Herrnstein Smith goes on to explain how contingent value becomes conflated with objective truth. Here she examines "Hume's Natural Standard" (55–64) and "Kant's Pure Judgments" (64–72) and concludes that logic about matters of value inevitably comes down to contesting one person's authority over another's. All values and truths, for that matter, are pretty relative things; there is no bottom line, no ultimate truth. The fact of this matter, indeed, is quite inescapable and oppressive, as can be assessed from the tone of her concluding argument:

> There is thus no particular single dimension or global parameter, whether "biological"/"material" *or* "cultural"/"spiritual"/"psychological," with respect to which entities can be tagged or tallied as, "in the last analysis," good or bad—profit or cost, reward or punishment, pleasure or pain—for any subject or set of subjects, much less for man in general. There is thus also no way for individual or collective choices, practices, activities, or acts, "economic" or otherwise, to be ultimately summed-up, compared, and evaluated: neither by the single-parameter hedonic calculus of classic utilitarianism, nor by the most elaborate multiple-parameter formulas of contemporary mathematical economics, nor by any mere inversion or presumptive transcendence of either. There is no way to give a reckoning that is simultaneously total and final. There is no Judgment Day. There is no *bottom* bottom line anywhere, for anyone or for "man." (Herrnstein Smith 149)

If the "bottom line" isn't—if there is no supreme value and no uncompromising truth—what *is* there? Well . . . what there is is our own personal standard of truth, which we establish according to criteria that, again, are personal and have personal value. Truth is relative and relativism cannot "deduce or demonstrate its own rightness." Instead, relativism "recognizes . . . that 'the way' will be perceived and pursued differently by each to whom it is pointed out" (Herrnstein Smith 183).

Having accepted relativism as the natural state of things, we also have accepted that value and truth are in constant flux and multiply various. Forevermore, we must conceive of the "irreducibly various as irreducibly various, and of the multiply configurable as always configurable otherwise" (Herrnstein Smith 183). What keeps things in this state of constant flux is the fact that value and truth are always relative to the conditions of the moment which affect the cost at which they are purchased; things always change into something else because we perpetuate an endless system of "(ex)change" (144) in which, as Herrnstein Smith suggests, one good is purchased at the cost of another. Hence, all human activity, including the desire to locate a value or declare a truth, consists of "a continuous exchange or expenditure (whether as payment, donation, sacrifice, loss, or destruction) of goods of some (but any) kind, whereby goods of some other (but, again, any) kind are secured, enhanced, or produced" (Herrnstein Smith 144). She interprets truth as a real-world commodity constructed by individuals and groups and bought, paid for, and traded as a way of maintaining integrity and authority.

Contingencies of Denial

To deny that anything but relative truth can be obtained through writing (as does Neel) because nothing but relative truth can be found in human experience (as does Herrnstein Smith) is to deny the organic, developmental, and evolutionary nature of all human activity. It is to conclude that all human activity, including truth seeking and writing, is meaningful only in its singular moments, a conclusion that makes life akin to a chess game in which one piece is continually poised to wipe out or replace another in the next move. This is a very old and seductive idea; it is derived from a limiting belief in three epistemological perspectives: ideological historicism, essentialist objectivity, and fundamental temporalism. In the sections that follow, I examine these perspectives as they both motivate Neel's and Herrnstein Smith's support of philosophical relativism and limit their theoretical construct of truth.

Ideological Historicism

If the past drives the future, then whatever dreams we have must be restricted by history, and likewise, future truth must be contingent on prior knowledge. A deterministic view of history is fundamental to philosophical relativism.

Ideological historicism leads Neel and Herrnstein Smith, for instance, to predict with absolute certainty the future course of human activities and to stalwartly deny any other possibilities; our potential to find truth is relative to our failure to secure it in the past. For Neel, historicism refutes the power of the polis to determine the truth through rhetoric. History demonstrates that we did not arrive at truth through argument in the past, and hence, we cannot do so in the future. For Herrnstein Smith, historicism supports and refutes her central thesis that people and values are multiply various and everchanging; in a world historically determined, variety may be sustained but change is an illusion, as it but marks the return to something prefigured by the past. For both of these critics, historicism is an ideological prerogative that corroborates their denial of human growth.

Neel's historicism is disguised by his continual talk of dismantling what is fixed, of replacing supplements with supplements, old beliefs with new beliefs, arguments with counterarguments. Such talk apes the continual movement of narrative and suggests that an unpredictable future overshadows the past. But in fact, Neel himself has not escaped from a worldview that insists on a prefigured future. In attempting to describe how Derrida's vision of the apocalypse differs from that of his Southern Baptist tradition, Neel holds on to the notion of a prefigured event moving toward a predetermined end. Here is how he describes the apocalypse as explained in the religion of his childhood:

> This whole scenario is logocentric because in it Christ constitutes a beginning, an ending, an absolute authority, and an origin of meaning. When Christ speaks, at least in the Southern Baptist theology of my childhood, he speaks absolute meaning. In effect, what he says *goes*—no equivocation, no ambiguity, no margin for error. In that scenario, the trumpet on the last day needs no interpretation. (Neel 102)

In the fundamentalist interpretation of spiritual truth, the meaning was clear in the beginning and remains clear in the end—nothing changes.

In describing how Derrida counters the foundationalist belief in the certainty of meaning, Neel sticks to the same historicist perspective. Instead of the Word, which had a meaning at the beginning that will remain the same at the end, there "will always be the play of signification, as signifier refers to signifier in an endless chain that never leads back to an origin" (Neel 103). Neel interprets Derrida's vision of the endless "play of signification" as an "apocalyptic" (103) vision of another sort. Instead of fundamentalist belief in an absolute end dispatched by an eternal God, we now have deconstructionist belief in endless ends determined through eternal agon. Being uncomfortable with the ethical paucity of this perspective, he concludes that there is purposefulness within this destiny of eternal contest. It is to express and discern sophistic truth through the practice of strong discourse. The virtue of strong discourse is its distinction as the most persuasive voice heard "in a cacophonous plurality of other voices, many of which are also strong" (Neel 208–09). The messianic vision of the fundamentalist is portrayed as false truth to be overcome in this new vision of the apocalypse. For Neel, the false messiah is the presence of a truth that silences other voices; this

> weak discourse . . . always presents itself in the guise of the messiah or the philosopher-king—the one who claims to offer truth but in fact supplies only the silence that must occur when rhetoric, persuasion, writing, and sophistry, those most human of things, have been precluded. (209)

So the possibility of truth for Neel shatters the possibility of rhetoric, and the possibility of rhetoric obliterates the truth. An apocalypse—historically determined—is at hand in either case. To preserve the possibility of rhetoric, Neel opts for a position of relativism, which accepts that apocalypse is inevitable and that whatever truth emerges from the external confrontations we are historically destined to experience must be considered the best truth, if not the only truth.

Herrnstein Smith's relativism is also conditioned by historicism. For her, history of social class, family relationships, religious persuasion, and aesthetic training determine the future, endlessly maintaining diverse and equally valid human perspectives. Her fierce individualism and egalitarianism shape this conclusion. Unwilling to say that a single, final authority born of human will resides with someone or some group and no one else (individualism), she concludes that multiple authorities determine history for everyone (egalitarianism). There is no subject who wills absolutely for Herrnstein Smith, because to recognize a subject who wills absolutely she must recognize a subject to whom she might be subject. In her view, the subject may have a "*particular* . . . identity/economy/perspective," but this "individuated" state is "not in all respects unique" (175). Further, there can be no transcendental objective reason that justifies one subject's choices and "no other subject's choices" (Herrnstein Smith 176). Yet the individual's choices are dictated by something, and if that something is "not transcendental, then it must be historical, and if the justification is not universal and unconditioned, then it must be restricted, partial, and local" (Herrnstein Smith 175). In other words, conditions as they were, have been, and are right now determine an individual's choice; there is no choice without the conditioning of history and hence no truth that transcends this contingency.

Ideological historicism excludes the possibility of human will. It discounts the originary power of the human subject and hence the hope of the subject attaining truth through lived experience. As Karl Popper maintains in his critique of the role of the polis in an open society, historicism obliterates responsibility for action in society. Plato's historicism bound him to the view that "social change was degeneration" (Popper 16, italics removed). In positing the past existence of ideal, perfect forms of government, society, law, and other social systems of which real systems in the current world are degenerate copies, Plato had to conclude that ultimately change must halt in order to prevent further degeneration. This belief in a disembodied perfection in an irretrievable past makes human alteration of this ideal a corruption to be stopped at all costs. A similar condemnation of human activity results from the Marxist project, which Popper characterizes as a social science initiative driven by historicism. Popper holds that the social science perspective fosters a kind of "methodological essentialism" (26). The method by which one determines a social truth is to determine the nature of what is to come on the basis of how one has named or interpreted events in the past. If revolution in the past is interpreted to have come about because of class struggle, then this identified principle will determine the nature of revolutions to come. Far from viewing truth as open or even shaped by human will, the historicist perspective closes truth and takes it out of the realm of human action; thus, any discussion humans may have about truth is relative to the exclusion of truth from their daily lives.

Essentialist Objectivity

To the relativist, truth can be none other than an object, a commodity subject to barter and exchange. In order to interpret truth as subject to displacement or replacement, it must be characterized as having an essentially objective presence. Neel, for instance, strongly opposes the possibility of conceiving of truth as anything but an object, stating that if truth is not an object, it is but an "opening"; to attempt to find it in writing is indeed hopeless:

> By "taking" *Phaedrus* as the source of the *possibility* of truth, not the closure of truth . . . the writer can open the possibility of dialectic within the writer's own self. Rather than a place or a destination, rather than the shelter of some closed and complete revelation, truth becomes an *opening*. Any writers who agree to enter Platonic writing will find themselves in just such an opening; thus, most struggle with all their might never to go there. (82)

The only alternative to jumping into the "opening" that Neel projects as Plato's "truth" is to write as a "psophist," Neel's term for those who "present any position [one chooses] as the closure of truth" (81). This unfavorable alternative, which Neel attributes to Plato, is not noticeably distinguishable from the "sophistry" Neel advocates in the practice of strong discourse. The latter is more worthy presumably because it stands the test of public scrutiny, the acumen of which—if we are to believe Barbara Herrnstein Smith—is of relative value.

Plato's truth lacks an objective presence that Neel longs for it to have, as is apparent in his analysis of a portion of *Phaedrus* in which Socrates speaks about truth, beauty, and moral value; the text is presented below:

> *Lucidity* and *finality* and *serious importance* are to be found only in words spoken by way of instruction or, to use a *truer* phrase, written on the *soul* of the hearer to enable him to learn about the *right*, the *beautiful*, and the *good;* finally, to realize that such spoken truths are to be reckoned *a man's legitimate sons,* primarily if they *originate* within himself, but to a secondary degree if what we may call their *children* and *kindred* come to *birth,* as they should, in the *minds* of others—to *believe* this, I say, and to let all else go is to be the *sort of man,* Phaedrus, that you and I might well *pray* that we may both become. (secs. 277e–88a, qtd. in Neel 88–89)

This text is objectionable, Neel says, because "the whole paragraph presents itself as an emptiness waiting to be filled through the process of dialectic" (89), and further, he claims, the words that he has italicized—in fact, all nouns, verbs, and modifiers in the passage—hide "an unending series of questions, uncertainties, replacements, deferrals, differences, and supplements" (89). Neel complains about the uncertain meaning of words in themselves, apart from the context of the narrative they develop. To define those italicized words, he says, would open "an unclosable dialectic" (Neel 89). This activity somehow seems unnatural and heinous to him, as well it should. It is certainly not how we go about interpreting communication in our daily lives.

If we go beyond Neel's treatment of the words of Socrates' speech as separate objects, we see that the story told here is not equivocal, uncertain, or deferential in any way. Truth surely is not presented as an object, but just as surely, it is not presented as an opening or void. Socrates' tale of how truth about the right, the beautiful, and the good gets made is rooted in the very concrete material of human flesh and the factual event of human growth. Truth is born with humanity, is learned by way of instruction, is passed on to others, and grows in them as well in a continuous cycle of birth, growth, and regeneration: an endless, yet constructive, narrative. What could be more common to human experience than this familiar progression? What could be more certain than birth, growth, and regeneration? More substantial than the reality of progress through learning? Neel's truth consists of continual replacements and deferrals, whereas the truth of which Socrates speaks is embodied in the process of living and, being so, is as material and vital as the human body. Neel's truth—which he believes to be Plato's truth—is an abstract and motionless entity, a mathematical place holder waiting to find its real object or substitute. It remains the same, never changes, and never progresses. It is an object never to be touched by people, yet always already to be replaced by them.

Herrnstein Smith's objectification of truth is similar to Neel's, yet it is motivated by her attachment to an economic model of value. For her, truth is a good on the open market, subject to free exchange. This analogy forces her to misconstrue the exchange of goods itself as the ultimate function of human existence, obviating activity motivated either by self-conscious will or disinterested altruism. A "good"—such as truth, for example—resists analysis and hence is affirmed only by what other good can be exchanged for it. Herrnstein Smith describes the exchange of goods that establishes what we value as follows:

> Goods, either one by one or collectively (as in "the good"), are not reducible to anything else *in particular,* such as pleasure, the enhancement of survival, or the promotion of communal welfare. . . . The irreducibility is a function not of objective qualities but, rather, of Western (perhaps human) thought and language within which "good" or some counterpart term or set of terms [such as truth, we might surmise] operates conceptually and discursively as *a generalized positivity* that can be locally specified but not further analyzed: in other words, (one) "good" can only be exchanged for (an)other good, in discourse and otherwise. (146)

Although Herrnstein Smith claims that the exchange of commodity for commodity in the search for value in discourse may be necessitated by limitations of our linguistic resources, that is, language cannot always describe exactly what we mean, she also suggests that in some essential way the exchange of good for good simply defines all activity in human experience. It is *the* way we live out our lives in linguistic and other human action. An exchange of good for good even explains our altruistic behavior. To prove it, Herrnstein Smith argues against Bataille's attempt to demonstrate that humans in some circumstances will pursue an "irresistible impulse to reject material or moral goods that it would have been possible to utilize rationally (in conformity with the balancing of accounts)" (Bataille 128–29, as reported in Herrnstein Smith 143). As she interprets Bataille, an individual's seeming altruism is motivated economically because he or she willingly suffers loss or degradation in exchange for an *"ultimate value,"* which is "the unlimited exhibition of his irreducibly sovereign free will, his insubordinate subordination of matter to spirit, and thereby his uniquely and definitively human transcendence" (Herrnstein Smith 144). In other words, a person will suffer loss and degradation to help others in exchange for retaining his or her belief that humans are superior beings with the freedom to choose. Confident that altruism, too, is accounted for in her system of exchange of truth for value, Herrnstein

Smith advocates her own brand of absolutism, declaring that to conceive of all good in terms of exchange is not only a Western phenomenon but also "perhaps human" (146). In short, she declares absolutely that all we value, whether it be a material good, an aesthetic ideal, or a moral principle, is but an object subject to replacement and exchange for another object.

   An essentialist vision of truth as an object cannot be confirmed by empirical or other evidence. Nor can objective presence be assumed for anything that we identify as a material or ethereal substance. Nonetheless, as D. W. Hamlyn, a philosopher of metaphysics, has explained, a belief in objects or substances is necessary "to sustain our ordinary talk of and belief in change and the identity over time which is the correlate of change" (66). In other words, our need to see ourselves and our ideas as identities that change within a history of time sustains our desire to think of both material and abstract phenomena as objects. There are other possibilities; for instance, we can conceive of truth (and even physical substances) as a process or event and thus defined as a fluid continuance rather than objective presence. Science has taken this route, as Hamlyn notes: "Scientific views of the world give plausibility to the belief that the best terms in which to speak and think of the world are not those of substance, identity and change, but, for example, events or processes" (66–67). Neel and Herrnstein Smith, however, do not attempt to consider truth as a process, but rather limit their discussion of truth to its depiction as an objective presence. Hence, to disprove the presence of truth in human evaluation or in writing, they demonstrate that it is not an object to be found. It could be argued that their essentialist rhetoric does not lead them to conclude that objectivity is a metaphysical necessity, that is, an absolute quality of truth or anything else. But it does overtly lead them to rely on objectivity as an "epistemic" or *de dicto* necessity, that is, a necessity for the way they talk about truth (Hamlyn 79). Such apparent essentialist objectivity has serious implications for the way we approach truth as a goal of rhetorical practice, as I shall consider in the closing pages of this chapter.

Fundamental Temporalism

Relativism also presumes that events over time reflect no direction or progress. Each moment makes sense only relative to some other, with the accumulation of events triggering no progress toward a discernible goal. To view time and human activity in this way is to assume that time's cyclic function obliterates individual intervention in the course of cosmic events. This belief goes beyond the imperative of historicism, which limits the future to events prefigured by a past to suggest that time itself has no forward direction, no aspect that marks events as progressive. Without a conception of human experience as marking progress over time, relativists must reject the conclusion that events may occur that define human activity as purposefully progressing toward an understanding of truth.

The textual examples cited earlier confirm that Neel defines truth seeking as the historically determined endless task of replacing a supplement with a supplement, never reaching the truth. This view of truth seeking is similar to Herrnstein Smith's tale of the endless balancing of accounts. Movement from one account to another is motivated only by what is better or worse in a given situation; the sands of value shift as needed to maintain her desert ecosystem of exchange. Both theorists have assumed not only that human activity is determined historically but also that it fundamentally lacks direction over time. Their way of looking at time, truth, and events is consistent with ancient metaphors of time and destiny that have both dominated and constrained scientific explanations of natural events. As Stephen Jay Gould asserts, time has traditionally been conceptualized in terms of two controlling metaphors, the "arrow" and the "cycle":

> At one end of the dichotomy—I shall call it time's arrow—history is an irreversible sequence of unrepeatable events. Each moment occupies its own distinct position in a temporal series, and all moments, considered in proper sequence, tell a story of linked events moving in a direction.
>
> At the other end—I shall call it time's cycle—events have no meaning as distinct episodes with causal impact on a contingent history. Fundamental states are immanent in time, always present and never changing. Apparent motions are parts of repeating cycles, and differences of the past will be realities of the future. Time has no direction. (10–11)

Employing the temporal metaphors of both the arrow and the cycle to describe a single ceaseless dynamic, Gould notes, can help one explain and interpret the world as a system progressing toward an end while maintaining a singular identity. But kept ever separate, these metaphors can prevent one from interpreting change as growth (being blind to time's arrow) and from interpreting pattern as evidence of immanent identity (being blind to time's cycle). Through examining the writings of early geologists, Gould demonstrates how belief in the ancient metaphor of time's cycle led them to interpret the earth as a machine that regenerates itself, despite the lack of empirical support for this notion; this theory was confirmed empirically at a much later date. However, he shows further that this same belief in the cyclic nature of events over time led scientists to reject the possibility of unexpected catastrophic events changing the direction of earth's geologic development, a theory confirmed in later investigations.

Neel and Herrnstein Smith, like the early geologists cited by Gould, discount the complementarity of the dual conceptions of cyclic and directional time. Both interpret events over time as an endless cycle of exchanging supplement for supplement, good for good, truth for value, and writing for truth, without possibility of intervention, catastrophic or otherwise. They deny the possibility of directional change, maintaining that human behavior will continue to reflect the same cycle of searching for truth, yet getting nowhere. At best, men will be able to determine what is better or worse at a given time, which is what they have always been able to do and will do endlessly. The possibility of directional progress is absent in both theorists' worldviews; hence, they fail to interpret the cycles they have inscribed as having a purpose. For both, human activity results in infinite diversity and plurality of purposes and values, and the ceaseless activity they project has no overriding goal. Consequently, it suggests nothing about the viability of truth when one person's relative truth A prevails over another's relative truth B, because the truth is fundamentally determined by the cyclic event of one argument appearing more persuasive than another in a given circumstance. The possibility of people behaving differently than this pattern suggests is also unthinkable, because it is unthinkable either that events may occur over time that would move them to behave otherwise or that they themselves together can control directional progress. This interpretation of human existence suggests that there can be no ultimate purpose to the public and private experience of truth seeking, since the prospect of controlling the diversity of future events is nil. This perspective effectively dismisses human agency as a factor that might direct and enable social change for the common good. Here is where I believe relativism most seriously misses the mark: It categorically denies that human activity, both public and personal, has anything to do with finding common truth, an exclusion that I argue later is not only false but also damaging to our collective enterprise.

Restoring Truth to Writing

As I have proposed, three rational assumptions behind philosophical relativism deny the relationship between writing and truth. Ideological historicism rejects the malleability of the future and denies the possibility of human agency that both embraces *and* overcomes the past. Hence, truth that has not yet been found is seen as unattainable in human experience and thus in writing. Essentialist objectivity makes of truth an exchangeable, displaceable, replaceable object; it encourages the belief that observable and discrete differences in individuals' values deny the possibility of a truth held in common. Such a view of truth limits human discourse to continual position taking, in which belief in something now presupposes the replacement of a former belief ad infinitum, with no replacement ever having a claim to truth and no hope of a truth encompassing all human activity. Fundamental temporalism denies the possibility that human activity is evolutionary, developmental, and progressive. It interprets the pattern of exchange of value for truth as perpetual and purposeless, unable to move in a direction. If human activity is direction-less, then seeking the truth through writing is essentially purposeless and merely substitutes change for progress, as one discourse continually replaces another through besting an other.

In order to transcend the implications of the relativist philosophy of truth for a rhetoric of writing, we must resist relativism as a guide for producing and evaluating written discourse. Resistance to relativism involves interpret-ing strong discourse—that method of resolving difference through conflict and conquering—as a rejection of human experience and ultimately a rejec-tion of knowledge and learning. Relativism dictates that we must conquer for truth. We must do so because our personal history is something to be over-come lest it dictate our future, because what wins our belief does so only at the cost of displacing some other "truth," and because the very best we can hope for is to exchange our current fate for some other. We can behave and believe otherwise if we reject the very premises that limit truth to a historical contingency, a singular presence, a random event. We can make of truth some-thing that is essential to our subjectivity, that lives in the dynamic of human interaction, and that is attainable through our own efforts. To do so, we must reconstruct our notion of truth as separate from the present life we experi-ence, and thus hope to find it not in the ideal, but rather in the personal; not restricted and objectified, but rather open and dynamic; not outside of our knowledge and control, but rather integral with our purpose and within our reachable grasp. The consequence of reconstruing truth in this way is not to separate our rhetoric—that is, our writing and speaking of truth about the world—from philosophy, but rather to practice philosophy, that is, the seeking of truth, as rhetoric.

In an illuminating essay on Plato's *Gorgias,* James L. Kastely remarks that scholars have repeatedly misunderstood Plato's concern about rhetoric as a practice divorced from philosophy. He concludes about Plato's *Gorgias,* for example, that the outrageous arguments presented by Socrates there force us "to question Socrates, Plato, and ourselves" (107). This condition of "ques-tioning," he finds, is highly relevant to the situation of dialectic as Plato con-ceived it. Kastely explains the role of the teacher in facilitating dialectic as a phenomenological enterprise like this:

> Being a teacher can no longer be read as a professional role that one assumes; rather, it marks one of two positions in the dialectic. To teach is to question. . . . To fulfill one's position as a teacher is to practice philosophy as rheto-ric—to understand the particularity of the other member of the refutation (that is, to recognize the historical, passionate, and rational elements of the other person as they have been brought together to constitute an individu-

ality), to be sensitive to the language and the commitments informing that particularity, and to induce reflection on the language lived with and by the other individual. (107)

The notion of practicing philosophy as rhetoric is not a dangerous enterprise, one that may leave us floundering in a void without seams or structure. Our lives are not seamless, nor endless; they are shaped by our friends, relatives, schools, churches, homes, and nations, and their meaning is reflected in our decisions and actions. The truth we seek through such interaction with others is subject to memory and learning and opens us to the possibility of a better life.

Relativism sets up a condition for distrusting our memory of past experience as a contingency that taints our perspective on a world that is construed to be something more. We see this distrust in both Neel and Herrnstein Smith's expressed suspicion of memory. Neel protests that Plato ruined writing for the West through insisting that truth comes from memory of the past carried in one's soul; this places a stranglehold on the "endless possibility" (73) that writing affords. It is the separation of writing and self, Neel argues, that allows systematic control over one's soul, to get a "*fixed* idea" (75) about it. Detachment from writing may indeed create the dialectic of self and other that puts one on the journey toward knowledge, as Neel claims. But knowledge has no meaning for us without the personal memory of what shapes it, the consciousness of having experienced what we ourselves know *as* someone. As is suggested by his personal rejection of his spiritual past, the substance of memory is for Neel a restrictive censure on the possibility of speaking a truth in writing, rather than a clue to its meaning.

Herrnstein Smith also makes memory a thing to get past rather than the substance of meaningful truth. Memory determines us, she claims, rather than frees us to act individually while celebrating a common heritage. She characterizes the moral behavior of the relativist—one who understands that there is no objective basis for truth, but only a history or tradition of value upheld by a community—as behavior that in essence puts memory in its place. The relativist sees one's moral principles "as having no other basis than [one's] 'personal feelings' "; hence, as she herself says,

> While [one] may have organized and evaluated some of the latter into rela-
> tively general and verbally articulated 'principles,' [one] might also continue
> to conceive of them as a more or less scrappy assortment of memories, hab-
> its, unconscious associations and identifications, . . . and so forth. (165)

For relativists, memory represents a kind of unfortunate dyspepsia rather than the sustenance of meaningful experience. A private understanding of who we are gives us the desire to respect and cooperate with others to learn about the world we share. Far from denying our personal history, rhetoric should build it into our future with others. It is this desire, for instance, that has inspired Peter Elbow's commitment to private writing. Elbow has long been fascinated with the writer's struggle to express what is held in consciousness, that is, with the effort, as he puts it, "to break free from what feels like the heavy mud and clinging seaweed that are clogging my ability to *say directly* what I already feel I know" ("Toward a Phenomenology" 61).

Writing is a means by which we get in touch with our personal history, the substantial experience that grounds our belief. That contact can be expressed publicly, but it must be experienced privately; it is what we experience deep within us that connects us to others in public. In asserting this view of the importance of personal experience to public understanding, Elbow quotes the following passage from Thomas Langford's and William Poteat's introduction to an anthology on Michael Polanyi's theory of personal knowledge:

> [The ancient model of the confession] can be seen as a disclosure to oneself of one's basic beliefs, grounded, first, in one's own personal history, with its roots in a pre-personal somatic appearance in the world, bearing its genetic inheritance; and secondly, in a native language upon the insinuations of a larger coherence of which one has trustingly and acritically relied as the conditio sine qua non of one's coming ever more fully to possess one's human being. (Langford and Poteat, 17–18, quoted in Elbow, "Forward" 16)

It is through disclosing the private in language, then, that we come to understand our personal history, our memory, as having a larger meaning shared by others. This discovery does not come from the effort to make a case for a truth that will win out over someone else's vision of reality, but rather from the effort to understand what we know privately so that we can engage with others in shared understanding. This is the value of private writing; Elbow tells us:

> In the safety of private writing, people usually discover and articulate things for themselves which they find a way to offer into the public discussion. When there is no private writing first, people tend to play it safer and engage less with each other—which . . . leads to more domination by strong voices and good arguers. ("Forward" 18)

A private understanding based on personal memory is one that is truly free, that is, unhampered by the objective of taking someone else's place, or more likely, of preventing someone from overtaking ours.

Relativism is unable to reconcile this kind of freedom with truth seeking. Truth can be free *because* it is created from memory and a substantive past shared with and shaped by the pasts of others. Further, truth can be both a singular goal and a boundless, continuous, and malleable process. Memory is the record of our progress toward truth; it is evidence not of our failure to know in the past but of our continuing to know in the present. The relativist perspective cannot acknowledge the overriding persistence of truth seeking; it can only regard one interpretation of reality as temporarily overtaking another—it cannot regard true knowledge as both persistent and dynamic. Herrnstein Smith illustrates this failure, dismissing her own capacity to grow toward truth through experience. She opens her treatise on literary value with a recollection of a personal dilemma, an account of her changed perception of the value of Shakespeare's Sonnet 116. Reporting the history of her appreciation of that sonnet, she claims:

> For a long time, I didn't much like it at all. As a discriminating young snob, I was predisposed to find the value of any poem inversely proportional to the frequency of its appearance in anthologies. . . . So it stood until several years ago, when I was immersed in teaching the plays, editing the poems and rereading the critics, and immersed also in my own life and a second marriage—of true minds, of course, or maybe . . . or maybe not. And, at that point, I discovered an altogether different 116. . . . To be sure, the arguments are frail and the sentiments false and strained: but this is nonetheless a powerful sonnet because, among other things, that very frailty and strain and falseness are expressive of what is strong and true, namely the impulse *not* to know, *not* to acknowledge, not to "admit" what one does know and would wish to be otherwise. (Herrnstein Smith 6–7)

Although she narrates a series of events in her own process of evaluating Sonnet 116, she does not see these "parts" of her history as they contribute to a seamless whole. She chooses not to acknowledge that she incorporated her earlier pejorative assessment of Sonnet 116 in her later belief that its "frail" and "false" arguments serve admirably to express the difficulty of being straightforward about what one knows, the important meaning she claims to have found anew when she reevaluated Sonnet 116 in her later years. Her more recent judgment did not wipe out or change her earlier belief, rather it subsumed it, incorporated it, expanded it, and even blessed it; the seemingly diverse claims grew into one complex evaluation. Yet the model Herrnstein Smith proposes to explain these events does not account for them as a narrative of growth. And it is this choice not to view evaluation as a process that leads her to see value and truth as local, contingent, locked into the framework of time and place. It is what leads her to declare that diversity obviates truth and contingency displaces universality. It is also what leads her to conclude that human activity as a whole is nonevolutionary and essentially directionless.

We can avoid this failure by reconceiving of truth as living in continued human interaction; thus, truth finds no victory in declaring a single argument wrong or its author in error. Nor does it deem it necessary that we seek the final word, for such finality only forecloses the possibility of truth by dismissing someone who may yet speak. And further, such silencing of others threatens the essential direction of all our activity, which is toward more perfect interaction with an other, that is, with all we perceive to be outside of ourselves, in order to know all that is other as well as we presumably know ourselves. We reach out toward the world, take it in, and make some sense of it for ourselves; we produce a necessary order that preserves both our identity and that of the world in which we reside. It is this necessary order that gives human activity its direction.

The critic Mario Vargas Llosa explains that while "the evolution of our species in the past does not allow us to deduce a direction in human activity" (1023), human creativity nevertheless designs a direction. Such can be discovered in a great novel, Llosa argues, which can help us deal with the truth of being ultimately free beings. A great novel, he tells us, provides us with

> rigorous and intelligent order, where nothing is gratuitous or incomprehensible, where life flows in a logical and inevitable channel, seduces us because it calms us[,] . . . rationalizes and orders our surroundings, giving us back that confidence which human beings only with great difficulty resign themselves to renouncing: that of knowing what we are, where we are, and—above all—where we are going. (Llosa 1024)

This consciousness of a necessary order that makes sense of the contact of one with an other is denied by Neel and Herrnstein Smith. For they are unable to acknowledge the overriding order of a discourse that is a dynamic engagement in purposeful truth seeking.

Purposeful truth seeking through interaction demands shared consciousness; it demands intimacy. The relationship between the intimacy of shared consciousness and Plato's conception of truth is explored by Susan Miller in *Rescuing the Subject*. In her analysis of *Phaedrus* here, she recounts how Socrates speaks of the soul as a being in action, moving in constant progression toward heaven. Interactive discourse between men who seek the truth moves "toward divine insight." In the process of speaking, the "lover improves the soul of the beloved" (Miller 116) and both move closer to truth.

The image of soul improving soul through dialogue is intimate, powerful, and grounded in human experience. As Miller explains, it is not writing itself that destroys the truth seeking of human souls, but rather the fact that writing, which addresses specific contexts and cases, can be taken to address all contexts and cases. The only way that knowledge can be found is through "discussion—immediate interactions between individuals" (Miller 120); it is through this discussion that the soul is accessed and its progression toward truth can be shared with the soul of another. The potential evil of writing, according to Miller's interpretation of Socrates' words in *Phaedrus*, is that it disembodies speech from the soul of the person (121). Yet *this* is what Neel celebrates about writing. He argues that the permanent form writing takes allows everyone to look equally at the rhetoricity that is exposed when speech is removed from the soul intending to tell the truth by it. One could contend that in taking this distanced view of writing and speech, we remove them from the realm of human consciousness, from the possibility of purposefully connecting one soul to another. It is this connection and intimacy that frees us to seek a common truth, to find within a past something to bring us closer to rather than further away from others.

Thus, as an antidote to endless dichotomization, to representing the world endlessly in terms of differences, opposites, and polar tensions, we need to return to the possibility of universal meaning—of believing that we ourselves and our writing make a sense that is shared and lived through our contact with others. Ann E. Berthoff claims that resistance to dichotomous thinking in rhetoric requires us to "reconceive of rhetoric as a hermeneutical enterprise" (281). The process of using language itself creates the "third" element, interpretation, which frees us from dividing the world into sign and referent, thought and language, and self and other. For Berthoff, "the mediating idea held by an interpreter" (281) links a symbol to its object and also motivates the dynamic that makes meaning possible and makes "the linguistic process itself the great heuristic" (282) that allows us to create meaning, and, one might add, move us toward truth. The very generality and universality of this process, its catholicity, if you will, joins all of humanity, past, present, and future, in a community concerned with making meaning. Invoking Charles Peirce's interpretation of the "ongoingness of the social process," she explains:

> The community of which we are a part had its beginning in pre-history; the community which each of us represents stretches into the future. . . . As they spread in the community of those concerned, our ideas develop generality; as we interpret our interpretations, we advance toward generality, gaining the power to compare and differentiate, to name and define and to form. (Berthoff 285)

The process of meaning making in this community of humankind is dynamic, formative, and developmental, not substitutive, supplemental, and displacing. Language is not a weapon to destroy meaning, displace truth, and supplement reality, but rather, as Berthoff claims, it is "the instrument of one's becoming, at once, one's self and representative of humanity" (286). It is this intense attempt at representation that makes writing essential to both individual freedom and social life. It is this process, I would add, that is its truth.

In short, to seek truth through writing or speaking, we must be engaged without apology in the act of trusting the human enterprise. This means giving up the notion that writing is primarily a site for struggle. To do so, we must abandon what Barry Weller has described as "our current critical practice," that is, those "tacit or explicit ideologies [that] advance one discursive pole—the active exercise of a writerly will—not merely in preference to, but at the expense of, the other, a kind of readerly receptiveness and self-surrender" (12). In other words, we must abandon a philosophy that invests the will with the power of resistance and robs it of the power to embrace the ideas of others. If we do so, we can finally claim that life itself has some purpose and that it is what we hold in common—our common aspirations—that gives humanity expression. We can decide finally that writing—like all of our discourse—is provisional, marking a path toward the goals of our various enterprises and contributing to our common humanity, rather than bringing conversation to a halt in a final word that becomes a final deed. And we can begin judging the written work of others as it aspires to be part of that conversation seeking truth, rather than as it aspires to win an argument.

Restoring Truth to Ourselves

The program I suggest for restoring truth to writing requires what in the current climate of textual criticism might be considered a leap of faith. Though some may generously concede that we would indeed get along better if we stopped arguing about what is true and treated the views of others more charitably, few would concede that this practice would lead us to truth without fail. And I would be among them. What is required is an essential change in our perspective on the self as arbiter and purveyor of truth. If we were to cease believing that history determines our future actions, that truth has bounds, and that we have no capacity to change our environment, we would still be no closer to finding truth. We would yet have to be persuaded that truth is indeed within our palpable grasp—that the potential to find it resides within us. In short, we would have to interpret truth phenomenologically, that is, as it has come to have meaning for us as part of our lived experience. But to do so within the context of current textual theory is a challenging task. Our predominant theories of self-representation have removed us from the potential of approaching truth as a phenomenon of human experience, and consequently from regarding human experience as its foundation.

As I shall show in the next chapter, critical and rhetorical theory, for the most part, not only accedes to the relativist claims that I addressed in this chapter, but also further excludes truth from human experience by accepting a construction of individual identity that defines the self in terms of its resistance to its physical and social environment. In short, textual theory interprets the aim of both expression and interpretation to be the preservation of self-identity through rejecting the influence of the outside world. A self that remains separated from the world where it dwells can never hope to understand it fully. In chapter 2, I address the loss of the truthful self in critical theory and the implications of that loss for rhetorical practice. I also call also for a reinterpretation of the self as empowered by an *acceptance of* rather than *resistance to* the world it seeks to know—a reinterpretation, which I show in chapter 3, is made possible through adopting phenomenology as a guide for a practical rhetoric.

2

The Problem of Conceiving
a Phenomenological Rhetoric

Rejecting Resistance

IF WE BELIEVE ourselves to be inevitably incapable of finding truth, then we cannot trust rhetoric to lead us to truth. As I have argued in the previous chapter, philosophical relativism, a conviction that removes truth from human experience, is a fundamental critical prejudice supporting this perspective. To counter the idea of relativism is not a straightforward matter; it requires us to accept truth as something *not* determined by historical or circumstantial conditions, *not* realized as an object with boundaries and limits, and *not* defined outside the realm of human activity throughout time. In short, we must believe that truth does, in fact, come forward through the process of our being and living in the everyday world. Yet to concede that this is so, we must believe our conscious selves to be capable of comprehending truth, that is, of interacting with the things of the world in such a way that we can fully understand their vast possibilities, effects, and consequences. In other words, we must accept understanding the truth of our existence as an essential phenomenon of our living in the world as human beings, a principle that, as I shall discuss later, is developed and elaborated in phenomenological philosophy. Only through accepting truth as phenomenologically integral with world experience can we develop a theory that names truth as the goal of rhetorical practice. This latter step requires not only that we alter our notion of truth, but also that we radically adjust predominant theories of the function of textual reception (criticism) and production (rhetoric) as these practices interpret and articulate truth.

The project of radically adjusting current textual theory requires not only abandoning the epistemology of relativist truth, but also reconceiving the role of the self in relating to the world. At present, the predominant conceptions of self in critical and rhetorical theory stake individual identity, and thus the power of personal expression, on the ability of a subject to resist or to counter influences that are external to it. Expression is deemed more legitimate and authentic if the subject positions himself or herself in opposition to socially constructed views, or at the very least distances himself or herself from the

31

world as it is directly observed or interpreted by others. This stance is most commonly defended with the philosophy of humanist individualism, the belief that individuals achieve agency, power, and knowledge through practicing skeptical inquiry. The parallel rebuttal to the agentive optimism of humanist individualism is social determinism, the belief that personal agency, power, and knowledge are necessary fictions that support culturally based institutions through subjecting individuals to ideological forces. Although individualism and social determinism are often thought to be mutually exclusive, they are founded on a shared premise: The human self or subject thrives through contest with and resistance to its context.

The consequences of defining the human subject solely as a product of resistance are devastating to a quest for truth through rhetoric. If individuals indeed express selfhood only through resistance, instead of interpreting the rhetor as open to knowledge, we must cast the rhetor as a political strategist, intent on gaining or maintaining power over or through others in order to resist their influence. Or if the self is believed to be totally constructed by external influences, then individuals' inability to resist such influence constrains their efforts both to speak truthfully and to discern truth from relative belief. In this chapter, I aim to illustrate the problem for rhetoric that is posed by these philosophies of self-representation. My point is to present the individualist and social determinist positions on the self as controlling metaphors with implications for how we define the limits of language use. In exploring the relationship between language and self-identity that these positions present, I turn to work by Karl Popper and V. N. Volosinov; first, to illustrate the rift between the individualist stance on human agency and the social determinist stance on the subjugation of self; and second, to articulate their common ground in the ideology of resistance. Then incorporating Paul Smith's efforts to mitigate these polar views, I explore briefly the powerful grip that the notion of resistance holds on textual theories of self-representation.

In the last half of this chapter, I correlate the individualist and social determinist perspectives on selfhood with Julia Kristeva's psychological characterizations of self-representation in discourse practices. Through exploring two psychological traits, *narcissism* and *fetishism,* and their discursive realizations, I define these traits as rhetorical practices linked to the investment of self-identity in resistance. Narcissism and fetishism, I contend, underlie authorial voice and professional stance, valued rhetorical strategies for self-representation that have been defined by scholars in rhetoric, composition, and related disciplines. These strategies demand that authors distance themselves from the world they experience not only in order to determine its truth, but also in order to define themselves within and distinguish themselves from the world where they dwell.

The valorization of rhetorical strategies that demand we distance ourselves from the world in order to make valid claims about it has resulted in a forced rejection of personal knowledge about this place that shelters us. Resistance by definition limits experience and consequently limits knowledge. I believe we can work to remove the barriers presented by critical and rhetorical theory that valorize resistance against truth seeking; we need only to show that the human self develops and achieves agency through *accepting* rather than *resisting* its worldly environment. This conception of self-identity demands a new philosophy of truth and selfhood, an ontology of both that does not dispense with one in order to create the other. As I propose in chapter 3, phenomenological philosophy helps us meet this challenge.

Self-Representation and the Necessity of Resistance

Resistance figures in our predominant contemporary theories of selfhood as *the* force that both carves out a person's identity and protects that identity from dissolution. Individual agency *is* the power to resist. If on the one hand, the individual is regarded as an autonomous entity, totally free to act within a context of numerous other individuals and forces of nature larger than himself or herself, then the individual must attain this freedom through some will to resist external influence. If on the other hand, individual agency is constrained and constituted by external forces that not only conflict with individual consciousness but also define it, then the distinguishable characteristics of individuals must be realized only when individuals resist some constraints only to be overtaken by others. Before offering an alternative to regarding resistance as the essential force that shapes self-identity, I wish to explore here how resistance has figured within two polar conceptions of selfhood that have girded much of critical theory, that is, humanist individualism and social determinism, and further, to suggest how resistance continues to define other postmodernist, antifoundational perspectives on meaning and identity. As I hope to show in the brief sketches that follow, both conceptions of human agency stand as powerful controlling metaphors for our behavior toward others in our endeavor to validate a common and truthful understanding of the world we share.

The individualist view of agency suggests that human beings can act and, in fact, *are obligated* to act freely in society; the individual's actions are determined neither by historical necessity nor social forces. Free agency is gained through the conscious practice of skeptical inquiry, which has been touted as the basic technology of humanist philosophy in its various articulations from the Italian Renaissance to the present. Humanist philosophers since the Enlightenment have emphasized secular methods of seeking knowledge and truth as opposed to positing an absolute truth or omnipotent God beyond the scope of human inquiry (Batchelor 299). Belief in humanist individualism removes the human subject both from its dependence on the absolute governance of an omniscient being, whether that be God or some other idealized abstraction such as Plato's "pure forms," and from the local influence of culture and history, as is projected by its opposing theory of agency, social determinism. To elaborate humanist individualism more fully as a representational stance, I rely here upon Popper's *The Open Society and Its Enemies*, one of the better known arguments in its support. This work specifically celebrates the free agency of the individual and his or her power to achieve moral integrity through adopting an independent perspective within a cultural environment that supports conflicting intellectual and moral interpretations of reality.

As Popper notes, the individualist perspective on human agency finds skeptical inquiry to provide the appropriate balance to our collective impulse to rally behind a socially favored position, an impulse reflected in many of our social institutions, such as government and public education. Popper finds collectivist interests to be suspect because such interests often direct their charity "towards anonymous groups rather than concrete individuals" (88). As a defense of the moral rectitude of charity toward individuals as opposed to groups, Popper notes that charity toward individuals is favored in Christian humanism and reflected in its altruistic aim: " 'Love your neighbour,' says Christianity, not 'love your tribe' " (89). Humanist individualism also declares moral actions pursued for collectivist ends to be valueless because they ignore the interests of the individual. From the individualist perspective, then, Plato's decree that the duty of every person is to serve the state is clearly in error. For Plato, "the criterion of morality is the interest of the state [italics removed]." If we accept this criterion, claims Popper, "morality is nothing but political hygiene." When the state is deemed superior to the individual, moral actions become those that contribute to the well-being of the state, regardless of the interests of individuals within it (Popper 94).

A modern threat that the state poses to the aims of humanistic individualism is its support of public vocational education. Public education discourages the development of individual character and inquiry in favor of developing serviceable skills that prepare people to enter careers: "The student is encouraged to study for the sake of his personal career; he is led to acquire only such knowledge as is serviceable in getting him over the hurdles he must clear for the sake of his advancement" (Popper 119). From the perspective of humanist individualism, the tribalist, collectivist urge to serve professions discourages individuals from behaving with moral purpose. The professions, like Plato's philosopher-king, foster a neat, controlled authoritarian state, a closed society. Humanist individualism projects as a moral ideal an open society, that is, one not governed by collectivist interests; individuals' needs can be served only when they must compete for a place, rather than when they accrue privileges by virtue of membership in a specific group, whether that be defined by race, creed, politics, or profession (Popper 153).

Humanist individualism promotes skeptical inquiry not only as a means to develop individual character but also as a moral quest that supersedes even the pursuit of aesthetic values. Individual character formed through skeptical inquiry both resists sociocultural and biological influences and stands above the influence of abstract philosophical ideals of the good, the beautiful, and the true. Individuals practicing skeptical inquiry can and must stand against the political agenda of collectives such as political parties, religious groups, and professions; and furthermore, they must resist the aesthetic agenda of radicalism promoted by intellectuals and "philosopher-kings." Radical idealism, Popper concludes, can lead only to violence:

> The artist politician has first to make his canvas clean, to destroy existing institutions, to purify, to purge. This is an excellent description of all political radicalism, of the aestheticist's refusal to compromise. The view that society should be beautiful like a work of art leads only too easily to violent measures. (146)

Those who foster political radicalism destroy social systems through insisting upon maintaining the purity of an idea, such as communism, at the expense of individual freedom (Popper 147).

Humanist individualism construes skeptical inquiry as both more moral and more rational than either collectivism or intellectual radicalism. The stand to assert the validity of individual skepticism is a moral stand against tribalism, a false belief that "unity and beauty and perfection" (Popper 176) can be attained in an oligarchic society, one dominated by a privileged group whose interests prevail. It is also a stand against sacrificing individual need to a radical ideal; the intellectual's dream of a perfect society is one in which we have forgotten our responsibilities to others in need. The goal of skeptical inquiry is to secure a better truth for all. The only humane choice of action for each individual seeking the truth is to try to secure a just society, to personally take on the burden of designing a better world:

> If we dream of a return to our childhood, . . . if we turn back from the task of carrying our cross, the cross of humaneness, of reason, of responsibility, if we lose courage and flinch from the strain, then we must try to fortify ourselves with a clear understanding of the simple decision before us. We can return to the beasts. But if we wish to remain human, then there is only one way, the way into the open society. We must go into the unknown, courageously, using what reason we have, to plan for security *and* freedom. (Popper 177)

The only route toward the good society is the choice to assume individual responsibility for this end. Although the state or collective must exist in order to provide an environment in which the individual can choose to act in a responsible manner, the fate of the individual faced with the task of choosing to act responsibly within society is a fate similar to that of Adam and Eve having been cast from Eden; redemption occurs only through individual struggle against the odds. Although individuals thrive in collective institutions, they must resist and hold suspect the very world that supports them. Self-reliance is the moral standard for humanist individualism and skeptical inquiry is the intellectual foundation of this virtue. The skeptical inquirer resists collective interest with the aim of becoming a better, more perfect— and thus more responsible—individual. In short, humanist individualism defines men and women as truly on their own, fighting against the influence of society, religion, and even the biological susceptibility of their human nature to do the right and responsible thing.

The consequences of humanist individualism are presumed to be benign and most certainly supportive of the common good. The individual who is active in a participatory democracy guards it against the mindless sway of collectivist tribal interests. Yet the power of the individual to do so is not adequately articulated in this philosophy nor practically substantiated. The individual persists through competing with others and struggling to take their place and to displace their ideas (Popper 153). When individuals fail in such struggles to change societal conditions, they are enjoined to blame themselves for societal failure to support the common good. As Popper notes: "Democratic institutions cannot improve themselves. The problem of improving them is always a problem of persons rather than institutions" (111). The technology through which a society of individuals—all acting responsibly to defend their own actions, which are evaluated autonomously—is supposed to cohere remains tellingly absent from the philosophy of humanist individualism. Furthermore, its vision of how verbally constituted cultural institutions such as laws, policies, agreements, and procedures come to reflect both public and individual good is impoverished. In a society in which individuals are valued solely for their distinguishing traits, distancing self-reliance becomes the best and most moral response to collective initiatives (Popper 163). The value of investing in public policy and assuming it as part of one's personal identity is clearly secondary to the value of critiquing it from the dispassionate perspective of a spectator.

At bottom, advocacy of self-reliance, like the image of tribal collectivism, is a radical ideal, one that limits our freedom rather than secures it. Through skeptical inquiry, the individual seeks the ideal of complete autonomy; the skeptical inquirer alienates himself or herself from collective interests with the aim of becoming a better, more perfect individual. Though the professed aim of skeptical inquiry is knowledge acquisition, its focus is on the attitude, character, and desires of the individual observer. When the world without is rejected by the skeptical observer, it fails to be recognized, let alone understood.

The failure of humanist individualism to account for how the external world integrates with individual consciousness is both countered and reversed in the social determinist account of human agency. Not only does this latter perspective refute the possibility of skeptical inquiry, through claiming that pervasive ideologies deny the ability of individuals to distance themselves from societal institutions, but social determinism also dismantles the very idea of individual autonomy. Despite its counterperspective, social determinism, like humanist individualism, touts resistance to external forces—ultimately, resistance to some social values as opposed to others—as *the* force that defines personal expression and enables identity to emerge within the realm of competing social constructions.

Social determinism, as it is represented, for instance, in Volosinov's *Marxism and the Philosophy of Language,* attacks the humanist ideal of a skeptical individual acting consciously to change or shape a collective interest. Symbolic action, language in particular, is not the tool of an independent agent, but rather it is the fabrication of an all-embracing culture. In its spontaneous use by individuals, language appears to assert their independence; however, linguistic signs merely maintain an illusion of agency and personal identity in order to perpetuate and generate social ideology: "Wherever a sign is present, ideology is present, too. *Everything ideological possesses semiotic value*" (Volosinov 10). Language is one specific means through which individual consciousness is controlled by ideology. In contrast to the humanist ideal of an individual consciousness that remains aloof from the influence of collective interest, social determinism defines consciousness exclusively in sociological terms:

> The only possible objective definition of consciousness is a sociological one. . . . Consciousness takes shape and being in the material of signs created by an organized group in the process of its social intercourse. . . . If we deprive consciousness of its semiotic, ideological content, it would have absolutely nothing left. (Volosinov 13)

Psychological experience is not within the control of an individual's consciousness, but rather is marked by social conditioning; no psychological experience is independent of the sociologically determined sign (Volosinov 26). In fact, what individuals may perceive as a separate, distinct psyche is the result of a process through which what one believes to be subjective individual experiences are first transformed into ideological signs and are then absorbed and "read" as part of one's psyche. It is through this interactive process that ideology remains vital and capable of development:

> Between the psyche and ideology there exists, then, a continuous dialectical interplay: *the psyche effaces itself, or is obliterated, in the process of becoming ideology, and ideology effaces itself in the process of becoming the psyche.* . . . The ideological sign must immerse itself in the element of inner, subjective signs; it must ring with subjective tones in order to remain a living sign and not be relegated to the honorary status of an incomprehensible museum piece. (Volosinov 39)

The successful integration of social ideologies within the individual psyche occurs when social struggle brings them to the fore and permits their dominance (Volosinov 23). This view, of course, diminishes the value of social traditions over which there is no quarrel and elevates conflict, not harmony, as a necessary element for creating meaning. But unlike the individualist claim that meaningful truth results from the conflict between a free agent and an institution, the social determinist position holds that truths that are accepted as meaningful result from conflict between ideologies that absorb and define individual psyches. And it further holds that communication about these truths, including artistic production, becomes meaningful only when it has achieved a place within a social ideology. Volosinov explains the relationship between meaningfulness in art and social ideology like this:

> In each period of its historical existence, a work must enter into close association with the changing behavioral ideology, become permeated with it, and draw new sustenance from it. Only to the degree that a work can enter into that kind of integral, organic association with the behavioral ideology of a given period is it viable for that period (and of course for a given social group). Outside its connection with behavioral ideology it ceases to exist, since it ceases to be experienced as something ideologically meaningful. (91)

This view of the integrity of individual communication virtually denies the possibility that what one says can have viability outside that permitted by the social system and historical period in which it is addressed or received. There is no capacity to mean meaning that is not constrained by time and place. Those who do not speak to a situation remain virtually unempowered, and those who are empowered to speak do so only because the situation allows it. There is no individual in the speech act: "*The structure of the utterance is a purely sociological structure.* The utterance, as such, obtains between speakers. The individual speech act (in the strict sense of the word 'individual') is *contradictio in adjecto*" (Volosinov 98).

Where the individualist position places the human agent in contest with a society in which the moral good of the whole rests upon one's capacity to remain separate from the rest, the social determinist position defines the human agent as a product of competing societal forces; one's sense of identity remains secure and intact when social forces support it, and it is threatened with obliteration or redefinition when social forces change. Where humanist individualism projects the romantic ideal of personal identity without context, social determinism denies this premise regardless of its influence on the way individuals conduct their daily lives. It is useless for the socially determined agent to speak out to others with the expectation of gaining a unique place within the social situation they both share. Speech does not articulate a place for individual consciousness, but rather creates, delineates, and constrains consciousness:

> Language lights up the inner personality and its consciousness; language creates and endows them with intricacy and profundity—and it does not work the other way. . . . Consequently, *a word is not an expression of inner personality; rather, inner personality is an expressed or inwardly impelled word.* (Volosinov 153)

Thus the individual comes to life as a speaking subject by virtue of having been given the words to speak and having assimilated them within his or her vision of a personal self.

Within the social determinist scheme, social speech establishes individual skill in rhetoric as the measure of an agent's social authenticity within the realm of competing ideological forces. As Volosinov notes, rhetoric provides the scene for certain social transactions, identifying the "boundaries" of authority implied, for instance, by an official court ruling versus a lawyer's interpretation of or commentary on a court case; in short, "rhetoric . . . is marked by an acute awareness of property rights to words and by a fastidiousness in matters of authenticity" (Volosinov 122). Rhetoric can thus be antithetical to dialectical struggle that creates the conditions for change. By virtue of its "transformation of the word into a thing" (Volosinov 159), rhetoric can serve to mummify an ideology, rather than subject it to dialectical struggle. The irony for the individual is that rhetoric is the only tool to resist ideology, and resistance to the determining force of ideology is the only hope for change or for discovery of a truth that differs from what current social forces dictate. To achieve individual agency as a socially constructed being, the individual must use rhetoric to resist rhetoric and is left in the end not with truth but with only rhetoric. The social determinist position on agency, like humanistic individualism, limits human discovery to what is learned through resistance, but it also further limits discovery to the articulation of competing ideologies rather than the formulation of all-embracing truths.

In short, both humanist individualism and social determinism suggest a relationship of the individual to the world that validates resistance as the act that protects and defends personal identity from dissolution. This is so regardless of whether the subject is defined as an intellectually free agent or a socially determined functionary of ideological forces. Of course, it must be acknowledged that the assumptions of these opposing critical perspectives are not as monolithic and mutually exclusive as they are presented here. Yet even where attempts have been made to account for individual agency within the framework of social institutions, that is, to reconcile the opposing concepts of individual freedom and social determinism, contemporary theorists have been reluctant to deny that individuals are alienated from an external reality they resist in order to survive.

For instance, phenomenological hermeneutics, a humanist approach to knowledge formation, displays modified claims about the freedom of the individual to interpret the world but defines valid interpretation as an act of resistance. Phenomenological hermeneutics both celebrates individual interpretation and concedes the influence of community and consensus on individuals' aesthetic and moral values. Deference to communal values is foregrounded as a condition for determining truth in the interpretive process. But in the act of hermeneutic interpretation, the individual's initial encounter with a text is viewed as an alienating experience: Meaningful interpretation results only when readers resist and thus appropriate the alienating contours of a text, transforming them to match their own self-image. The success of appropriating the text and thus overcoming initial alienation is measured by one's ability to remain distant and distinct from it and through this distancing transform the text into something that contributes generally to human understanding (Valdés 61–64). Resistance is the essential key to maintaining the integrity of one's self and of one's interpretation.

For those Marxist theorists who have made modified claims about the influence of social forces on cultural practices and the determinacy of meaning, resistance remains the only valid means of achieving human agency. Neo-Marxists theorize that individuals articulate cultural practices within social formations in ways that are *not* predetermined by social forces but rather are concretized at specific moments. A particular utterance or act results from a particular struggle between contradictory subject positions—for instance, between that of the masses versus the ruling classes—brought together at a particular point in time. In this scheme, personal expression, no longer thought to be predetermined, results from the tension and conflict between competing ideologies, each resisting the other (Trimbur 36–42).

The tendency of contemporary theory to define the self, or the subject who interprets, as a product of resistance is exemplified most tellingly in Paul Smith's *Discerning the Subject,* a carefully conceived effort to resolve the conflict between individualist and social determinist theories of self-representation. Smith attempts to recover individual agency in the aftermath of structuralist and poststructuralist critique. He sets out to "dis-cern" the subject, which in Marxist theory is *cerned,* that is, inscribed by a cultural heritage that defines individuals and gives them a " 'real' existence" (5). Individuals exist in a dialectical struggle with the environment that ultimately shapes them, but at the same time this struggle is somehow unique for each person:

> The subject/individual participates in a dialectical relationship with the social but also lives that relationship *alone* as much as interpersonally or as merely a factor within social formations: alone at the level of the meanings and histories which together constitute a *singular* history. (6)

Smith finds the Marxist position on individual agency to be essentially contradictory because it interprets the individual as a product of conditioning forces who attains identity through engaging in a struggle against these forces. The individual is supposed to achieve some potential for agency, which is at the same time unavailable to him when a revolutionary change in social forces takes place. The prospect of a fully realized individual emerging from the dialectical struggle with social forces is nil because, in the end, the individual remains within a social structure that defines his existence. This vision of dialectical struggle not only excludes the possibility of an improved condition for the individual, but it also overlooks the obvious instances of individuals who fail to be fully interpellated by ideology (Smith 3–13).

Yet the problem of fully explaining individual agency in textual production and reception is not addressed adequately by contemporary theories that oppose Marxist criticism. Deconstructionism is inadequate, on the one hand, because it ignores the role of the interpreter in making meaning and can be construed as "a patent eschewing of responsibility, . . . in terms of explaining the way in which the subject/individual acts" (Smith 50). On the other hand, the individualist view that human will defines a coherent agent who can oppose societal forces ignores the diversity and changeability of individual human behavior. To address these problems, Smith proposes to view the individual as a subject position one takes that may alter from instance to instance, incorporating societal influences within a singular history. He thus argues against what he calls the " 'entire subject,' " an abstract vision of the individual as either fully constituted by ideology or fully independent and conscious. Individual agency, rather, represents a subject position that is activated when an individual who is constituted by "ideology-in-general" is able to make a " 'choice' or conscious calculation" because of the process of negotiating among multifarious "subject-positions" (Smith 40). It is the recognition of a difference in subject positions that motivates individuals to make a choice and hence activates personal agency. Thus human agency can be "dis-cerned" in the moment of choice when one ideological construction takes precedence over another—a dialectical choice predicated by competing discourses:

> The human agent can be dis-cerned from the "subject" (indeed, perhaps the notion of the "subject" can altogether be abandoned) at the point where

the contradictions between different ideas and positions of the "subject" are recognized and privileged; that is, at the point where the negativity contained in and by social discourses and systems is once again allowed the right to work. (Smith 151)

The "dis-cerned" agent is not an entity that reconciles individuals' freedom of choice with their social conditioning. Rather, the human agent is a power external to the individual that is embodied in social discourses and recognized by the human speaker whose identity is subject to the occasion of having to make a choice. The world without (discourse) creates the occasion for a world within (individual consciousness) through the mechanism of resistance. Self-identity is realized only through the circumstance of being compelled to choose some occasion for meaning over another. The individual agent must assume the existence embodied in a discourse in order to both render a social environment meaningful and achieve an identity within it. In doing so, the individual resists one identity only to become subject to another: Agency is subject to resistance.

Resistance, whether in the form of skeptical inquiry, social conflict, or ideological choice, defines individual agents and makes life meaningful for them, or this is how much of contemporary critical theory, at least, would have it. To link self-expression and identity with resistance results psychologically in the validation of this self-preserving mechanism as an appropriate social practice. The interpersonal effect of resistance is not only to pit one set of social values against another but also one social group against another and, ultimately, one person against another. In short, resistance to ideas, to social values, and to institutions is realized concretely as resistance to persons. A theory of self-expression that champions resistance fundamentally denies communication or rhetoric as activity directed toward a common truth: If resistance is a necessary condition for self-realization, then we are from the get-go positioned to resist certain interpretations of experience, interpretations that may be essential to expressing a shared truth.

The strong figure of resistance not only underlies theories of verbal self-representation but also guides and validates certain communicative practices. In short, resistance both serves as a model of the ways in which we interact with the world in order to establish an authentic identity and validates defensive communicative practices as appropriate strategies for interpreting the world. As I will show in the next section, to declare resistance the only means to agency is to valorize what scholars have assessed psychologically as narcissistic and fetishistic behavior—behavior that has a correlate in valued rhetorical practices. Both humanistic individualism and social determinism link individual authenticity to the practice of resistance. By extension, these theories validate psychologically defensive rhetorical practices as both authentic and appropriate forms of communication. Rhetoric that endorses individual skeptical inquiry as the only path to credible meaning can be insidiously self-absorptive and socially alienating; rhetoric that valorizes only social ideology as the source of meaning can be hegemonic and normalizing. Neither expressive approach assumes an openness to world experience and its common meaning to all who potentially might share it.

Narcissism and Fetishism: Rhetorics of Resistance and Barriers to Truth

Where critical theory has valorized the role of resistance in securing self-identity and authenticity of personal expression, psychoanalytic theory likewise has exposed resistance as a defense mechanism protecting the individual against feelings of alienation from others. Two such behaviors, narcissism and fetishism, represent, respectively, the individual's resistance to an alien other and the individual's obsessive attachment to an object representing an idealized self. These postures parallel, I would like to suggest, the critical stances of humanist individualism and social determinism, and they underlie valued strategies in rhetorical practice. In the pages that follow, I discuss the psychological defenses of narcissism and fetishism, showing how they are realized as socially accepted forms of self-representation reflected within specific rhetorical practices.

Narcissism: Disguising Emptiness

Narcissism, or one's sense of reflecting back on oneself with satisfaction, disguises the "emptiness of separation" one feels from objects outside oneself (in Freudian psychology, the images of mother and father). According to psychologists, it represents a stage in our development which precedes our ability to function as social beings, that is, to use language to both connect with and separate from others. The developmental stages of narcissism as they are reflected in individuals' use of language have been explored by Julia Kristeva in ways that have particular relevance to critical and rhetorical theory. Kristeva tells us that narcissism is the driving force creating "the whole contrivance of imagery, representations, identifications and projections [as] a means of exorcising that emptiness [that is, that separation from others]." The separation of self from the objects it desires becomes "our opportunity to become narcissists or narcissistic, or at any rate subjects of representation" ("Freud and Love" 257). Our induction into the symbolic order, that is, our ability to use language that accompanies the development of mature consciousness, at least allows us to "block" up our "narcissistic emptiness and its surfaces composed of imaginary recognitions and cathexes" ("Freud and Love" 258). In other words, the ability to create in language objects of desire, which we can control ourselves, soothes our anxious and unrequited desires to fully assimilate the world and others in it. The fact that others in the world are external to us becomes an opportunity for us both to represent ourselves to them and to have as an object of our consciousness and desire not only the others we recognize as separate, but also our own personal representations of an ideal self.

Prior to making use of the power of symbolic reasoning, our narcissism represents a primitive attempt to preserve a naive perception that "we are" beyond what language creates us to be, that is, *negated* by the very fact of being represented, Kristeva notes:

> Woe unto him who thinks that you *are*—in good part or in bad, no matter. First, narcissism crumbles and the superego says, "So much the better, there's one problem out of the way." But the body seems to need an identity, and it reacts—matures, tightens, like stone, ebony. Or else it cracks, bleeds, decays. All according to the symbolic reaction that is more or less likely. Then, the symbolic covering (constituted by acquired knowledge, the discourse of others, and communal shelter) cracks, and something that I call instinctual drive (for lack of a better term) rides up to destroy any guarantees, any beliefs, any protection, including those comprised by father or professor. An aimless drifting ensues that reconciles me to everything that is being shattered—rejecting what is established and opening up an infinite abyss where there are no more words. (Kristeva, "The Novel" 162–63)

It is a reconciliation with our negativity, our solitary emptiness, that in the end compels us toward symbolic expression, toward an anchor in the discourse and community of others. Relishing the comfort of narcissism is a retreat from public life to the imaginary. A failure to move beyond desire for the imaginary, that is, failure to move from the perfect image of ourselves that we project in order to spare us from a separation from others, is in effect fatal, resulting in the death of the social self, or psychosis.

Narcissism can be the motivation for love and often takes this guise in adults who have not fully developed beyond this stage. The "amorous hysteria" that a lover experiences is evidence that one has transferred an image of the "ideal other"—who is none other than himself—to another. As Kristeva explains: "It is essential for the lover to maintain the existence of the ideal other and to be able to imagine himself similar, merging with him and even undistinguishable from him" ("Freud and Love" 250). This kind of attachment can result only in ill; in order to preserve the image of the ideal lover, the narcissist must do away with anything that threatens perfect assimilation of self and other. The other cannot be represented as something less than or different from the ideal of a perfect self. The story of Romeo and Juliet illustrates the dilemma of narcissistic attachment. As Kristeva explains,

Romeo cannot see Juliet other than be blinded by her, and he can only perpetuate that ecstatic state by "dedicating his body to death, in order to become immortal within the symbolic community of others restored by his love precisely" ("Freud and Love" 253).

Narcissism can drive far less dramatic antisocial acts than a lover's suicide. So much so, I would argue, that it threatens not to be recognized as the true motivation for seemingly altruistic behavior. The individualist projection of self as the responsible skeptic, resisting the collective interests of groups that fail to account for the interests of individuals, can function as a screen for narcissism. Under the guise of protecting oneself and others from evil—or at best unhealthy—external influences, the individual strives to trust himself best, that is, to regard his own judgment as a perfect ideal. One perfects oneself through remaining unsullied by the influence of popular ideas, or in the aesthetic humanism of Christian and Platonic philosophy, undistracted from one's attachment to God or to reason—with either goal being formed in one's own self or soul. The ideal intellectual pursuit is one that allows no intrusion from the outside. Humanist individualism, like narcissism, is a closed system; it delivers the satisfaction of an incestuous infatuation.

Rhetoric governed solely by the philosophy of humanist individualism, I would argue, is subject to the seduction of narcissism. Freud explains narcissistic love as the quest for perfection, a search for the ideal self, and he goes so far as to suggest that the state of being in love with another is but another manifestation of narcissism, for one "in love" has reopened the door to perfection through, as Lacan puts it, "a veritable subduction of the symbolic, a sort of annihilation, of perturbation of the function of the ego-ideal" (Lacan 142). The ego-ideal, as Freudian psychoanalysis informs us, is supposed to function as a socializing element. Our imaginary perception of an ideal allows us to see ourselves in a symbolic relationship to others, locating our different imaginary subject positions in the environment of others (Lacan 140–41). Narcissistic love destroys this symbolic functioning, giving us the illusion that what we imagine ourselves to be—perfect in relation to others—is somehow real. In effect, narcissistic love destroys the symbolic relationships that we develop with others and confuses our desires with the object of our desires.

Rhetoric that is dominated solely by humanist individualism encourages us to engage in the pursuit of self-perfection, that is, to validate narcissism as an ethical social practice. It places the speaking subject in contest with others, while forwarding the contradictory aim of improving conditions for all humankind. Narcissistic rhetoric enjoins us to present ourselves to others as unified wholes, single-minded in our philosophy and untroubled by doubt, uncertainty, and an unsavory tendency toward inconsistent behavior. Rhetoric governed by this narcissistic ideal presents the self as perfect, coherent, and fully committed to an ideal stance, a position, or warrant. The rhetorical task for the speaking subject is to position himself as a perfected, consistent self, or, as Wayne Booth described this image some thirty years ago, as "an ideal, literary, created version of the real man" (Booth 74–75; quoted in Coney 164). In short, I wish to argue that the ideal "implied author" of literature is the "rhetor" of narcissistic rhetoric. The skill of the rhetor is determined by his or her ability to manage separate identities or rhetorical selves for separate purposes. The task of choosing a particular self to portray (or the audience's decision to assign such a role to a rhetor) is not only a function of the way we construct truth in a world where truth and value are relative, but in such a world, it has also become essential in order for us to communicate to others through text. As Mary B. Coney suggests: "To posit the concept of implied author is to suggest that the requirements of the text demand a being different in significant ways from the actual author" (163).

Various pragmatic considerations govern the construction of the ideal rhetor or implied author, many of which, on the surface at least, appear motivated by concern for others rather than self-interest. Among them are: the need to present a unified point of view when a text is multiply authored; the need to identify oneself as the plural ("we") or a member of some larger community sharing similar values; the need to present oneself differently to different audiences; the need to eliminate personal bias when reporting findings; and the need to express certainty in order to move an idea forward so that its significance may become clear (Coney 165–66). And perhaps the most significant pragmatic justification for the rhetor's presentation of a unified singular self is the belief that one's very subjectivity may impose upon the reader or listener a version of reality that is wrapped up in the author's personal sense of self rather than appropriately related to the context it is called upon to address. As Coney puts it:

> Without such a rhetorical voice, authors would have no filter, no selective device to shape the language in a text for a reader. They would be hopelessly ensnared in their own subjectivity, unable to free themselves from the context, and, more importantly, free the context for the reader. (170–71)

In short, the effort to extract one's presentation of self from one's personal subjectivity is interpreted as resistance to narcissism or, as Kristeva might say, resistance to the semiotic, or the domain that expresses self-desire, in favor of embracing the symbolic, or the domain of public and political discourse.

But I wish to argue that the very effort to construct ourselves as implied authors embracing the conceit of a unified self with the presumably selfless aim of communicating more clearly to others is a covert surrender to the seductive sway of narcissism. Indeed, rhetoric that promotes the ideal of a single public voice can threaten to institutionalize narcissism, a fact that has been perhaps more overtly recognized in the past than it is today.

In a review of the role of rhetoric in the politics of the Tudor State, Linda Gregerson tells us of the link between narcissistic eroticism and the political position of the courtly subject. Gregerson renders an interpretation of the speeches given by Robert Devereux, second earl of Essex, at the annual Accession Day tilts. The tiltyard scene was a stage for dramatic entrances by the queen's courtiers, who, while dressed in regalia and riding their chariots, gave speeches to the queen that expressed their devotion and sang her praise. The speeches often employed allegory to depict the political relationship of the speaker to the queen. Narcissus was a common figure in these displays. In one staged by Devereux, he enacts a contest in which Devereux, posing as the knight of love, devoted to the queen, is tempted by others to follow Philautia, or self-love. As Gregerson explains the scene:

> The choice confronting the Knight of Love is the choice between two derivations of service. Will the path of ambition be self-motivated and self-referential, or will it be mediated by the Queen's patronage? Will public and private labor be derived from the Queen's bounty and refer its progress back to her, or will profession take its shape from self-interest alone? (5)

The tiltyard allegory of the earl of Essex creates a double subject position for the earl in relationship to his patroness: Should the queen endorse him, he will serve her resolutely; should she not, his only choice is to honor Philautia. Yet at the same time, in serving the queen, should she endorse him, the earl too serves Philautia, or the queen's self-interest. The queen, love's object, is the foil for Narcissus. Gregerson notes that the "derivation of subjectivity and public career from erotic paradigm . . . was in fact the dominant trope of courtly patronage in Elizabethan England" (8). The connections among self-love, public service, and political rhetoric were most unabashed in this context. Far from interpreting public service as selfless devotion to some altruistic end, the courtiers of the Tudor State regarded public service, and the rhetoric that instantiated it, as fully motivated by personal gain, ambition, and fulfillment. The gesture of presenting a public self as devoted to love was an exercise in self-preservation, a means of establishing one's position as subject to the patroness, the queen.

In Tudor politics, the behavior that overcomes the sway of Philautia is civic activity. As Gregerson notes, the Tudor ideal of public service rests upon Bacon's description of the mature self as active in civic life; those who fail in civic service "live a solitary, private, and shadowed life . . . and besotted at last with self-admiration, they fall into such a sloth and listlessness that they grow utterly stupid, and lose all vigour and alacrity" (Bacon 13:89–90; quoted in Gregerson 23). Yet as Essex's tale reveals, public service serves ambition, too, and cannot be easily disjoined from self-interest.

Contemporary interpretations of the presentation of self in rhetoric confirm that the very act of projecting a unified self in our public contact with others is irrevocably self-interested. Kenneth J. Gergen notes that by positing a conscious self or "mental world" behind a specific rhetorical identity, groups are able to position themselves in such a way as to justify their particular account of the world to others (72). If one's view of the world is construed so that it is acceptable to others, the benefits accrued to oneself are considerable (Gergen 73). In rhetoric, mental characteristics attributed to the speaking voice often determine whose voice is heard; hence, rhetoric becomes the vehicle that instantiates the mental self. For instance, the discourse of science that explains the external world in terms of hierarchically organized classes and categories serves to echo the "image of the good scientist," whose business it is to prove rhetorically some correspondence between external reality and our mental perception of it (Gergen 79). Mental attributes are certified rhetorically to serve personal as well as professional interests:

> If a mother can convince her children that sharing is a virtue, she may enjoy hours of tranquility. If a suitor can demonstrate that he is replete with fine qualities, he may win the love he so desires. . . . And if the scholar can make a clear and compelling case, he or she may enjoy position, and respect (one dare not add "fortune"). (Gergen 72–73)

Self-interest is the foundation of the rhetorical presentation of a unified mental self that, if judged successful, prevails over someone else's vision of a valid mental self. Base self-interest is the conscious aim of the rhetor's effort to present a unified self, and this objective is interpreted as just, ethical, and moral.

The moral aim of presenting a unified self to an audience is defended most ardently in the rhetorical practice of developing authorial voice. Indeed, in institutionalized visions of the mission of rhetoric, particularly the vision of rhetoric promoted in composition instruction, development of a distinctive verbal identity has been associated with both rhetorical expertise and ethical behavior. And further, the cultivation of personal identity through rhetoric is simultaneously promoted as a moral and practical aim. Development of personal integrity and honesty has been associated in composition pedagogy with the creation of a distinct authorial voice. In a recent critique of such teaching, Lester Faigley questions some pedagogues' preference for personal writing in an "authentic voice" about private experiences, asking, "Why is writing about potentially embarrassing and painful aspects of one's life considered more honest than, say, the efforts of [a] student . . . who tries to figure out what Thucydides was up to in writing about the Peloponnesian War?" (121). In addition to privileging individual, private experience as more authentic, pedagogy in favor of cultivating personal voice ultimately places an emphasis on personal difference, strategic positioning, and pride in performance that parallels psychological investment in the narcissistic impulse. For instance, Ken Macrorie, a well-known advocate of developing students' capacity for personal expression in writing, asks composition teachers to demand "honest" writing that aims for the truth. The honesty and truthfulness of the individual is presupposed to be self-evident in his or her rhetorical production. Macrorie advises teachers:

> Ask for honesty. Say you know school doesn't often nurture it, that at times you will be dishonest, as everyone is without realizing—but you will try to speak the truth. Pass out an example of phony writing—pretentious, empty:
>> But the area which caused Henry and I to become steadfast friends was outdoor sports.
> Also pass out an example of honest writing, like this:
>> He doesn't have legs. Not ones that feel or move. It's been that way four years now. Wheels. I was scared to talk at first, felt like a kid asking what it is that everyone's talking about. But we did. We used to goof around and tell dirty jokes. I always felt a little fake. Dan and I took him to the bathroom every day. Had to be done in a special way. We were there once, Dan asked a question—I don't remember what it was—something involving my ability to work.
>> "What do you think I am, a cripple?" That's what I said. I didn't look at anyone, just the wall. For about half an hour, I felt very whole, but my stomach was tin foil. They were quiet, both of them. Quiet as being alone. I wished someone would cut off my arms. (82)

A great many philosophical presumptions about the nature of truth and the validity of identity underlie Macrorie's advice. Notably, this advice reflects a prior judgment that writing can be assessed accurately to reflect the moral intent of the author. Furthermore, it equates a narrative of identity, in this case an assumption of physical ability as opposed to disability, with a discourse of truth telling. At the same time, it presupposes that public environments for rhetorical expression, particularly the public school setting, actively work against one's telling the truth because they suppress self-identity. Nevertheless, Macrorie presumes an institutional setting can help writers develop a voice of identity that will make them appear honest within a scene that dismisses honest expression. All of the themes of psychological narcissism come to play in Macrorie's scenario: The student subject discovers his separateness from the world (the school) around him and, as a way of both validating and consoling himself, claims his self-revelation is the best and true object of his love; he thus works to express this identity in his writing as the logical end point of a quest for truth within the school setting.

Rhetoricians' emphases on personal voice are redolent with narcissistic overtones; this is perhaps most evident in Peter Elbow's narrative of self-discovery subtitled "How I Got Interested in Voice," which appears in his composition textbook *Writing with Power*. Elbow's more recent writings have not favored the development of voice over attention to the mutual interactivity of author and audience, but his framing of this argument in the past is a particularly useful illustration of the problems connected with valorizing authorial identity as a measure of rhetorical authenticity. In some twenty pages that report in confessional tones his assessment of valued writing, Elbow in his textbook tells would-be writers of his struggle to determine why some kinds of writing had always appealed to him and others had not. Writing with "voice," Elbow tells us, "had a kind of resonance, it somehow rang true" (283). Voice is "what most people have in their speech but lack in their writing—namely, a sound or texture—the sound of 'them' " (288). Good writing, writing with voice, says Elbow, "has the lively sound of speech" but also gives off "a solid thump that I can trust" (292). The art of distinguishing that trustworthy "thump" comes down to intuiting from the style of the writing that a real person with a singular identity is behind it. This "voice" is not only what speaks the truth, but also that which gives the speaker the power to be perceived as truthful:

> Most of us . . . neglect this power of real voice. . . . Sometimes it takes a kind of crisis situation for us to take the wraps off our power: perhaps we are backed into a corner and have to speak out to save our self-respect; perhaps it is an important letter. . . . We notice the surprising impact of our words on the listener or reader. For once our words *work*. Often it is startling or even frightening when other people actually feel the full weight of our words: it so seldom happens. (Elbow 294–95)

To be powerful is to assert a self that is recognized as distinct. As Elbow says, "The words somehow issue from the writer's center . . . and produce resonance which gets the words more powerfully to a reader's center" (298). The point is to target an effect, to "go deep" and to do so by asserting "sound, rhythm, energy, and individuality" in writing, all the qualities that are missing from writing "without voice" (299). Writing with "voice" has as its object the development of the person; it centers on this object, in fact, with all of its attention.

Elbow asserts that the quest for voice is distinct from the relativist claim that we use a particular voice—in fact many voices—to achieve a specific purpose in a specific situation. Yet his elaboration of this concept, dotted with caveats and uncertainty and punctuated regularly by his use of "I," is not substantially different from Walker Gibson's argument a decade earlier for the importance of developing a writer's persona. And for Gibson, this was clearly an effort to play a role. For him, writing "honestly and candidly" has little to do with finding the real self Elbow asks writers to seek. Honest writing is an honest act, with emphasis on "act" in two senses of that word: a "forthright and affirmative" action, "calculated to bring order into a situation," and a kind of "playacting, since the means of communication we choose, the roles we play, the language we use, are creative decisions we make, even though we usually make them quite unconsciously" (Gibson 4). The fact that someone is perceived as a "phony or hypocrite," is not the fault of having not used one's real voice, as Elbow might have put it, but rather the result of playing "a wrong role, an inappropriate or misleading one" (Gibson 4). Although one's attention to real or genuine identity is not the focus of Gibson's rhetoric, identity as a person with feelings is designated to be the key to effective expression. The purpose of adopting a persona is to convince the reader of one's attitude toward or engagement with the subject under study. The writer through voice projects an attitude onto a subject, projects a self, if you will, which in turn becomes his and the audience's object of attention in viewing the subject. Gibson notes:

> If we stand, say, on the lip of the Grand Canyon and we call the scenery beautiful, we are probably speaking like any tourist, and we are certainly saying the obvious. The persona is a bit dull; we become, in the comedian's expression, a "straight man." But if, facing the town dump, we say "beautiful," we become immediately a more complicated person! (Gibson 67)

The importance of an expression lies in what it says about the speaking subject, though its object is to interpret what is observed: Expression interprets the world as it is meaningful to the self. But it does more than this. Verbal expression projects the self onto objects that give it identity, interpreting them as they substantiate and secure the self's place in the world. An essential purpose of asserting self-identity rhetorically is not only to convince an audience of the sincerity of one's conviction but also to assimilate the world observed as part of oneself. Rhetorical identity involves more than presenting the image of an ideal, coherent, or honest self to another; it behaves hegemonically to appropriate the world without and bring it to terms with the world within. The gesture here is unidirectional: The rhetor interprets the world to make it his, rather than interprets himself to the world. In the act of interpreting the world, the rhetor subordinates that which is external to his internal perfect vision; he forms an attachment not to the world, but to the world as he himself represents it. Attachments to objects outside oneself as representations of oneself figure psychoanalytically as yet another aberration, namely, fetishism. As I shall argue next, this tendency, like narcissism, also has a specific manifestation in valued rhetorical practices.

Fetishism: Displacing Love

Fetishism is the displacement of narcissistic attention onto an object. In her complex reinterpretation of Freudian and Lacanian psychoanalytic theory, Kristeva identifies fetishism as a failure to incorporate the symbolic and thus a failure to project a thesis, whether linguistic or other. Unable to do this, a subject may imagine an object as a substitute goal on the way to the process of signification, that is, the process of interpreting the world to others. Through this substitution the subject "shifts the *thesis* onto *objects*":

> Fetishism is a compromise with the thetic; although erased from the symbolic and displaced on to the drives, a "thesis' " is nevertheless maintained so that signifying practice can take place. . . . [It] is a displacement of thetic on to the realm of drives. (Kristeva, "Revolution" 114–15)

Fetishism, like narcissism, protects one from the loss of identity threatened by the discourses of the symbolic order. In the psychoanalytic tradition of Freud and Lacan, Kristeva interprets the development of a thesis in symbolic discourses as a submission to the dominance of the phallus, or the father. Fetishism displaces the need for the phallus or symbolic order with some other object that figures as an attachment to the imaginary maternal phallus.

To examine how fetishism functions in expressive acts, we can turn to Kristeva's interpretation of da Vinci's artistic technique as an enactment of fetishism. Expanding upon Freud's analysis of da Vinci, Kristeva notes that in his quest for "a maternal phallus, the painter never stopped looking for fetish equivalents in the bodies of young people, in his friendships with them, in his miserly worship of objects and money, and in his avoidance of all contact with and access to the feminine body" ("Motherhood" 244–45). Da Vinci as a child was dominated by the power of the symbolic in the person of his father, who was a distinguished authority in public life (Kristeva, "Motherhood" 244); further, he was removed from his mother as a child and raised by a dominating stepmother. These influences, concludes Kristeva, led him to go "in quest of fantasies that insure any group's cohesion [and to reveal] the phallic influence operating over everyone's imaginary." Da Vinci's art represents objects that reflect the influence of authority on imagination (Kristeva, "Motherhood" 245). He reduces the potentially threatening and gratifying exploration of artistic expression "to a simple, technical device, destined to give the effect of representable, desirable, fetishistic forms" (Kristeva, "Motherhood" 245). This reduction is confirmed by his obsession in his later years with science. According to Kristeva, da Vinci's fetishism is realized through his reducing artistic expression to the reproduction of "bodies and spaces as graspable, masterable *objects*." This limited approach to art parallels da Vinci's role as the "complex-ridden center confronting that other function, which carries the appropriation of objects to its limit: science" (Kristeva, "Motherhood" 246).

Kristeva finds a similarity in the aim of da Vinci's fetishistic representational art and science's reduction of the world to objects. She asserts that science through a technologized representation of reality mistakes the objects it produces for things that are real outside the realm of science itself. Marxist critics have explained this link between science and a tendency to reduce malleable environments to a collection of circumscribed objects. Max Horkheimer and Theodor W. Adorno, for instance, assert that the scientist's tendency to reduce the world to graspable objects reflects bourgeois economic objectives to dominate through ownership. Science, the epistemological technology of bourgeois society, is privileged as the mechanism by which things are found to be equivalent and ultimately by which society will achieve a state in which "there is no longer anything unknown" (Horkheimer and Adorno 16). In promoting technical equivalence rather than exposing difference, the ultimate effect of scientific thinking is the reduction of the complexity of the world and all in it to a technical apparatus. This results in the self-alienation of "individuals who must model their body and soul according to the technical apparatus" (Horkheimer and Adorno 29–30). Individuals' reason, in effect, serves as a general tool, useful for the manufacture of all other tools (Horkheimer and Adorno 30).

To demonstrate the pervasiveness of reductionist thinking, that is, the tendency to reduce the unknown to graspable objects, Horkheimer and Adorno reinterpret the Odysseus myth as a parable of bourgeois technicism. The hero, Odysseus, must try by all means to know all that can be known, taking all risks in the name of possible success (Horkheimer and Adorno 62). The road to success is acquisition, that is, the subjugation of anything in the world that is foreign or different from oneself to the status of an object that is fully subject to one's recognition of it. The subjugation of women is justified because women represent the difference that must be eliminated if Odysseus is to conquer the world around him. Hence, Odysseus abandons Penelope and rejects Circe's charms in the manner he might treat property that serves his interest: The wife is the husband's possession and the courtesan sells herself for his pleasure (Horkheimer and Adorno 71–74). The systematic technicism of such rationalization is figured by Horkheimer and Adorno as equivalent to male identity; and male identity levels and conquers to avoid both recognizing something other than itself and redeeming or changing its own nature:

As a representative of nature, woman in bourgeois society has become the enigmatic image of irresistibility and powerlessness. In this way she reflects for domination [the male] the pure lie that posits the subjection instead of the redemption of nature. (71–72)

To make woman/nature the object of male/scientific attention, one must subject her to reason, in effect harbor her within the limited understanding that defines oneself as in control of a system in which she is one of the world's objects:

> Prostitute and wife are the complements of female self-alienation in the patriarchal world: the wife denotes pleasure in the fixed order of life and property, whereas the prostitute takes what the wife's right of possession leaves free, and . . . subjects it again to the order of possession: she sells pleasure. (Horkheimer and Adorno 73–74)

Initiative has no place in the bourgeois technicist system; instead, domination and system displace enthusiasm and openness to knowledge—they displace love. In an economic system in which all is a matter of the expediency of an exchange, nothing is at stake. Likewise, in the technicist model of reality fostered by Enlightenment thinking, "the general has no advantage over the particular fact, and all encompassing love is not superior to limited love" (Horkheimer and Adorno 102). In short, obsession with the technique of one's pursuit of truth—in this case, obsession with the system of scientific reason—has no less real value than truth itself.

Fetishism, as a substitute for love, mistakes an aspect, feature, or structure of the thing desired for the thing itself. Marxist criticism itself can reflect epistemological technicism, that is, one's absolute reliance on a chosen method for obtaining and validating knowledge. The "sociotechnical determinism" of Marxism, for instance, brings the actual world within perfect predictable control of the theorist. Once having empirically analyzed the modes of production and accompanying social relationships, Manfred Stanley observes, the theorist has determined through technique "the forms and contents of the more abstract world of ideas and intentions" (7). In effect, technicist Marxism subjugates ideological abstractions to the rubric of its own preeminent ideology. This result is ironic indeed, given the intent of Marxist technicism to expose ideologies that dominate and constrain individual action.

The fetishistic attachment to epistemological method reflected in scientific method and the technicism of Marxism has its counterpart, I contend, in rhetorical practice that controls truth telling through declaring where and how truth may be spoken. Fetishistic rhetoric functions like a dominating ideology, socially determining the possibilities for constructing truth and subsuming the conscious perceptions of the authors who adopt it. In this respect, fetishistic rhetoric enacts cultural and ideological control over individual agency, functioning as a mechanism of social determinism. Fetishistic rhetoric establishes a social territory in which an individual can realize authority over others. One rhetorician, Nevin K. Laib, has claimed that ideological territoriality marks a rhetoric that "is not based on informational content, on logic, on genre, or even on effectiveness and purpose" but rather promotes a set of attitudes or beliefs (582). Laib's territorial rhetoric, like what I have called fetishistic rhetoric, not only rationalizes "social and territorial issues," but also presents "opinions, observations, and hypotheses [as they] express desires as well as informational content" (583). In short, it stakes a claim on the universe of information, impression, sensation, and interpretation by subjecting it all to a controlling image that marks it as possessed by the speaker and some higher authority to which the speaker is privy.

Fetishism operates most notably in the rhetoric of the professions, guiding the way professionals seek knowledge and present what they know as truth. Professions can and do stake an exclusive claim on truth by asserting that a certain epistemological method is the only valid means to explain the world and individuals' place within it. Science, for instance, not only advocates the scientific method as the path to truth, but also presumes that its deterministic descriptions of present reality can both predict any future reality and explain any past. Stanley notes that the technicist goal of science is to reduce the world to objects under mechanistic control:

> The scientific project . . . is to search for evidence relevant to the construction of deterministic models of nature. This requires a mechanistic view of the world in the sense that any explanation of a scientific sort is mechanistic. The ultimate test of understanding something scientifically is the ability to deconstruct and reconstruct the object of understanding at will. (13)

Science makes the world at large conform to a perfect model. The scientific method is flexible enough, John Ziman notes, to allow the scientist to alter various constructions at will. While in some instances science works to account for reality within a predetermined scheme, in others "science seeks out situations where there is a direct contradiction between theory and experience, and then modifies theory in the light of experience" (Ziman 47). In either case, faith in method dominates the choice and the presentation of investigative results. As a linguistic representation of the scientific method, science writing appeals to a "hypothetical, very sceptical reader"; presents impersonal arguments in the passive voice; and is dominated by "quasi-logical" conclusions stressing "the rational necessity of [a] particular outcome" (Ziman 62). Attachment to the rubric of the scientific method can be obsessive, that is, application of the method can negate or dismiss perceptions and observations that are not compatible with scientific epistemology. The device of the method can dominate to the extent that observation that cannot be measured is simply not recognized as valid information.

A fetishistic attachment to method as a means of knowing the world is not exclusive to the rhetoric of science, although it is perhaps more easily detected in that domain. In a study of technology as it defines contemporary life, Albert Borgmann claims that the device paradigm now dominates our access to information in all spheres of life. Devices that range from technical instruments that measure physical phenomena to political institutions that offer a means of shelter and livelihood have become the tools by which the goods of the world become available to us. What characterizes all devices that allow us access to knowledge or other commodities is their ability to make something available with minimal investment or skill on our part and minimal acknowledgment of their role in doing so:

> The machinery [of a device] makes no demands on our skill, strength, or attention, and it is less demanding the less it makes its presence felt. In the progress of technology, the machinery of a device has therefore a tendency to become concealed or to shrink. (Borgmann 42)

The scientific method has become invisible as a device for determining the laws and regulations of the physical world to the extent that the characteristics it defines are assumed to account fully for reality. A desire for this kind of control can accompany the uncritical application of a device or a method that makes knowledge available. Such has been the case in the social sciences. Even though human behavior is inherently complex and often defies reduction to a set of laws, social science attempts to classify it. The motivation behind this continuous attempt to classify the unclassifiable, Borgmann claims, is control. He offers the following example:

> If mental well-being is defined as a kind of euphoria induced by direct stimulation of the brain, then we may well be able to devise a function of contentment. If the work world is taken over and streamlined by a state apparatus, we can design regulations to control employment and productivity. The success of such social theories will depend on the extent to which we accept an equivalence of the reduced and the original phenomenon. (Borgmann 70–71)

Whether or not we accept Borgmann's claim that a hegemonic quest for control underlies the epistemologies of the social sciences, it is fair to say that the rhetorical task for those who practice the profession of science is to prove to those who read or hear of their findings that the scientific paradigm fully explains reality. Within the profession itself, this involves using rhetorical devices that assert that conclusions reached are explained fully by the scientific paradigm, and further, that they parallel scientific findings by others whose work already is accepted by the scientific community. Hence, scientific progress is often marked by voluminous and meticulous citation, and this practice in itself serves as a means of continuously validating work. The choice not to cite a relevant work is in effect a signal that it is not acceptable to the scientific community. Ziman notes that "in the diplomatic language of scientific discourse, silence speaks against assent" (66). And in contrast, numerous citations of one's findings by others and inclusion in lectures, textbooks, and course syllabi take these findings further from the scene of debate and make them eventually "immune from criticism" (Ziman 67).

Outside the profession of science, the rhetorical task of convincing an audience that scientific findings are true becomes a matter of asserting the complexity of the subject matter and the special ability of the scientist as expert to interpret it. In popularizations of science, there are but two appeals, as Jeanne Fahnestock notes: One cites the wonders of nature as they are revealed by the "breakthroughs and accomplishments of the scientists themselves," and the other cites the application of scientific findings to more mundane or practical uses (279). Both appeals valorize science as a device by which the audience might obtain a commodity, either an understanding of the mysteries of nature or a product to improve one's way of life. In short, they bring the world under the control of those who speak about it, thus protecting them from feelings of alienation and separateness. Scientific rhetoric presents a defense against the unknowable, and if accepted without dissent, displaces the need to understand anything beyond what it displays. It reduces reality, as Kristeva has said of da Vinci's realist art, to "representable, desirable, fetishistic forms" ("Motherhood" 245).

Although I have chosen the rhetoric of science as a particular example of the fetishistic appeal, I must acknowledge that the use of reductive devices to make reality accessible pervades discourse in many professions, and the legitimacy of this reduction is defended both by professionals and those who use their services. Professionals delegate their authority to judge to the rubric of a discipline or institution, and nonexperts delegate their authority to judge to the experts. Stanley notes that "the acceptance of 'expertise' may be defined as the conscious or unconscious delegation of one's cognitive authority over some part of the world to persons one regards as more competent than oneself in the exercise of cognitive judgments" (97). The expert stands between the nonexpert and the alienated world, bringing it to him in terms he can understand. Whether one reduces reality to an epistemological paradigm or hands over its interpretation to an expert, one ultimately defends the self against engagement with the world. This is the ultimate ploy of fetishism, to substitute a device for true, total, selfless attention to what one desires, to, in effect, remove the self from the possibility of discovering truth unmediated, that is, from experiencing the world without protection from it. Whether we attribute the tactic of ceding all authority to a dominant epistemology, to the forces of social determinism, or to the psychological aberration of fetishism, the outcome is the same: The self resists experience in its obsession with a dominant perspective that comfortably reduces all that is inaccessible to something that can be possessed within this perspective.

Both narcissistic and fetishistic behavior is reflected in our valued rhetorical practices. Writers are encouraged to adopt a personal persona that establishes their identity as separate, distinctive, unified, and coherent, a perfect narcissistic image of the self projected against the world that threatens to consume it. And they are enjoined to fetishize the epistemological methods of a profession and thus control reality through both subjecting it to reductive principles and disguising its true diversity—variety that threatens to make it unknowable. Certainly both of these rhetorical strategies have had and do have pragmatic value. To present a stable, coherent persona to an audience is to ensure some level of communicative authority; one hopes to be perceived by the reader/listener as a trustworthy, competent bearer of a message that likewise can be assumed to be truthful and accurate. To present a reductive model of reality by applying the scientific method, a sociological or critical theory, or some other epistemological technique is to define a complex world in terms that can be shared by those who have put faith in that way of knowing, thus ensuring their common progress toward understanding the world in these terms.

I cannot help but acknowledge overtly that in making this very case for a new approach to rhetoric, I myself have chosen to present a fairly standard argument, following the established epistemological tradition of making claims and backing them with evidence that I demonstrate to provide support for these claims. I have aimed to present my arguments in a consistent manner, to maintain integrity in my use of terminology, and to project an unwavering personal commitment to my ideas within the rhetorical stance I have maintained. In short, I have aimed to present a unified authorial voice within the rhetorical tradition of argumentative prose. I have chosen this time-honored strategy because it allows me to communicate my views to others in terms that are familiar and that give some assurance that my words and others' interpretation of them are being generated and received within the same interpretive framework. I make no apologies for this approach (a topic to which I shall return in chapter 6); however, I also do not wish to assume that my delivery of a coherent persona and explanatory epistemology supersedes the need to recognize or admit experience that does not fall within these self-imposed limits. To do so would be to flatly deny that acknowledging such "other" experience would lead to the truth. There are other ways than I have chosen here, certainly, to picture a world and its meanings. The fact that there are other ways, however, does not in itself counter the validity of *this* way of attempting to express a common truth. At the same time, I must acknowledge that a dogged attachment to only favored or accepted argumentative methods can and perhaps has imposed limits on our potential to discover knowledge that might improve our common lot.

We might consider, for instance, whether the medical profession would be more equipped to handle diseases of women, children, and the aged if researchers were as responsive to the anecdotal and "unscientific" complaints of such patients as they are to empirical evidence gathered under controlled conditions. We might consider, too, whether those legislating our tax structures might be able to devise a more comprehensive model for reducing the effects of poverty than welfare if poverty were defined legally not only in economic terms but also in psychological, sociological, and ethical terms. If in speaking and listening to others we choose to value *only* rhetoric that adheres to the constraints of demonstrating intellectual coherence and of supporting a single, preferred epistemology within a single knowledge domain, we will ultimately face a wholly untenable result: denigration of human value, paucity of spirit, and wholesale dismissal of the complexity of the very world we live in. I believe this is the path that valorizing resistance to some kinds of experience can threaten to carve for us. And this is the price to be paid when we maintain the illusion of projecting a single and fully coherent self-identity in a single and fully transparent world.

Beyond Resistance Toward Acceptance

We can and do feel trapped by theories of self-representation and rhetoric that assert that we achieve integrity of identity through selectively denying some effects that the world and others in it have upon us. In an essay on literature and value, J. Hillis Miller records a poignant personal experience of our communal dilemma through reflecting upon a recent trip to Moscow to study with Russian scholars. Miller notes the deep gulf dividing the Russian scholar's pursuit of a spiritual truth that unites a people and the American scholar's commitment to individual points of view that deny an overriding value. He is personally troubled by diversity in values—American versus Russian as well as American versus American. These differences perplex a man who claims that "recognition and tolerance of difference, along with a conviction that one is really right, is a central component of Western-style democracy" (Miller 26). Unable to make rational sense of his experience in its totality, Miller admits that though "a cheerful man," his own "cheer is darkened by a small shadow of foreboding as [he peers] into an unpredictable future, like someone trying to steer a sailboat into the fog" (26). How can he make sense of these contradictions, particularly as they point to the "radically different assumptions about the social values of literature" (26) that can exist among reputable scholars in different cultures?

Academic rhetoric leads Miller to assess the individuals he met and interacted with in terms of their differences, conflicts, and distinctions. The comfort his Russian friends felt with ideology, honoring its capacity to both support and eliminate diversity, produced in him a disquieting fear. But at the same time he hints that Americans in pursuing skeptical inquiry have lost their spirituality and respect for historical tradition (Miller 22–23). Miller avoids any reflections on this experience that might lead him to an enfolding truth. His critical impulse is not to assimilate the diversity he perceives, but rather to distinguish, dissect, segregate, and categorize difference. It is an impulse rooted in our rhetorical tradition of distinguishing perspectives by defining contrasts and ignoring the ties that bind over difference. The effort to resist results in a constraint against expression; Miller cannot say what he really knows about the gap scholarship forces him to maintain between others and himself. He does not admit that opposition to the Russians' perspective keeps him from truly knowing what he experienced; and ironically, it is that very opposition that defines him as an individual. Miller only can note his dilemma as a dilemma. In effect, he is kept from fully expressing himself by the very rhetoric that displays his identity to the world both as a man and as a scholar.

Our dominant critical and rhetorical theories of language and identity simply do not permit the conscious self, the individual, if you will, to be entirely truthful. The self cannot be truthful without risking individual integrity and identity; to face the world without resistance is to give in and give up—both ways are repugnant to Western ideals of individual empowerment and authority. On the one hand, we cannot ignore the advantage that this distancing and positionality affords. Our ability to back away from a stance, to resist the impulse to assimilate it and instead to endeavor to treat it as something disconnected from our individual integrity, keeps us from acting only to please or strengthen ourselves and from evaluating the discoveries of others only in terms of how they conform to our own beliefs. But on the other hand, we cannot expect to find an encompassing truth if we accept such resistance as a condition for meaning and self-identity. It would seem that the only way to resolve the dilemma of achieving selfhood while pursuing truth that goes beyond it is to redefine individual consciousness as something that does not come to life by resisting external influence, but rather thrives by integrating the external world as part of its developing identity. But we must ask ourselves, in practical terms, whether such a shift in perspective is philosophically defensible, and further, what is at stake in entertaining it.

The angst Miller feels over the scholarly gap between American and Russian literary theory is in its most direct sense an academic issue: No one is getting hurt by the lack of coherence in these scholarly perspectives; each camp's resistance to the other is not overtly compromising a larger good. It would be nice, certainly, if we could feel more connected to those whose experiences and worldviews differ from ours. But is it equally satisfactory not to be so connected? I strongly suggest that it is not. Scholarly disputes such as the one Miller describes strike us as harmless enough, but the consequences of such investment in identity can be costly in practical terms.

One of the more well-known accounts of a scholarly rivalry is Bruno Latour and Steve Woolgar's *Laboratory Life,* a tale of the truth telling of two top scientists in competing laboratories, each racing to isolate a particular hormone. The decision of one scientist at one point in his research to accept as firm a conclusion that he had previously claimed to be uncertain allowed both labs to begin pursuing a course that, in fact, had been identified by the lead scientist in the rival lab several years earlier. The decision to resist compromise for years allowed each scientist to maintain separate reputations and to accrue separate economic support to expand facilities and hire personnel. It was only when that external support dried up for both laboratories that one player dropped the effort to maintain competing projects in favor of a course that might generate new funds for both (Latour and Woolgar 124–47). The resistance to knowledge in order to preserve separate reputations and support chronicled here cost the unsuspecting public a very great deal. But the cost of resistance can be far more devastating than losses of time and money.

As I write, the scandalous civil war in Bosnia strikes me as pressing evidence of the failure of resistance either to preserve identity or to ensure progress. Here the world watched a nation that once hosted the Olympic Games in a city of culture, peace, and dazzling beauty tear itself in two, sacrifice its men, women, and youth, and destroy its accomplishments in order to claim that what once was identified as one should now be indissolubly two. Is this what resistance to the influence of the other must mean if carried to its bitter end? Certainly, some will say that we can avoid another Bosnia and preserve difference too; we can decide rationally not to let our differences bring us to blows and patiently stand beside one another, tolerating differences we find mutually untranslatable by maintaining separate lives. I myself have witnessed this kind of compromise as a white, reasonably well-to-do resident of the city of Detroit. This city's failure to thrive as a place where men and women of different ages and ethnic backgrounds gather to work and celebrate the many pleasures of a diverse, yet shared, culture can be attributed to many material woes—the deadening dominant influence of the automobile industry, the popularity of suburban life, and the fear of crime and its companion, poverty, among them. But most important, in the end, Detroit's failure has been the result of a society's inability to reconcile differences between people whose identities and self-worth are staked on their skin color. The difference in values associated with these identities indeed have been well honed: The desires for privacy, excellent schools, and barrier-free commerce compete with the desires for mass transportation, more jobs, and drug-free streets—all these aspirations, equally valid, are grouped and pitted against each other in a ceaseless identity with race.

Being unwilling to consider a larger truth does have consequences for each and every one of us, even scholars who some say idly ponder ideas while dispensing with the practical problems of real people. Just what does it cost *not* to reconcile the Russian's spiritual faith in ideology with the American's pragmatic belief in those ideas that prove to be most plausible or useful? Perhaps little. But we might also consider that if we cannot reconcile difference here, where the outcome affects only a change of outlook, we certainly have no chance to do so where the material stakes are high and dearly felt.

We need a way to champion the self as integral with all we conceive as reality, a way to accept a deepening relation to and acceptance of our environment as a mark of both personal growth and our progress toward knowledge that enfolds all we experience. And we need a philosophy to guide our efforts to reflect on the world as it appears to us, to help reveal the meaning of difference and lead us to change ourselves in order to accommodate its sense. It is to this end that I am proposing a phenomenological approach to subjectivity and identity as one that not only validates and preserves the conscious self, but also articulates how consciousness is laid open to new possibilities for meaning. As I shall show in chapter 3, phenomenology describes how the world constitutes or shapes us through consciousness and how we consciously intersect with the world. Phenomenology limits truth neither to ourselves nor to the world we perceive to be outside ourselves, but rather finds it in the dynamic of our engagement with this world. Consequently, phenomenology permits us to regard the search for truth through rhetoric as a natural function of our everyday existence. Our search for truth does not begin or end with a definitive, single perception or declaration, but rather continues always in our daily activity of speaking/writing/living. Our increased understanding of this activity as truth seeking quiets our compulsion to claim a single unique voice and to reduce all diversity to laws or patterns. Truth seeking instills the desire to interpret our personal history as it reflects and accumulates the larger experience of the community of humankind. This alteration of one's personal perspective does not ask that we abandon individual beliefs, nor does it threaten individual integrity. Rather, it replaces our impulse to resist with a steady embrace of the world where we dwell. It is the meaning of this process that we shall explore next.

3

Developing a Phenomenological Rhetoric
Lessons from Husserl and Merleau-Ponty

To SEEK TRUTH through rhetoric, we must believe, first, that truth is fully accessible in human experience, and second, that individuals reach truth not through resisting, but rather through fully embracing the world outside. In this chapter, I propose phenomenology as an alternative to the limiting philosophy of relativism and the constrained constitution of authorial identity in resistance. As I have discussed at length in chapters 1 and 2, both theories are supported by much of current textual criticism. I advocate phenomenology both as a philosophy and as a rhetoric. As a philosophy, phenomenology presents a guide for living reflectively, that is, a guide for gaining a true understanding of all that we experience through attending to its meaning. As a rhetoric, phenomenology grounds our consciousness within the world where we may both experience and express truth more fully. Phenomenology differs radically from philosophical relativism and the rhetoric of resistance: It establishes an essential relationship between individual experience and truth and thus validates expression that embraces the world rather than remains distant from its influence.

In advocating a phenomenological perspective, I have chosen to revisit a theory of being and meaning that has been rejected outright by some scholars and transformed to meet the constraints of philosophical relativism by others. This return to phenomenology is grounded explicitly in the need to restore rhetoric as a truth seeking practice. I hope to demonstrate here that postmodern rebuttals of phenomenological philosophy have dismissed its potential to offer an alternative to both absolutist epistemologies, which equate truth with dogmatic method or religious faith, and the antifoundationalism of philosophical relativism. My arguments rely upon an interpretive reading of the phenomenological philosophy of Edmund Husserl and Maurice Merleau-Ponty. In addition to providing a broad outline of phenomenology's guiding principles as articulated by these philosophers, I entertain counterperspectives offered by Jacques Derrida and Jürgen Habermas with the aim of showing them to neither adequately represent phenomenology's project nor effectively foil it. In the main, my discussion focuses upon three principles in phenomenological philosophy that together define our lived experience within the world as the means through which truth is found; they are:

1. all essences or truths are located in subjective experience;
2. truth is an outcome of intersubjective understanding; and
3. intersubjective understanding progresses toward truth through expression (writing/speaking).

Each of these assumptions suggests a way that rhetoric works or ought to work to further our endeavor of making sense of the world. Following my explanation of these premises and my consideration of objections to them, I conclude by refashioning them as operational guidelines for a phenomenological rhetoric—a rhetoric that both validates and motivates truth seeking in human experience. These guidelines in turn are developed separately and in greater detail in chapters 4 and 5.

As readers encounter this chapter, I ask that they consider "phenomenology" as a concept in development; it refers both to a philosophical tradition of examining meaning in human experience and to my adaptation of this tradition to suggest a rhetoric of truth seeking. It does not refer to phenomenological theories of reading or criticism. Although phenomenological theories of textual interpretation are based on some premises of phenomenological philosophy—in particular, the notion of subjectivity as it explains how the world is perceived in consciousness—these theories, as expressed in the work of Roman Ingarden and Wolfgang Iser, among others, have had the limited aim to explain reader response as it relates to and impacts upon the meaning of a literary text (see Ray 8–40). Phenomenological criticism aims both to distinguish the separate roles of the text and the reader as defined by linguistic or psychoanalytic structures and to explain the contribution of such structures to an eventual meaning. My concern is not to distinguish the structures of either language or consciousness but rather to explore the implications of siting all meaning within consciousness. Phenomenology accounts for consciousness as it is constitutive of both meaning and the implicit object of meaning—truth. My aim is both to explicate a phenomenological view of truth and meaning and to suggest that it points to a reconstrual of the purposes of rhetoric as it is currently theorized and practiced.

Through Subjectivity Toward Truth

Phenomenology locates truth in subjective human experience through equating the study of being with the study of meaning; it rejects a dualistic distinction between the world as it exists and the world as we interpret it. This basic premise unites a great variety of phenomenological theories that are vastly divergent and have been applied to fields ranging from psychology to literary criticism. In the main, for the phenomenologist, to examine the meaning of the world is to examine the world itself. There are no gaps, differences, or distinctions between one and the other. Furthermore, phenomenology projects human consciousness as *the* agent that gives meaning and shape not only to social ideologies or operational systems that direct and motivate human action, but also to the existence of the world itself. It explains "humanity in the world" not in terms of humanity's history of being but in terms of what our existence in the world means. Abstract terms that address being conceptually, such as "absolute being," "truth," and "objectivity," are articulated in phenomenology as they have meaning within human consciousness and not as ontological concepts. From the phenomenological perspective, the only possible origin of absolute being, truth, and objectivity is human experience. To believe otherwise is to attribute these concepts to a consciousness that resides outside of human will and directs human consciousness (theism), or it is to reject the existence of the external world and thus claim it unknowable, except through representation (idealism).

For instance, to assume that truth expresses an essential meaning of reality beyond the grasp of human consciousness is to assume necessarily that the world outside of oneself is one kind of reality and that our consciousness of this reality is in effect another reality. To evaluate our consciousness as a measure of external reality, one must assume a mediator, since reality as it exists outside us is never given. Our belief in this never-given reality is justified in Cartesian epistemology by the existence of God, who "validate[s] our 'natural' beliefs" (Nakhnikian xvi). The alternative to assuming a God responsible for reality and our conscious belief in it is to deny the separate reality of material substance and propose an idealist epistemology in which all existence has reality only in human consciousness (Berkeley's solution) (Nakhnikian xvi).

Phenomenological philosophy attempts to explain the relationship between self (consciousness) and other (external reality) in another way. Rather than describing what we know about the world in terms of concrete and abstract things, it defines knowledge as a relation between self and others resulting in meaning. Hence, phenomenological philosophy has as its end point not being but rather the essence of being, which is meaning. A philosophy of meaning implies a relationship between a mind and an other; thus it rejects the purely idealist stance that views knowledge as self-contained in individual consciousness. In explaining the phenomenological investigation of meaning as the basis on which to evaluate being, Cornelis A. van Peursen, a modern-day interpreter of Husserl, notes that "meaning . . . is never a self-contained entity but always implies a relational structure, a reciprocal reference between consciousness and world" (30). Thus, meaning through which we know of being and being through which we know of meaning are entirely a function of human subjectivity:

> Man is man only with and through reality and this reality has meaning only as human reality. That's why man can only be described in connection with the total structures of reality. Similarly, reality can only be described in relationship with man. (van Peursen 18)

The basic phenomenological premise that reality has meaning only as it stands in relationship to the self is congruent with postpositivist interpretations of the relationship between language and reality. Rejecting the positivist notion that words have a direct relation to external things, phenomenologists interpret language as a symbolic medium reflecting a relationship between individuals and their environment that is developed in subjective consciousness; the meaning of language resides in consciousness, where it is developed intersubjectively. As I noted in chapter 2, current critical theory endorses the idea that truthful meaning is created intersubjectively; however, the dynamic for developing intersubjective truth is described as a dialectical process in which opposing forces of "individual self" versus "social other" are either eliminated through contest or neutralized through consensus. Truths produced as the result of contest and consensus are by these circumstances necessarily limited, contingent, or both. The phenomenological perspective on rhetoric that I shall propose avoids limiting truth not only through placing it within subjective experience, but also through defining intersubjective knowledge as open, inclusive, and noncontestual.

Phenomenologist philosophers assert that all essences or truths are established in subjective experience; hence, truth is integral with rather than separate from human activity. The argument that truth is a function of human experience has been developed most specifically by Husserl and has been extended by modern-day interpreters who hold that human experience can be processed by human consciousness to arrive at an essential meaning (van Peursen 35–39). Husserl distinguishes between a psychological interpretation of meaning in consciousness that is based on empirical observation and a psychical interpretation of meaning that is based on intense inner reflection. It is the interpretation born of inner reflection, the psychical interpretation, that forms the subjective field where truth exists and truth seeking takes place. In exploring the major tenets of his theory here, I shall address postmodernist objections to Husserl's perspective articulated by Derrida and Habermas and at the same time suggest how Husserl's view has more significant consequences for the practice of rhetoric.

A major premise of Husserl's phenomenology is that to arrive at the essential meaning of the world as we experience it we must eliminate our presuppositions about the nature of that very world. The method he developed for accomplishing this task is complex, almost mystical. He employed several metaphors to describe its components. David Stewart and Algis Mickunas provide a straightforward explanation of these metaphors, describing Husserl's three main processes for deriving meaning: the "phenomenological reduction," which refers to the means by which we reduce "a complex problem to its basic elements"; the "phenomenological epoche"—the latter word borrowed from the terminology of the ancient Greek skeptics—which refers to the process of suspending judgment in order to open oneself to the "full range of the different dimensions of experience"; and finally, "bracketing," a mathematical term harking back to Husserl's first career as a mathematician, which refers to the process of putting a supposition or perception aside to be dealt with differently in the process of arriving at the essential meaning of a phenomenon (Stewart and Mickunas 26–27).

Husserl elaborates how essential meanings, that is, truth about the world as it exists, become known to the individual through reflection upon experience. He posits that the individual is capable of discovering truth through intentional attending to the meaning of the world as he or she experiences it. This intentional attending is the operation of consciousness that Husserl dubbed the phenomenological reduction, the mental technique through which one locates the essential elements that have meaning for human consciousness. The phenomenological reduction obtains "absolute evidence" of what is meant by a " 'real datum,' " that is, the true meaning of things we perceive to exist (van Peursen 45). Husserl illustrates this through conducting detailed analyses of the essence of what we mean by a phenomenon such as a "real object." Through concentrated attention one can deduce that the essential meaning of the term "real object" is entailed in a "certain continuity of time." Van Peursen explains the process of reaching this conclusion thus:

> One sees an object, closes the eyes, opens them and then again sees the object. . . . Even though the question about reality is eliminated [in the phenomenological reduction], the object presents itself in temporal duration with the "pretention" of being something that lasts and is real, precisely because it has the time-form of not disappearing when I close and reopen my eyes. Phenomenologically, then, a certain continuity in time is implied in "real object." (van Peursen 45)

While he identifies consciousness as the seat of the meaning discovered through the phenomenological reduction, Husserl simultaneously denies that reduction of perceived experience must result in some evidence that is contingent upon environmental factors, such as culture, history, or even biological influences. The individual derives essential meanings through articulating the relationship between consciousness and "givenness," that is, our sense that the real or material world exists prior to ourselves. Husserl approaches givenness not as a naturalist, who describes empirically the world outside of consciousness, nor as a humanist, who defines reality historically in terms of conscious observations reported in different times and circumstances. Rather, he explains "givenness" through the meaning of "objectivity," the perspective in consciousness that is believed to define "given" reality:

> To study any kind of objectivity whatever according to its general essence (a study that can pursue interests far removed from those of knowledge theory and the investigation of consciousness) means to concern oneself with objectivity's mode of givenness and to exhaust its essential content in the processes of "clarification" proper to it. (Husserl, "Rigorous Science" 90–91)

What are the processes of "clarification" proper to exhausting the "essential content" of objectivity? According to Husserl, the phenomenological reduction, when performed consciously as a heuristic, is the means by which to access the essential objective meaning of all things in the world as they are revealed in human experience.

Given that Husserl claims that all there is to know about the world is a function of the mind, he has been accused of idealism. Furthermore, his phenomenological reduction, quite aside from its enormous complexity, has been rejected outright by some as a scholastic exercise, particularly since Husserl claimed the reduction to bear no relation either to natural science or to idealism but rather to represent a truly essential subjectivist approach to philosophy (Farber 5–7). Aside from these difficulties, Husserl's "reduction" merits serious attention as a method of interpreting reality. The phenomenological reduction is based on a study of the concrete; Husserl maintains that the world experienced in its diversity is a "particularization" of the essential structure that defines meaning in consciousness (van Peursen 48). Hence, he does not deny psychological or social influences on interpretation of meaning, but like relativists, he claims that these meanings are not essential. By essential, we mean not reliably accountable for our complete experience of the world as a lived-in reality. He goes further, however, to claim essential meanings *are* available through attending to pure consciousness. Consequently, these meanings can be expressed—an assumption that gives credence to the possibility of obtaining truth through rhetoric.

Expression of essential meanings is animated solely by consciousness; language for Husserl is merely the technology that functions to mean as long as intentional consciousness stands behind it. It is here that Derrida's theory of language and meaning stands in stark contrast to Husserl's. Derrida makes no distinction between language as reference and language as sense (Garver xiii–xvi). He faults Husserl both for separating language as indication from language as expression (Derrida, "Speech and Phenomena" 17–26) and for presuming that a theory of knowledge has "the authority to determine the essence and origin of language" (Derrida, "Speech and Phenomena" 7). At the same time, however, Derrida finds no difficulty in suggesting that a theory of signs preempts a theory of knowledge. Derrida echoes the phenomenologist perspective in suggesting that meaning is subject to the play of differences noted within a language system and between expressions spoken and interpreted at different times and places; this account of language function grounds meaning phenomenologically in language as it is experienced. But Derrida is not interested essentially in meaning *as it is experienced,* aside from how language technologically sets the scene for meaning. In Husserl's philosophy, meaning as it is experienced differs from language's role in creating meaning in that it is not volatile, destabilized, and uncertain, subject to the constant play of differences. Rather, we experience meaning as sense that builds constructively toward something universally true.

Stability of meaning for Derrida is simply an illusion that language creates along with the illusion of being or "presence." Adopting, as he claims, Heidegger's perspective on the nature of being, Derrida aims to distinguish two meanings for "being" as a stable "presence": first, the process of living that brings us to experience a present that appears to stabilize meaning, and second, the stable objects we perceive to be present through experiencing them (Derrida, "Differance" 153–58). What we have forgotten, Derrida insists, is the fact that "presence," what we perceive as stable meaning in the process of living, is but a "trace," that is, "the simulacrum of a presence that dislocates, displaces, and refers beyond itself" (Derrida, "Differance" 156). *Differance* is the technology that produces the trace we believe to be "presence." There is no stable object or stabilizing process that is the goal of meaning suggested by *differance;* it is merely a characteristic of language systems that causes us to believe in a present. Language both defers to what appears to be external to it and differs so that we experience what appear to be changes, variation, and progress in a world of substance. In deconstructing this illusion, Derrida denies that truth can have a foundation in what we perceive to be present. For Derrida, the technologies of language and rationalized thinking (which are indeed required for the phenomenological reduction) bring about our belief in a stable presence; without these tools, presence has no existence because time has no existence. The phenomenological reduction implies presence through implying change over time:

The "world" is primordially implied in the movement of temporalization. As a relation between an inside and an outside in general, an existent and a nonexistent in general, a constituting and a constituted in general, temporalization is at once the very power and limit of phenomenological reduction. Hearing oneself speak is not the inwardness of an inside that is closed in upon itself; it is the irreducible openness on the inside; it is the eye and the world within speech. *Phenomenological reduction is a scene, a theater, a stage.* (Derrida, "Speech and Phenomena" 86)

But this interpretation of phenomenology as a stage upon which presence is created and the truth of presence is confirmed equates the stage with the dance performed upon it. For Derrida, the stage exists to create the performance that becomes reality. For Husserl, the stage and the performer relate to one another to create their reality. The human agent is for him absolutely central to the reality of the event. Derrida faults Husserl's claim that presence could be so absolutely within our control, rebuking what he interprets to be Husserl's conclusion that "the genuine and true meaning is the will to say the truth" ("Speech and Phenomena" 98). In other words, he denies that language and sense are correlated necessarily; that language, consequently, has an essential relationship to knowledge. Derrida deconstructs the stability of knowledge as a presence that is created by the capacity of language to point to a rational structure, a stable "present," if you will, behind the shifting and dynamic reality we experience in everyday living. But to say, as does Derrida, that stable presence is a mere illusion is not to account for its major significance to us. The deconstruction of presence is a less than satisfactory explanation of life as we interpret and experience it.

The limitations of a theory of language and meaning that focuses on instability of meaning rather than intent to share understanding are serious indeed. Such a conception threatens our faith in a future in which we might arrive at common understandings and beliefs that we trust as true. Admittedly, we need not think of deconstruction as an apocalyptic theory. As a mere technique, it does not threaten our ability to act in the service of the moral good. In an appraisal of the role of Derrida's work in a reconstrual of personal ethics, Dawne McCance notes that we can indeed regard deconstruction as a tool in the service of ethics. The fact that it "does not give us an ethics, an address of rectitude" (41) is not cause for believing that deconstruction is "an amorality or an immorality" or that it is "indifferent to questions of justice" (41). Wendy Farley, too, in reflecting upon the pursuit of truth in the aftermath of postmodern thought, notes that for critics "such as Derrida or Judith Butler," postmodern approaches to analysis of texts and societal structures provide the "radical exposure" that "is the prior condition for a more thoroughgoing effort on behalf of justice" (7). In its analytical application, deconstruction admittedly can reveal injustices, power plays, and hegemonic rule imposed upon the unsuspecting and the disenfranchised, yet there is no guiding presupposition behind deconstruction that makes its application in this service preeminent. Deconstruction, in its overt dismissal of a grounding in personal consciousness, has no overt ethical ground. Furthermore, without a presumed goal of some certain and shared knowledge, without the recognition of valid arguments for truth, deconstruction as a guide for rhetorical action can become a mere game. The one who ceaselessly deconstructs arguments to locate their origins in some false foundation or presence plays what Gadamer has called the role of the "spoil sport," someone who does not take arguments seriously as arguments for a possible truth. This dismisses human interaction and the accumulative sense it builds as a valid component of meaning, one that joins us to the concerns of others (see Crusius 46; Gadamer 41–42).

Recognition that human interaction builds accumulative and shared sense is important, but this too is insufficient to explain our individual motivation to contribute to such an enterprise. Habermas presents a theory of communicative interaction that leans heavily on the philosophy of Husserl in specific and on phenomenology in general; however, he rejects Husserl's notion of the autonomy of consciousness and consequently fails to explain individual agency. Habermas asserts that knowledge and truth are indeed formulated intersubjectively through communicative interaction, but such communicative practice is not dependent on the conscious activity of a subject "relating to itself in an objectivating manner" (Habermas, "An Alternative" 323). Rather, intersubjectivity is a function of discoursing as a process in itself. He defines the goal of intersubjectivity to be "mutual understanding," and it is this goal that, when met, keeps the world before us as a present reality. Mutual understanding is achieved through language used communicatively, and in language so used "we can find . . . the structures that explain how the lifeworld is reproduced even without subjects, so to speak" (Habermas, "The Undermining" 149). For Habermas, consciousness is something beyond individual subjects and their persistent need to define an objective presence that gives them and the world identity. The philosophy of the subject, according to Habermas, cannot avoid a dichotomization that defines the subject in opposition to some external other that it either controls or is controlled by, whether that be society as a "normative order" or the subject's own physical body to which it is "related eccentrically." He concludes: "Thought that is tied to the philosophy of the subject cannot bridge over these dichotomies but, as Foucault so acutely diagnosed, oscillates helplessly between one and the other pole" (Habermas, "An Alternative" 317).

To avoid the limiting perspective of the individual subject, Habermas proposes that mutual coherent understanding or true knowledge is achieved not through internal conscious activity but rather through social discoursing. He advocates redefining rationality as a social rather than a cognitive process through which "various forms of argumentation" (Habermas, "An Alternative" 314) are viewed as interdependent and "participants overcome their at first subjectively biased views in favor of a rationally motivated agreement"

(Habermas, "An Alternative" 315). Focusing on the social process of intersubjectivity, Habermas gives no initiatory or ontological privilege to the individual subject as the seat of rationality, seeing, as he does, emphasis on the subject to be polarizing, contestual, and contradictory to the goal of mutual understanding (Habermas, "An Alternative" 315). But to submerge the relationship between individual identity and the perception or development of a valid truth is also an unsatisfactory position; this fails to account for individual agency as we believe it to operate in the everyday world.

Individuals *act as if* they are in control of their identity, albeit that their destiny is constrained by various social forces. They do so because they believe in the possibility of autonomous reflection, of thinking for themselves. For Habermas, autonomous consciousness is not a possibility. We are not consciously in control of anything, although we can "fault" ourselves for the world being as it is, that "fault" being "an involuntary product of an entanglement that, however things stand with individual accountability, communicative agents would have to ascribe to communal responsibility" ("An Alternative" 316). It would certainly be considered naive to suggest in these times that we can extricate ourselves from social influence and think truly original thoughts, as it were. However, it is equally naive, I believe, to suggest that individual subjectivity can or should be dismissed or even overcome in the process of constructing rational argument. Without individual reflection, what possibility indeed can there be for a new mix, a new approach, a new outcome in the communal quest for shared knowledge?

In contrast to both Derrida and Habermas, Husserl focuses on the process of individual reflection as it motivates the potential for mutual understanding and communal responsibility, seating that potential in consciousness. Hence, his work has much more to say about the process of communication as it is directed or manipulated by the individual. For instance, Husserl addresses the issue of how individual reflection leads to a truthful interpretation, that is, an understanding that is universally true. Individual reflection approaches truth through an intense attending to the meaning of lived experience. To engage in such reflection, one must disengage from all presuppositions about the nature of one's experience. As Marvin Farber explains the role of reflection in phenomenology, "one is concerned with the experiences themselves, without any metaphysical commitments about the objects of those experiences" (3).

What is meant by "the things themselves," the term Husserl often employed to stand for the gamut of phenomena in human experience, is difficult to understand and easily misunderstood as a reference to some positivist reality that matches up, one for one, with the thoughts or language we use to refer to it. Husserl meant "things" to refer to "anything of which one is conscious" (Stewart and Mickunas 22), the range of the term including such diverse phenomena as "natural objects, mathematical entities, values, affective states, volitions, melodies, moods, desires, [and] feelings" (Stewart and Mickunas 23). Husserl's concept of letting go of any preconceptions or commitments is even more difficult to comprehend than his "things." It rests on a distinction he makes in the way we apprehend the world in consciousness. Husserl identifies the psychical sphere as that in which subjective consciousness reflects upon and perceives the world directly, unfiltered by temporal and physical limitations of empirical observation or by social and psychological influences upon conscious interpretation of data. The psychical, in other words, clears a space for understanding that is pure, and because it is pure, it is shared universally. We shall explore the implications of psychical reflection for intersubjective communication later, but we first need to explore Husserl's notion of psychical consciousness in order to both explain this difficult concept and account for its apparent contradiction to current theory about the contingency of knowledge.

According to Husserl, psychical consciousness, as opposed to psychological consciousness, is the route by which we understand objectivity and arrive at an objective understanding of the natural or given world. Psychological and psychical consciousness constitute different ways of representing the individual's relationship to the world. Psychological consciousness assumes that the material world is represented as an "appearance," which differs from "reality." "Psychological appearances" are reported through empirical observation and comprise an incomplete picture of nature "out there." In contrast, psychical consciousness assumes no difference between appearance and nature. As Husserl claims, "there is, properly speaking, only one nature, the one that appears in the appearances of things" ("Rigorous Science" 106). One must remember that Husserl's aim is to study meaning, and this aim demands no dualist separation of consciousness and the external world since meaning captures the relation between these entities. The psychical sphere is composed of a continuous conscious impression: It is intuitive, appearing "as itself through itself, in an absolute flow, . . . as now and already 'fading away,' clearly recognizable as constantly sinking back into a 'having been' " ("Rigorous Science" 107). In short, the psychical is always already experienced, thus giving a true impression of the meaning of reality. And furthermore, the psychical is noncontingent; it is constitutive of being and meaning and not something independent of these phenomena yet related to them.

Husserl insists that psychical consciousness, the domain through which meaning is realized, is the route through which the "essence" of reality is understood, and further, that the psychical must be examined intuitively and not empirically. Thus, the "naive" data of individual psychological experience analyzed intersubjectively will not reveal a psychical or intuitive knowledge of reality. Nevertheless, intersubjective psychological experience in conjunction with intuitive knowledge comprises the complete experience of how things exist psychologically in human consciousness ("Rigorous Science" 115–18). Psychical knowledge, the result of intentionally attending to experience, is where the true meaning of that experience resides. For Husserl, psychical "intentionality" does not "bridge" the subject's consciousness and its object in the real world; rather, it forms "an interconnection which precedes the disinction between subject and object," and further, this "interconnection is not static but always in the process of being brought about" (van Peursen 47).

Given our rational tendency to separate ourselves from the objects we observe and to regard our actions as discrete, it is difficult to fathom psychical intentionality as Husserl must have conceived it. To recognize intentionality as a condition about us that is always active, we must begin to view ourselves as achieving our sense of presence and being through a continuous and intentional act of looking out toward what appears to us. From this perspective, every gesture, word, or act we produce forms the seamless whole that is our intentionality, that is, our looking out to the world, creating the view through which we shape ourselves. Stewart and Mickunas describe the difference between intentionality as it was described by the nineteenth-century philosopher Franz Brentano and Husserl like this: "For Brentano intentionality was a causal relationship to the external, concrete characteristics of things. For Husserl intentionality was not a causal relationship to objects but an activity of consciousness which is identical with the meant object" (8). Intentionality is not a concept that we can define psychologically, that is, through interpretation of our discrete personal observations. Hence, the intentional act of inner reflection that leads to the phenomenological reduction cannot be assessed psychologically, that is, through an assessment of our discrete observations of the world.

The aim of inner reflection is to concentrate upon one's "intentional interiority" as this reveals the essence of our consciousness of the external world. This intense reflection, which, as we noted earlier, Husserl has called the phenomenological reduction, involves inhibiting "every judgmental drawing-in of the world as it 'exists' for [us] straightforwardly" (Husserl, "Phenomenology" 24). Through this experience, the world as it "exists for the subject in simple absoluteness" is replaced "by the world as given in *consciousness* (perceived, remembered, judged, thought, valued, etc.)." The things of the world are in effect "replaced by the respective meaning of each in *consciousness* . . . in its various modes (perceptual meaning, recollected meaning, and so on)" (Husserl, "Phenomenology" 24; cf. Husserl, *The Paris Lectures* 12–13). In short, the phenomenological reduction is an intense attending to the world as it has meaning for us, as it shapes our consciousness of the world and ourselves in our perceptions, thoughts, judgments, and memory. Intentionality is the quite serious business of behaving as *the* agents who are constructing, shaping, and responding to reality. Furthermore, it is the act that validates our consciousness as the harbinger, stronghold, and perpetuator of truth. Far from being held captive to the constraints of biological or cultural influence, consciousness creates the condition for these meanings and the means for judging them as distinct. The essential meaning which consciousness attains through intense reflection, then, is the result of a perpetual assessment of worldly experience as this both differs from and accounts for static assessments rendered in biological or cultural terms at given points in time.

Husserl refuses to accept that cultural or biological history "out there" determines the conscious interpretation of reality achieved through inner reflection, for this leads to what he defines as "sceptical subjectivism." To accept the skeptical perspective would be to destroy "validity" as it has meaning in human experience. Husserl critiques this line of thinking as follows:

> [If we deny the meaning of validity, then to say] an idea has validity would mean that it is a factual construction of spirit which is held as valid and which in its contingent validity determines thought. There would be no unqualified validity, or validity-in-itself, which is what it is even if no one has achieved it and though no historical humanity will ever achieve it. ("Rigorous Science" 125)

In short, our capacity to understand the essence of validity as a concept establishes it as a meaning with existence in human experience. To eliminate validity would be to deny our experience of validity as it has meaning for us; in doing so, we thus reject the only validity or truth available to us, psychical meaning obtained through inner reflection.

Phenomenology asserts that both the existence of reality and our knowledge of it are affected by how we value it. For Husserl and phenomenologists in general, "there is no consciousness in itself and there is no reality in itself" (van Peursen 18). Just as surely, one does not exist without the other. Husserl asserts that the constant intention to know the truth permits one to distinguish true knowledge from idiosyncratic perception. It is this view toward experience that both allows and compels the possibility of sharing its meaning and value with others and that makes Husserl's phenomenology a particularly apt guide for rhetorical practice. Missing both from Derrida's theory of the signifying properties of language as they suggest a present reality and Habermas's theory of communicative rationality as it leads to mutual understanding is any sustained interest in the speaker as one *intending to know*. Quite aside from the metaphysical question of what accounts for being or directs human agency, speakers' everyday activities in the world presume an intention to know if for no other reason than to preserve their very existence. This subjective desire requires that we relate to others so that we make our intentions known. Husserl's phenomenology confirms this basic premise and further suggests that our intent to know is the catalyst and generator of knowledge, whether that be accomplished through the technology of Derrida's *differance* and/or Habermas's communicative interaction. In short, psychical reflection, as Husserl describes the intent to know, suggests a relation between the individual (self, internal consciousness) and his or her environment (other, external world) that has important implications not only for a philosophical theory of being but also for a rhetorical theory of communicative practice.

If we accept the phenomenological perspective that being is—or rather, *means*—an intuitive or psychic *consciousness* of being, then our quest to understand being must lead us to examine human consciousness as the ongoing process of determining being as meaning. If determining meaning is an intense introspective activity, highly personal, then it cannot deceive us. It cannot be something standing outside what we know, something that merely persuades us that what we know is the same as some different reality. What we know the world to mean *is* what it means. The phenomenological perspective, in short, offers us the potential to resolve the relativist's dilemma of accounting for truth. Since truth has meaning for us, it is, in effect, within our grasp. Truth is not relative to a set of constraints, whether biological, psychological, or social, nor is truth an exclusive possession of a group, a religion, or a science. Rather, truth is achieved consciously through careful attention to the meaning of lived experience. There can be no objective truth "out there" because the very idea of truth and its objectivity lies within our consciousness; hence, it is there that we must look for hope of its articulation. At the same time, the search for truth is not solipsistic, wrapped up in one's knowledge of self; rather, truth seeking entails the interaction of the conscious self with the lived-in world. The freedom of this process, as this implies both freedom of the subject to interpret and freedom of the subject's environment to change, is addressed by the phenomenological process of intersubjectivity, the concept we shall explore next.

Seeking Truth Through Intersubjectivity

Phenomenologically speaking, truth can reside nowhere else *but* in human experience since it is conceptualized entirely within human consciousness. Nevertheless, the mere activity of consciousness does not necessarily lead it to truth, that is, to define a complete and continuous understanding of reality in all its complexity. This potential, however, exists in the interactive relation formed between the subject and the lived-in world, that is, in intersubjectivity.

Phenomenologists explain intersubjectivity as a relation that generates consciousness and can lead us to truth. Husserl, for instance, defines intersubjectivity as the psychical functioning of consciousness that relates the individual to the environment. Merleau-Ponty expands Husserl's description of psychical activity to explain: first, how we intersubjectively derive a unified or shared understanding of the world as it has meaning for ourselves and others; and second, how speech functions to help us achieve this understanding. In presenting the views of both philosophers here, I shall interpret intersubjective consciousness as it might figure in a rhetorical epistemology, that is, a way of finding truth through rhetoric.

As I noted in the previous section, Husserl distinguishes a psychological or empirical assessment of reality from a psychical or intuitive assessment. The former is based on an evaluation of discrete observations within a given epistemological framework. For instance, the observation that a desk is an inanimate object relies upon epistemological assumptions about what does and does not constitute an animate object. A psychical assessment, according to Husserl, requires that we abandon all preconceived epistemological frameworks when examining a new phenomenon to get at the essence of what something means in our experience. Hence, we would examine the "desk" of our example as it functions as a meaningful reality within the world we live, breathe, act, and interact within, *without presupposing* something about its ontological substance, that is, about its origins in a real or ideal world. The psychical assessment is not limited to a discrete observation, but rather reflects the whole of our lived experience; psychical consciousness of meaning develops within us as we continue to relate to the world.

For Husserl, intersubjectivity is defined as the intuitive "pure" relationship of consciousness to its environment that results in a direct experience of things as they are, freed from the contingent influences of biological, psychological, or social constraints. In short, intersubjectivity can be assessed as suprapersonal, that is, functioning beyond the meanings we project on our environment that reflect idiosyncratic experience or sociocultural interpretations. Hence, intersubjectivity accounts for the possibility of consciousness achieving a "directly given" experience of reality; it is the unadulterated, "pure" relation of self to environment that enables consciousness to perceive what is essential about what it observes. All this may seem contradictory within our current scheme of viewing the world and our perceptions of it as totally separate—the premise of Cartesian dualism. But Husserl sought an entirely new ontology by which what we have defined as universal and existing free from the influence or interpretation of individuals is found only within reality as it is lived by us. As van Peursen explains, Husserl's ontology privileges consciousness as the catalyst of being; within consciousness, "self reflection becomes a never-ceasing movement which constantly reveals new horizons of the given reality." In other words, "logical possibility and factual reality then appear to belong together" (van Peursen 110).

Consciousness always implies "consciousness of." Therefore, we cannot speak of consciousness as an entity without referring to that which is the focus of its meaning making activity, the lived-in world. Likewise, we cannot speak of the being or presence of the world without referring to consciousness, for the very notion of being is a product of consciousness. Therefore, our sense that our lives have a place in the world and that our activity in the world changes the world's objective reality is generated in the *relationship* of our consciousness to the things it is conscious of. Intersubjectivity does not presume the social interaction of one consciousness, which is developed psychologically within an individual, coming into contact with and being influenced by another individual consciousness, nor does it presume the social development of shared consciousness. Husserl indeed addresses the social phenomenon of communicative interaction among individuals and groups, but not as this is essential to his notion of intersubjectivity. Again, for him, intersubjectivity constitutes a pure relationship between consciousness and the things it is conscious of that is not subject to psychological or cultural influences.

One can, of course, argue convincingly against Husserl's insistence that individual and cultural interpretations can be divorced from the intersubjective relation that forms consciousness of the essential meaning of experience: Our "situatedness" makes a conscious separation from cultural influence difficult, if not impossible, some would say. However, one must remember that the phenomenological perspective does not recognize a distinction between consciousness and the things one is conscious of; situatedness *is* consciousness, not a mere contingency of consciousness. Individual and cultural interpretations are for Husserl empirically devised observations, subject to historical and biological contingencies rather than essential meanings generated by the ongoing phenomenon of lived experience for which there is no contingency. One also can object that Husserl inadequately explained how language conveys the meaning of consciousness. Derrida, as I noted earlier, interprets Husserl's inadequate explanation of language in meaning development as an overt result of having separated language, a worldly phenomenon, from meaning, a transcendental phenomenon. However, one also could treat Husserl's failure to account for language as an embodiment of consciousness as an omission rather than a misunderstanding of the function of language. Such is Merleau-Ponty's reasoning.

Merleau-Ponty addresses concerns about Husserl's idealism through designating communication as a necessary condition for consciousness, and consciousness in turn as a necessary condition for communication. His work toward a philosophy of communication has been interpreted by some critics as a needed corrective to Husserl's idealism (Farber 9–11; van Peursen 37). Yet Merleau-Ponty has himself countered this claim. In the preface to his *Phenomenology of Perception*, Merleau-Ponty contrasts Husserl's concept of consciousness with transcendental idealism. The latter position asserts that the world conceived in one's own mind and the minds of others is all part of the same noncorporeal idea; as Merleau-Ponty puts it, "the I and consequently the Other are not conceived as part of the woven stuff of phenomena; they have abstract validity rather than existence" ("Preface" xii). Merleau-Ponty argues that Husserl rejected the notion that everything within and outside us is part of a unitary transcendental ideal; if this were so, one could not conceive of the Other as someone who has a vision of one's self that differs from one's own vision of self. To truly assert the cogito—that is, the subject's power of intentionality or of fixing attention on the lived-in world—one "does not define the subject's existence in terms of the thought he has of existing," nor does one displace the world with "thought about the world" or "the world as meaning." Rather one "recognizes my thought itself as an inalienable fact, and does away with any kind of idealism in revealing me as 'being-in-the world'" ("Preface" xiii).

Moving from his argument against pure idealism as the foundation for the phenomenological perspective, Merleau-Ponty goes on to explain the phenomenological reduction as an exercise that is constituted in psychical intersubjectivity but that can never be made complete in thought. It is important to explore this notion here, for it is the foundation upon which Merleau-Ponty explains consciousness as the intersubjective interaction of the I and the Other. The phenomenological reduction, Husserl's mental heuristic for getting at the essence of our perception of things in this world, cannot be made complete in thought, Merleau-Ponty speculates, because if it could, we would be "absolute mind," and if that were true, we must again face the paradox of our perception of the Other and its gaze upon us. The aim of the reduction, then, is not to reduce the world to ideas, but rather "to make reflection emulate the unreflective life of consciousness" that finds meaning in being in the world ("Preface" xvi). There is, then, no absolute being that is made explicit by means of material senses or conscious thought; rather, our consciousness achieves the "laying down of being" ("Preface" xx). To understand this difficult concept, one might turn to the analogous situation of the "laying down" of meaning in speech. In the act of speaking or listening, meaning is not captured, fossilized, and preserved, but rather is set forth, activated, and enlivened. This point has important implications for the function of philosophy as it uses language to study truth and being. "Philosophy," Merleau-Ponty concludes, "is not the reflection of a pre-existing truth, but, like art, the act of bringing truth into being" ("Preface" xx).

Merleau-Ponty attends specifically to the role of language in "bringing truth into being" through making explicit the interactive relation of the I and the Other in the lived-in world. For Merleau-Ponty, to examine consciousness as it reifies being is to investigate consciousness as an embodied phenomenon. Precisely this orientation has led scholars of phenomenological philosophy to distinguish his view of the phenomenological reduction from Husserl's.

Husserl appeared to make the goal of the reduction "an impersonal and ideal subject" (van Peursen 37). In contrast, Merleau-Ponty clearly grounded the reduction in lived experience. For the latter, the most direct evidence of consciousness "in the flesh" is communication. It is communication that articulates the interpersonal process of coming to the meaning of being. Merleau-Ponty reveals, as Richard L. Lanigan notes, "the process nature of personal and interpersonal *Being* by examining the lived-encounters of perceptive and expressive *signs* that are experienced as communication" (45). He concretizes Husserl's notion of the essence of meaning by locating essence in communicative signs, that is, in gesture and expression (speech). For Merleau-Ponty "essences are signs reflecting and constituting meaning-as-lived" (Lanigan 46). Following Husserl, Merleau-Ponty regards meaning as a function of experience as it is contextualized personally and interpersonally, yet he explicates this theme far more concretely. For him, meaning is, in a sense, acting who one is. The overt evidence of meaning as action is speech communication.

Speech echoes back our reflection on the lived-in world so much so that we understand ourselves not as thought, but rather as speech. Merleau-Ponty demonstrates this by reminding us that children understand the social meaning of language before they understand the world they direct their speech toward:

> [The fact that a child understands himself as a "member of a linguistic community" before he understands nature] is conditional upon the subject's being able to overlook himself as universal thought and apprehend himself as speech, and on the fact that the word, far from being the mere sign of objects and meanings, inhabits things and is the vehicle of meanings. ("The Body" 178)

The meaning of speech is gestural, in the sense that words gesture toward a "context of action" in which they make sense ("The Body" 179). Further, speech gestures toward others through "taking up of others' thought"; speech creates "an ability to think *according to others* . . . which enriches our own thoughts" ("The Body" 179).

It is important to put Merleau-Ponty's views of speech within the perspective of our larger claim that both meaning and its truth lie in an intersubjective relation, that is, in the interaction of consciousness with the world to which it attends. Rather than asserting that true consciousness is defined by "pure reflection" that is removed from both psychological perception and natural language, as does Husserl (van Peursen 55–59), Merleau-Ponty posits that true consciousness develops through communication. Understanding, then, comes about through communicative involvement with the world. My consciousness of the world is the result of my speaking in it, and thus reaching toward it and defining myself through it. Speaking is a fully interactive state in which self-realization is simultaneous with world-realization in a mutual involvement of mind, body, and language (Merleau-Ponty, "The Body" 184–87). This mutuality of involvement extends to others as speech activates meaning that is shared in intentions and gestures recognized throughout a community:

> The sense of the gestures [words, for instance] is not given, but understood, that is, recaptured upon an act on the spectator's part. . . . The communication or comprehension of gestures comes about through the reciprocity of my intentions and the gestures of others, of my gestures and intentions discernible in the conduct of other people. (Merleau-Ponty, "The Body" 185)

Reciprocal sense developed between self and others is not static or discrete, but rather is continually moving, extending, and expanding through speech communication. Speech makes us conscious of meaning that transcends our individual empirical understanding of the world. As Merleau-Ponty explains it: "Speech is the surplus of our existence over natural being" ("The Body" 197). Through speech we can move beyond an empirical or psychological interpretation of lived experience to actively create new meaning. It is this function that he claims "conditions the child's first use of speech and the language of the writer" ("The Body" 197).

The embodiment of consciousness in speech is manifest during spontaneous conversation when physical speech appears to occur simultaneously with thought, and also in the act of writing when putting words down on paper stimulates ideas. Merleau-Ponty's notion of embodied speech differs starkly from Volosinov's conception of how consciousness is shaped by language as I presented it in chapter 2. In Volosinov's scheme, speech is the platform, unstable though it may be, upon which consciousness is built. The agent's relationship to speech is parasitical: Without speech assimilated from without, agency is mute. For Merleau-Ponty, speech instantiates a mind at work, interpreting and breathing life into language. This description of meaning-in-process is very close to the role assigned *writing* in current postpositivist critical theory. *Writing* is the dynamic process of creating an interpretation, rendering a conscious assessment of what is, whether that rendering is accomplished through the medium of speech, the medium of writing, or the media of listening and reading, acts that also entail active interpretation. However, the dynamics of this "writing" are not for Merleau-Ponty a function of signification, as they are for Volosinov or, more recently, Derrida, but rather a function of consciousness.

Derrida's argument that speech controls the interpretive process proceeds from the assumption that meaning is a presence created by language in itself, quite aside from its relation to objects or speakers' intentions. As Derrida claims: "The absence of intuition—and therefore the subject of the intuition—is not only *tolerated* by speech; it is *required* by the general structure of signification, when considered *in itself*" (Derrida, "Speech and Phenomena" 93). For Derrida, the disappearance of the writer or the objects to which a text refers does not prevent it from meaning something. He claims that Husserl's mistake was to consider difference to be derivative, to be a function of the gap between some absolute meaning and the real-world representation of that meaning in a text. For Derrida, the whole mechanism of perceiving being as a presence is derived from the essential difference language defines between one moment of reality and some other moment. The only event that ends this play of difference as it is perceived by the speaker is physical death: "Only a relation to my-death could make the infinite differing of presence appear. . . . *Differance* . . . becomes the finitude of life as an essential relation with oneself and one's death" (Derrida, "Speech and Phenomena" 102).

The "infinite differing of presence" (102) is a function of presupposing a death—each moment a death, and, finally, my death. The difference we see between one interpretation and another, or between interpretation and a perceived reality, creates the desire to project an end to difference that will produce a word, a voice, in which *differance* is not present. The absence of difference is for Derrida the condition for absolute knowledge, for "*within* the metaphysics of presence," absolute knowledge is "the *closure* if not the end of history" ("Speech and Phenomena" 102). In other words, we must believe in an end to any possibility of change or difference *if* what exists in the end is to be absolutely known. There is a price to pay for this absolute knowledge, as Derrida notes, and that is a loss of the very distinction that defines the present reality we seek to know: We are left with "*a voice without differance, a voice without writing,* [that] *is at once absolutely alive and absolutely dead*" ("Speech and Phenomena" 102).

In contrast to Derrida's theory of deconstructed presence, phenomenology presumes that consciousness makes use of its capacity to distinguish difference, to attend to the world as real and to the world as imagined, in order to maintain the relationship between self and world that is reality. So long as we maintain this relationship between the real world and the ideal, we create knowledge absolutely; to destroy that relationship would be in turn to end all knowledge absolutely. There is a subtle but important difference in these two philosophical perspectives. In the former case—that is, Derrida's—consciousness and knowledge are created by *differance;* in the latter case—that is, Husserl's—consciousness is the relation that creates *differance* and knowledge. Merleau-Ponty identifies speech as the physical expression of conscious knowledge: Speech compels consciousness to go beyond itself, to outstep itself, lose and regain itself through contact with others; it is both touch and text. And *as* both touch and text, that is, in its simultaneous function of being (or the self's experience of being) and interpretation (or the self's experience of meaning), speech (writing) is the means by which the self comes to believe its sense of the world can be true. Speech lays down the meaning of what it is to *be*.

To summarize our discussion thus far, the phenomenological perspective on meaning as it relates to one's lived experience suggests that: first, meaning and its truth are generated through consciousness that is embodied in the subject; and second, consciousness is not a static presence but an interactive relation through which human agents develop an intersubjective understanding of the world that can be declared true. Through attending to our consciousness of the world as we experience it, and through our exercise of speech (writing), we achieve the possibility of attaining an interpretation of the world that is true. In short, because nothing stands between us and the world we live in that can show us a "truer" meaning that is not available to us, we can believe there is no truth that goes beyond our grasp. This is not to say that our mere existence and our mere persistence with speech (writing) as the expression of our consciousness will lead us to truth, just as water will continuously seek its own level, or as the planets will continuously rotate around the sun. Rather, it is to say that truth can be made available to us through the activity of conscious reflection and speech communication.

What is it that directs speech (writing) toward the pursuit of truth? If attaining truth is not indeed the necessary outcome of our random acts of living and communicating with each other, what directs us toward truth? The answer to this question is suggested by a third premise of phenomenological thought, the notion that consciousness is purposeful, directed, and hence, capable of progress. This directedness moves humankind to compose together the meaning of our existence, to move through intersubjective consciousness toward a universal understanding of ourselves, our purpose, and our place on earth. We see purpose, I shall argue next, in participating together in *writing* the world; and it is in doing so that we move together toward writing truth.

Through Intersubjectivity Toward Writing Truth

The third premise of phenomenological philosophy to be explored here is the idea that intersubjective consciousness is a continuous activity that constantly progresses toward the goal of mutual and true understanding. Consistent with the objective of phenomenological philosophy to explain the world and humankind in it as it has *meaning*, phenomenological philosophers have tended to view human experience as purposeful, that is, as having the goal of increasing conscious understanding and of ultimately reaching truth. The essential meaning of *meaning*, if you will, is a "truthful interpretation." We behave as if the meaning we assign to our human experience *adds to* or *en-hances* our conscious understanding of the world. We behave as if meaning *is* truth or at least *can be* truth, in other words.

The notion that human agents have the capacity or will to achieve truth is justified phenomenologically by the fact that we behave and act in this world as if we have this power, and hence to deny it is irrational. A philosophical denial of human agency is unjustified because our conception of ourselves as conscious beings entails our capacity to make meaning and behave meaning-fully. To deny this conceptually would be to deny that a conception that is conceivable is in fact a conception. Similarly, as I noted earlier, some philoso-phers have denied "validity in itself," although, as Husserl has pointed out, this is, in fact, "what [validity] is even if no one has achieved it and though no historical humanity will ever achieve it" ("Rigorous Science" 125). Human existence has meaning for us as something purposeful, progressive, and direc-tional. Phenomenologists Husserl and Merleau-Ponty have argued this philo-sophically and have also cited empirical justification for their claims. Husserl addresses the philosophical grounds for viewing conscious activity as direc-tional, and Merleau-Ponty defines the role of speech in composing or *writing* this direction. Both apply their philosophical views to the world they live in, and in so doing suggest the role of rhetoric in our conscious pursuit of truth.

Husserl claims that the phenomenological pursuit of essential meaning is humanity's most important work and is the object of all quests for knowledge. In other words, in seeking knowledge we are always by definition seeking truth (essential meaning), and that task must be guided by phenomenology as an overriding science. He gives a concise rendering of this argument in an article over which he labored much, a shorter translated version of which first appeared as the entry for "Phenomenology" in the *Encyclopedia Britannica* of 1929. The unabridged version of "Phenomenology" has subsequently been translated and published by Richard E. Palmer. In this longer piece, Husserl argues that the scientific quest for knowledge can be addressed most ade-quately by the epistemology of phenomenology, which he defines as the sci-ence of explaining the world through the experience of inner reflection. Husserl views phenomenology as a possible universal science that presents the a priori ground for a "genuine form of an all-embracing science of fact" ("Phenomenology" 33). Phenomenology places fact within a hierarchy of kinds of knowledge, all embraced by *essence,* which is true meaning. Fact rep-resents an experiential or psychological assessment of reality, whereas essence represents a psychical or intuitive assessment of reality. As I explained earlier, the former is influenced by circumstance, the latter is forever true; essence transcends the perception of the moment because it is perpetual, living, on-going.

In the unabridged version of his *Britannica* article, Husserl explains the mediation between psychological and intuitive assessments of the world as "the transcendental problem." We must constantly distinguish between assessments of the world that are contingent and those that ring true. This is particularly difficult because the world is constituted both *by us* and *for us,* whether we are aware of that or not:

> Every acceptance of something as validly existing is effected within ourselves; and every evidence in experience and theory that establishes it, is operative in ourselves, habitually and continuously motivating us. This [principle] concerns the world in every determination, even those that are self-evident: that what belongs *in and for itself* to the world, is how it is, whether or not I, or whoever, become by chance aware of it or not. ("Phenomenology" 27–28)

If the world we perceive as real—or any other world, such as the world of fantasy or abstract ideas—seems unintelligible to us, we must ultimately go back to our consciousness of the world to understand it: "For [the world] is precisely as meant by us, and from nowhere else than in us, that it has gained and can gain its sense and validity" ("Phenomenology" 28). It is this fact that makes our conscious lives necessarily directed toward the pursuit of understanding and ultimately truth; our whole existence is consumed by the act of making conscious sense of the world and thus defining our place in it. At the same time, the very existence of a relation between psychological (or empirical) consciousness, which *is* contingent, and psychical (or intuitive) consciousness, which *is not*—as well as the possibility of variability in that relationship—requires us to pursue truth actively in order to achieve it. In other words, we can solve the phenomenological problem of distinguishing psychological perception from intuitive or true knowledge only if we work at it. Husserl argues further that this objective can only be achieved communally.

The communal aspects of the phenomenological pursuit of true knowledge are treated only fragmentarily in Husserl's *Britannica* draft. He does note here, however, that the pursuit of true knowledge through intuitive reflection is a spiritual matter, requiring the commitment of a community dedicated in spirit to this goal. In the final words of the *Britannica* piece, Husserl explains the intuitive reflection of phenomenology as "a function of the all-embracing reflective meditation of (transcendental) humanity" ("Phenomenology" 33). He characterizes this activity as a common effort of humanity "in the service of striving towards the universal ideal of absolute perfection which lies in infinity, [a striving] which becomes free through [the process of] disclosure" ("Phenomenology" 33). Husserl is unabashed in establishing a moral goal for this effort: It moves "in the direction of the idea (lying in infinity) of a humanness which in action and throughout would live and move [be, exist] in truth and genuineness" ("Phenomenology" 33). He ends his encyclopedia entry with the claim that "phenomenology demands the phenomenologist foreswear the ideal of a philosophic system and yet as a humble worker in a community with others, live for a perennial philosophy" ("Phenomenology" 35). This view of phenomenological philosophy as an endless truth-seeking task that is pursued in a community of others is discussed further in a later essay entitled "Philosophy and the Crisis of European Man," a work derived from a lecture given in 1935. It is here that Husserl conceives of phenomenology not only as a cognitive method for achieving true meaning, but also as a method for improving humankind, for setting the goals toward which human will should be directed in order to achieve truth and, ultimately, a better society.

In "Crisis," Husserl links his abstract technology of the phenomenological reduction to lived experience. He defines the act of inner reflection within the larger context of human social existence, moving from an ontological explanation of the essence of human consciousness as meaning to a teleological explanation of the essence of social consciousness as spirituality. In short, Husserl holds that the purpose of consciousness is to be directed toward spirituality, a condition shared by multiple consciousnesses with the object of uncovering ultimate truth. The major argument of "Crisis" is to establish European rationalism as the intellectual method that will eventually overtake all other methods of obtaining knowledge about the world and become the ultimate pathway toward truth. My object here is not to address or defend this argument in particular, but rather to focus on Husserl's definition of communal spirituality as the intersubjective scene in which truth is sought and progressively revealed.

In outlining his vision of communal spirituality, Husserl first defines truth seeking as a credible, definable enterprise that gives purpose to human existence; and second, he locates this enterprise within the context of a communal effort to link individual consciousnesses through a spiritual renewal. Husserl wrests truth from the dilemma of the relativists by establishing it not as an entity with changeless substance that exists outside of humankind, but rather as a dynamic and perpetual goal that both directs and gives purpose to existence—a goal realized through shared consciousness. As Husserl's translator notes, truth for Husserl is "a Platonic Idea, in relation to which any particular truth is but a participation" ("Crisis" 162 fn). At the same time, Husserl declares that this idea of truth "belongs also to what in the scientific sense 'really is' " ("Crisis" 162). The idea of truth is perpetual and, by extension, so is our relation to it.

Husserl sees the pursuit of truth as a normative goal toward which communal activity is directed or a community "attitude" is developed. This ideal "attitude" has origins in the behavior of the Greek philosophers who, in Husserl's view, like modern-day scientists and mathematicians, have worked together to discover truth. The collaborators' efforts result in their "growth and constant improvement," which "ultimately" produces "a will oriented in the direction of an infinite and completely universal task," that is, the seeking of truth. Growth toward truth is marked both by progress and improvement of the truth seekers whose "attitude bespeaks a habitually determined manner of vital willing" (Husserl, "Crisis" 165). The particular perspective that individuals have on existence, whether influenced by family, profession, or religion, allows them to link their experiences to those of others and thus make sense of communal experience as a whole. Individuals can bracket out particular influences and at the same time relate them to their individual identities. The object of phenomenology as a philosophical theory of truth seeking is to offer us a "practical" or "professional" means of achieving this capability of "bracketing out" individual experience to understand universal truth. Husserl defines this pragmatic aspect of his theory thus:

> It is a practical outlook whose aim is to elevate mankind through universal scientific reason in accord with norms of truth in every form, and thus to transform it into a radically new humanity made capable of an absolute responsibility to itself on the basis of absolute theoretical insights. ("Crisis" 169)

Some critics of Husserl interpret his attention to history and recognition of the contribution of individual perspectives to a socially held, yet absolute, truth to be a reversal or a contradiction of his theory of the phenomenological reduction and transcendent meaning. Stewart and Mickunas, however, claim that this view can be held only by those who mistake Husserl's philosophy for a version of idealism. In their view, "*The Crisis of European Sciences* was Husserl's final attempt to lay these charges to rest by showing that all philosophizing is rooted in the distinctions operative in experience of the lived-world" (Stewart and Mickunas 46).

Some phenomenologists, influenced by the postmodernist perspective, grant Husserl's call to bracket out some information in order to be more receptive to new experience, but they reject Husserl's view that one can, through the phenomenological reduction, approach an experience without historical presuppositions. James L. Marsh, for instance, in expanding Husserl's work to develop a theory of dialectical phenomenology, concludes that we can indeed "bracket" some overtly "dominant presuppositions" in order to approach experience in a more open way; for instance, we can bracket "the scientistic presupposition that persons are objective things" (38). While an essential, apodictic meaning may not be possible to attain, "apodicticity in a weaker sense is possible" (38) by "testing my eidetic [or essential] claims against a judicious selection of counter examples" (Marsh 39). Husserl himself might have argued, as claim Stewart and Mickunas, that his earlier doctrinaire approach to the phenomenological reduction was a necessary step, demonstrating the need to extricate "consciousness from the naturalistic assumptions of prephilosophical reflection," a process that makes the integral relationship of "consciousness and the world" more apparent (47). Husserl's latter work serves to show how phenomenological essences are distinct from psychological impressions and yet "experienced as being in the lived-world" (Stewart and Mickunas 47).

We can continue to argue, of course, that Husserl's later notion of "absolute theoretical insight" achieved through social interaction opposes his earlier dismissal of social or cultural data as the source of essential meaning and, thus, find his quest to determine absolute meaning through examining historical experience to be contradictory. This view ignores the accumulative and continuous nature of phenomenological reflection, which takes no stock in the validity of discrete impressions. Phenomenological truth is progressive and, as such, finds no discrete impression to be definitive. For Husserl, the very idea that truth is "a work in progress," so to speak, elevates human aims and consequently improves society. The possibility of truth is *the motivation* for humanistic value, for a spiritual outlook toward life that presumes we all are part of a common progressive enterprise. Husserl predicts:

> If the general idea of truth in itself becomes the universal norm of all the relative truths that play a role in human life—actual and conjectural situation truths—then this fact affects all traditional norms, those of right, of beauty, of purpose, of dominant values in persons, values having a personal character, etc. ("Crisis" 174–75)

In "Crisis," Husserl identifies a few of the human behaviors that would have to dominate in a world where truth seeking became the communal goal of the populace. He predicts the quest for truth to be potentially threatening and to result necessarily in a conflict throughout which pursuit of the truth will generally prevail over the forces of societal traditions that threaten it ("Crisis" 175–76). He insists that conflict must yield to cooperation; this will occur when humankind regulates destructive conflict, reducing it to an acceptable level of mutual criticism: "Inevitably there develops a particular kind of cooperation whereby men work with each other and for each other, helping each other by mutual criticism, with the result that the pure and unconditional validity of truth grows as a common possession" ("Crisis" 175).

To summarize, Husserl projects phenomenology both as a science of meaning that reaches essential truth through the technology of the phenomenological reduction (a precise method of inner reflection) and as a philosophy of living for the benefit of humankind. The pursuit of truth directs us toward common consciousness or spirituality, through which we achieve ultimately a mutual understanding of what is true. Phenomenology becomes a practice that drives us toward this end, primarily through regulating the conflicts that arise when we confront the differences in our individual or socialized perspectives and surrender to a cooperative, progressive enterprise to seek a common truth.

Standing in bold opposition to Husserl's somewhat idealistic explanation of how all of humankind will resolve their differences is the mundane fact of our obvious physical, social, and psychological diversity. How can we achieve a common spirituality, given the historically successful sway of biological and social influences on individual perception? How can we come to a shared understanding when our personal identity is defined by our unique individual perceptions? And even if we could overcome these social and psychological barriers to perfect and mutual agreement about what is true, by what technology can we link our various efforts to pursue truth through reflection? And how are we to ascertain whether that technology, like scientific reason, in itself limits our capacity to know? Certainly questions like these are at the base of postmodernist critiques of phenomenology, and they underlie revisionist reconstitutions of the basic premises of this philosophy. Most notable, in the light of our discussion of the shortcomings of the agency of resistance posed in chapter 2, is Jean-François Lyotard's reconstrual of Husserl's phenomenology, also entitled *Phenomenology*.

Lyotard values the basic aim of the phenomenological movement to restore attention to human consciousness, but at the same time he critiques the insensitivity of the movement to the material historical reality of cultural and economic modes of production. From Lyotard's perspective, phenomenology does not ignore historicity, yet its interpretation of history assumes that consciousness can transform its consequences in a way that ignores the material realities produced by dominant ideologies. As Lyotard explains, the phenomenology of both Husserl and Merleau-Ponty teaches that we can recover historical data through an intentional analysis that is not "read through any single 'factor,' be it political, economic, or racial" (*Phenomenology* 123). The situatedness of phenomenology in history is not considered by Husserl a fault, but rather a "safeguard" that enables this science to respond to the world as it is really experienced in time. As Lyotard summarizes, phenomenology "presents itself as a moment in the development of a culture, and does not take its truth to be contradicted by its *historicity,* since it makes of this very historicity an open doorway to the truth" (*Phenomenology* 123). Where Husserl's phenomenology fails, in Lyotard's view, is in masking the material reality of social structures and systems that are more than psychological presuppositions to be contradicted by the concentrated efforts of solitary thinkers. The belief that historical clashes between classes do not reflect the material realities of oppressive modes of production, the premise of Marxist materialism, but rather reflect clashes between "individual *consciousnesses*" (*Phenomenology* 132 fn) is considered by Lyotard to be a radical extreme. He calls for a balance in perspectives, realizing both the human freedom implied in a conscious attempt to analyze meaning without presuppositions and the historical reality of material forces that are already embedded in consciousness (*Phenomenology* 129).

From my own perspective, Lyotard's interpretation does not threaten the basic premise of Husserl's phenomenology, that our understanding of reality is rooted in conscious reflection. My objection is to the Marxist presupposition that ideological forces determine our freedom to change perspective. As I have argued in chapter 2, the powerful trope of resistance that dominates theories of social determinism in itself stands in the way of an openness to reflective thinking that is the foundation of Husserl's phenomenology. Husserl's dream of a community moving toward a common understanding must surely fail if we choose to believe that our differences are determined solely by social forces that we struggle to resist. And it must likewise fail if we interpret truth and its pursuit within the current populist framework of philosophical relativism, which takes cultural, physical, epistemological, and psychological diversity to be absolute barriers to achieving common ground. The reality of these differences can be handled within the framework of phenomenological philosophy without loss of its claim to universal understanding or acquiescence to a naive optimism about the power of individuals to change social realities. Our power to deal with both lies in the material reality of speech.

Merleau-Ponty focuses on speech as the technology that can lead us to interpret our diverse experiences as common. He identifies both authentic and empirical uses of speech: Authentic speech is "identified with thought" and corresponds to what Husserl might term intuitive or psychical consciousness, and empirical speech is "speech about speech," corresponding roughly to Husserl's empirical or psychological consciousness ("The Body" 178fn). For Merleau-Ponty, speech is both the authentic cause of humankind's common experiences and the empirical proof of those shared experiences: Truth is the presumptive goal of speech, truth being the thought held in common that supersedes all speech. Like Husserl, Merleau-Ponty suggests that the idea of universal truth is a powerful motivator. The idea that truth is possible cannot eliminate uncertainty, but it can lead us to deny false solutions and work together to move beyond impasses in the common pursuit of true knowledge. Unlike any other expressive medium, such as music or art, verbal language presumes a direct relationship to the world that we share with others. As Merleau-Ponty says of writing:

> Each writer is conscious of taking as his objective the same world as has already been dealt with by other writers. The worlds of Balzac and Stendhal

are not like planets without communication with each other, for speech implants the idea of truth in us as the presumptive limit of its efforts. ("The Body" 190)

Speech is the only expressive medium that can, in effect, "speak about itself" and that can improve upon itself. As Merleau-Ponty elaborates, this explains why "every philosopher has dreamed of a form of discourse which would supersede all others" ("The Body" 190), while it is not possible to think of painters or musicians creating a painting or composition that would "exhaust all possible painting or music" ("The Body" 190).

Although he demonstrates that the presumptive end of speech is to discover truth, Merleau-Ponty does not claim that reaching truth through speech communication is inevitable, just as Husserl does not claim that shared consciousness of universal truth can be achieved by random activity. In particular, he notes that we will not of necessity reach the truth through communication if we continue to fear and reject the ways that language, in joining us together, changes us. We must be open to the idea that our communication with others alters our private conception of the world:

> Language is that singular apparatus which, like our body, gives us more than we have to put into it, either because we apprise ourselves of our thought in speaking, or because we listen to others. For when I read or listen, words do not always come touch significations already present in me. They have the extraordinary power to draw me out of my thoughts; they cut out fissures in my private universe through which *other thoughts* irrupt. (Merleau-Ponty, "Man and Adversity" 235)

The obstacle to finding truth is not, as the relativists claim, the absence of a truth that is universally valid, but rather the unwillingness of those who seek truth to be changed by language, that is, to view truth seeking as bound up with our very being in the world, and to see the connection of our thoughts with those of others, past, present, and to come, and the development of ourselves as a result of that experience. A willingness to change, a willingness to engage with others, is central to the phenomenological approach, a factor that I discuss more thoroughly in chapters 4 and 5. More prevalent, it would appear, in our society at present is a willingness to defend a position, to resist change at nearly all cost.

Opposition to the idea that language connects us through changing us is reflected in the preponderance of adversarial language we observe in the personal and political communication that surrounds us. Applying his philosophy to his own times, as did Husserl, Merleau-Ponty notes that politicians cannot even speak of peace-making efforts without presuming opposition; a peace initiative is now described as a *"peace offensive;* to propose peace is to disarm the adversary, to win over opinion, and thus almost to win the war"

("Man and Adversity" 237). Human relations will remain adversarial until we fully accept that adversity denies the necessity of our living and working together.

Although Merleau-Ponty concludes that progress in human relations "is not a metaphysical necessity" ("Man and Adversity" 239), he dreams of a future in which progress will be made toward a shared consciousness through reflection, thus anticipating, as does Husserl, the possibility of spiritual renewal: "Sometimes one starts to dream about what culture, literary life, and teaching would be if all those who participate, having for once rejected idols, would give themselves up to the happiness of reflecting together" ("Man and Adversity" 242). At the same time, however, he sees little hope of this future arising in a society in which "the contingency of moral and social structures is clear" ("Man and Adversity" 241). Having discovered that our differences are rooted in or contingent upon the different ways we are situated in the world (born into an ethnic group, reared in a social class, trained in a religion, constrained by a profession), a fear of facing differences that is a "fear of the new," as Merleau-Ponty puts it, "galvanizes and reaffirms the very ideas that historical experience had worn out" ("Man and Adversity" 241). In other words, we retreat to absolute answers, sacred answers, solutions outside of humanity that reject the rich diversity of our lived experience in the world reflecting in and through others.

The philosophy of Husserl and Merleau-Ponty suggests that the goal of our conscious existence is quite simply to make meaning together. It is to continue a conscious expression of what the world means in the hope of touching, reaching, and joining with others to advance a mutual understanding; it is to participate together in writing the truth of our shared world. Through speaking and writing we make the effort to express what is beyond ourselves and to include others; it is through such expression that we create the relation that enables us to reach the truth we share. What we find to be true about our own condition is, in fact, only that which we have learned through our contact with and responsiveness to others. Merleau-Ponty declares this interpersonal nature of truth without equivocation:

> The movement of ideas comes to discover truths only by responding to some pulsation of interpersonal life, and every change in our understanding of man is related to a new way he has of carrying on his existence. If man is the being who is not content to coincide with himself like a thing but represents himself to himself, sees himself, imagines himself, and gives himself rigorous or fanciful symbols of himself, it is quite clear that in return every change in our representation of man translates a change in man himself. ("Man and Adversity" 225)

As long as we admit that the situation that we represent is indeed one we share with others and that consequently changes us, it should be possible to discover a way our experiences are circumscribed, if not by an idea that we share, at least by the prospect of the new experiences we create together: "Whatever our responses have been, there should be a way to circumscribe perceptible zones of our experience and formulate, if not ideas about man that we hold in common, at least a new experience of our condition" ("Man and Adversity" 225). The opportunity to create a new experience together is the opportunity to discover truth. We cannot deny the contingency of experiences that have shaped us and upon which our various belief systems and epistemologies are built. But we can create together a new experience, one through which we can declare a truth that moves beyond the constraint of contingencies that separate us.

Speaking together can create the scene for an intersubjective understanding that is universal, precisely because speaking is so bound up with our bodies, our situatedness, and at the same time so capable of extending beyond these contingencies to create the scene for new experiences that join us to others:

> As my body (which nevertheless is only a bit of matter) is gathered up into gestures which aim beyond it, so the words of language (which considered singly are only inert signs that only a vague or banal idea corresponds to) suddenly swell with a meaning which overflows into the other person when the act of speaking binds them up into a single whole. (Merleau-Ponty, "Man and Adversity" 235)

Thus, intersubjectivity—the active condition by which we become conscious of the world and its meaning—is maintained through our speaking with others. And further, it is through our speaking with others that intersubjective understanding has potential for universality, a potential that is realized by meeting one another openly, a ground that might well be reached, as Husserl might say, through spiritual renewal.

Phenomenology and Rhetoric

Phenomenology provides a foundation for human activity that is prerhetorical, that precedes our linguistic engagement with others in efforts to constitute together the world we share. Phenomenology asks us to view what is behind language, behind those cultural symbols that we often equate with the world as it is given to us. It does so by exposing how all that we perceive to be the objective world is made available to our own consciousness through subjective action. Phenomenology is suprarational; it moves beyond the rationalism of linguistic argument to the very engagement of consciousness. It is neither solipsistic philosophy nor self-interested rhetoric. Phenomenology makes no claim that the world is the sole construction of a single mind, as does idealist philosophy, nor does it aim to preserve or privilege psychological identity, as does narcissistic rhetoric. Rather, it proceeds from the disinterested and pragmatic presumption that human experience—being all that we can and do know—is primordial. To know the world, we must attend both to our subjective consciousness of it and to its intersubjective presence for us.

Husserl and Merleau-Ponty explain truth and humanity's relation to it as a phenomenon with meaning in human experience. In drawing out their arguments with some detail, I have attempted to suggest how the purposes of rhetoric are implicated by phenomenological philosophy. In the closing pages of this chapter, I wish to focus on this point by restating the phenomenological principles introduced here as they might guide rhetorical practice.

Phenomenology establishes as essential the individual's role in determining the meaning of reality; our capacity to understand its truth is linked necessarily to our intention to know. As *the* agents who are both constructing and responding to the reality they experience, individuals, construed phenomenologically, are capable of determining its essential meaning. To articulate that sense, however, involves more than a simple, passive acceptance of experience; it requires an active intersubjective engagement with everything one is conscious of. Meaning evolves from the continuous interaction of our consciousness with the world to which it attends. Sense develops within us as an organic movement of consciousness, embodied through speaking with others. Through writing, we create a relation with others that enables us to reach the truth we share; we create, in other words, a common, all-embracing context that subsumes the separate contingencies of our individual engagement with the world. A recognition of the reciprocity of our behavior as conscious beings directs us to move toward one another in a mutual effort to constitute the world as it means for us.

In practical terms, phenomenology allows us to view rhetoric as fundamental to truth seeking because it claims that *both language and identity are subject to a consciousness that constructs them while constructing the world they inhabit*. If the aim of rhetoric is "to persuade others" and if we further define this aim "to persuade others toward truth," we are caught in a bind if we believe that both our identity and our ability to use language are achieved through resisting our conscious experience of the world, for through such experience lies our only access to its truth. Yet resistance is precisely what predominant critical theory purports to be essential to identity and self-expression. In contrast, rhetoric viewed phenomenologically functions to establish our engaged relationship with the world; its aim is to move us from alienating resistance toward open collaboration, in short, to progressively take us away from indisputably valorizing the practices of narcissism and fetishism, which I presented in chapter 2, and toward accepting practices that leave us open to discovering knowledge in subjective experience and to changing ourselves as a result of attending to others.

If we yield to the presumption that all truth is found in subjective experience, then to use rhetoric to profess what we know is to express the truth that is within our grasp. Underlying every expressive act must be genuine understanding gained from reflection upon our lived experience, an open, dynamic understanding that overrides, as Husserl has said, "every judgmental drawing-in of the world as it exists for us" ("Phenomenology" 24). Our aim in using rhetoric to persuade, to move, to touch another with our experience of truth is then to continue an openness to experience that keeps us connected to its truth. To adopt a phenomenological perspective on rhetoric is to obligate ourselves to use persuasion to expand openness to the experiences of ourselves and others. Such communication is not about reducing the world and others in it to some vision that reflects an ideal invented by oneself. It is rather about belonging to the world and defining it through deep engagement with all found in it.

If we accept that truth is an outcome of introspective understanding of consciousness obtained through the interactive state of being in the world with others, then the purpose of truth seeking is to sustain that interaction that brings truth into being. Rhetoric aimed toward truth seeking, then, avoids preemptive closure, control of response, or fetishistic attachment to method as a defense against interaction that may lead beyond the parameters of the expected, the known, the accepted. Rhetoric that seeks truth complements our ability to go beyond ourselves through speech, to create meaning with others through allowing ourselves to change, to embody in language our shared consciousness of the world as it must be; it allows speech to express "the surplus of our existence over natural being," as Merleau-Ponty has claimed ("The Body" 197).

A phenomenological perspective, in the final analysis, inspires rhetoric that is purposeful as our existence is purposeful—to make sense of the world and give it meaning as long as we shall live within it. Such a rhetoric eschews relativism, elitism, and collectivism. It expresses rather an intentional effort to abandon adversity, to engage, as Husserl has asked, in an "all-embracing reflective meditation" that moves toward "the idea . . . of a humanness which . . . would live and move [be, exist] in truth and genuineness" ("Phenomenology" 33). Such a rhetoric would lead us, as Merleau-Ponty has suggested, "to discuss truths only by responding to some pulsation of interpersonal life" ("Man and Adversity" 225) and to create together new experiences of the world that move beyond the limitations of our separateness.

In the remaining chapters of this book, I develop these ideas further and propose a scheme for a phenomenological rhetoric. In the process of doing so, I revisit the phenomenological concepts introduced here as they suggest a theory of rhetoric as practice and as they offer an approach to seeking truth in human experience that simply has not been articulated in current cultural and rhetorical theory. This task in the main involves describing the processes of conscious intention and intersubjective interaction as they contribute to and are constitutive of rhetorical communication. In attempting this elaboration, I strive to move through the theoretical impasse that has kept rhetoric separate from truth by defining its practice as one of attending to and interacting with the world with openness and acceptance rather than positioning and resistance. Rhetoric, quite simply, is a conscious embrace of the Other.

4

Profession

Embodying Truth in Self-Expression

Natural writing is immediately united to the voice and to breath. Its nature
is not grammatological but pneumatological. It is hieratic, very close to the
interior holy voice of the *Profession of Faith,* to the voice one hears upon
retreating into oneself. . . .

—Jacques Derrida, *Of Grammatology*

IN CHARACTERIZING THE problematic relationship between truth and
writing, Jacques Derrida distinguishes "natural writing," taken as truth
given to us by nature or God and understood within our hearts, from the
writing we produce as an artifact in the material world, a writing that is exterior to us. He tells us: "There is . . . a good and a bad writing: the good and
natural is the divine inscription in the heart and the soul; the perverse and
artful is technique, exiled in the exteriority of the body" (Derrida, *Of Grammatology* 17). Natural writing conveys divine truth; it "is venerated." But more
than even this, "it is equal in dignity to the origin of value, to the voice of
conscience as divine law, to the heart, to sentiment, and so forth" (Derrida,
Of Grammatology 17). Natural writing is also always totally understood, existing as a kind of rubric, guiding our way of being: "The good writing has
therefore always been *comprehended.* Comprehended as that which had to
be comprehended: within a nature or a natural law, created or not, but first
thought within an eternal presence" (Derrida, *Of Grammatology* 18). Divine
or natural writing is embodied in consciousness as an absolute totality, as a
body of given understandings, to which everything else we presume to understand falls subject. Opposing natural writing and its embodiment as a totality speaking absolute truth is the writing through which we engage with
the world every day, a writing that is disruptive and creative, having no foundation in an external, divine truth or an internal, immutable idea. Rather than
representing a stable truth, it continually obviates the possibility of our very
belief in such a thing.

In the remainder of this book, I propose an approach to rhetoric that
mediates the gap between truth as totally understood and writing as perpetu-

ally disruptive, a rhetoric that interprets writing as both stabilizing and inno-
vative, akin neither to unwavering belief nor to boundless creativity, yet harnessing the productive aspects of each of these conscious activities. I attempt
to do this through describing writing as an embodiment of truth as we experience it, expressed through the self. Because the theory that I propose leans
heavily on phenomenological philosophy, particularly as inscribed by Husserl,
Merleau-Ponty, and their sympathizers, I have called my approach phenomenological and I have attributed my perspective to phenomenology, realizing, of course, that the method I am advocating is not compatible with all
philosophical and critical approaches to writing that have been gathered under
this umbrella. Nevertheless, the approach incorporates, as Husserl might say,
the essence of phenomenology, extending its reach to the problem of defining
a rhetoric of writing. This being so, and wishing not to be overly cumbersome
in referring to my approach each time as an adaptation of phenomenological
principles, I have employed the terms "phenomenology" and "phenomenological approach" to stand for the specific theory I am introducing.

The phenomenological approach to rhetoric assumes neither that there is
an external, divine truth that is revealed by writing, nor that writing merely
creates the illusion that truth exists; rather, it projects embodied consciousness
as the sole source of writing and its meaning and validates the capacity of
individuals to express the truth of their experience. Rhetoric approached phenomenologically attends to the linguistic expression of embodied consciousness as a faithful rendering of lived experience, as the voice of truth. Phenomenology's privileged view of consciousness expressed through language
does not declare naively that all conscious self-expression is naturally truthful
or, like Derrida's natural writing, that it appeals to some divine law that validates it as the very essence of lived experience, yet phenomenology does attribute to consciousness the potential to give rise to truthful expression. One's
personal sense of whether an expression is true or valid develops from constantly checking, evaluating, assessing, and adjusting impressions of one's past
and present experiences of the lived-in world to form a continually newer and
truer sense of what the world is. This activity is "natural" in that it occurs in
nature, within ourselves; at the same time, it is artful, improved upon and
made more effective with technique and practice.

The distinction between phenomenology's approach to truth and expression and Derrida's postmodernist view can be found in phenomenology's
overt claim that we make valid sense of lived experience as a totality, perhaps
an ever-evolving totality, yet a totality, nonetheless, one intimately related to
the totality we perceive to be ourselves. In this respect, phenomenology indeed
gives us reason to think of our attempts to convey meaning through speech
and writing as a "profession of faith," that is, like Derrida's natural writing,
a commitment to the idea of a totalizing sense of reality and its truth. Yet

the totality so professed is one gained by "drawing in" the world in a genu-
inely open way, rather than by "drawing up" the world, if you will, through
imposing upon it a prefigured conception of its structure as suggested by
divine, natural, or even scientific law. As I shall argue in the remainder of this
book, phenomenology can provide the technology for a rhetorical practice of
truth seeking by "drawing in" the world. It is through this "drawing in" of
the world that we can understand its disparate particulars as a totality and yet
retain the sense of these differences. Phenomenology articulates for us how
truth is experienced as a psychical phenomenon through our reflection upon
subjective experience, how it is brought into being through our intersubjective understanding, and how it evolves progressively as a common contingency
among us.

   In the several pages that follow, I suggest how phenomenological epistemology might translate into guidelines for an essentially noncontestual and
open rhetoric that personally engages us in truth seeking. In doing so, I show
how writers might apply phenomenological principles to transform rhetorical
practices that remove writers from engagement with the world they seek to
explain, as do the narcissistic and fetishistic rhetorics I described in chapter
2. Through adopting the phenomenological perspective, writers can move beyond and through the closed rhetoric of narcissism, which presents the author
as a perfectly composed, unidimensional entity, unwaveringly supportive of a
single point of view, toward the open rhetoric of *profession,* expression that
reflects their commitment to a truthful interpretation of life experience in its
complexity. Phenomenology likewise encourages writers to acknowledge the
constraints of fetishistic rhetorics, which bind them to world images constructed by ideology or science, and to interpret their experience of the world
with unaffected *altruism,* that is, through fully embracing its "otherness." The
metaphors "profession" and "altruism" are particularly apt tropes for the phenomenological approach because phenomenology establishes first, that a subject or author is the only concrete and categorical source of professed truth,
which is generated entirely through conscious attention to the world observed; and second, that the subject's effort to express the truth of his or her
experience is fundamentally altruistic, becoming meaningful only through activity shared openly with others for mutual benefit. I present a detailed elaboration of both of these perspectives in the discussions that follow.

   In this chapter, I focus in particular upon the first trope, rhetorical profession, casting it as a transformational alternative to narcissistic expression
that is based on resistance. Profession as a trope for rhetorical practice refers
to a way of engaging with experience that expands rather than restricts the
possibilities for expressing its meaning. Profession incorporates three conscious perspectives: first, intense *reflection,* a perceptual exercise through
which one attends to the world with open acceptance; second, reasoned *recep-*

tivity, a cognitive assessment through which one reconciles lived experience in the objective world with rhetorical interpretation of it; and third, conceptual *regeneration*, a process through which one's expressions simultaneously transform the world as seen and the "I" within it. I present here each of these activities as a self-directed, rhetorical expression of the phenomenological approach to truth seeking in consciousness that was outlined in the previous chapter.

Reflection

Reflection is quite simply the means by which we establish a conscious relationship to the world; it is also the act through which we understand the meanings of "self" and "world." As phenomenological philosophy posits, reflection is not a discrete activity; it is ongoing. Although it is subject to external influence, it is a product of individual consciousnesses engaging in the common processes that generate meaning for all human consciousness. We are all inherently capable of reflection, yet to reflect phenomenologically, with an aim toward understanding the truth of our experience, is not a naive act. It requires specific attention. Reflection is focused attention that, at the same time, does not reject any experience as irrelevant or meaningless. Described phenomenologically, reflection is the very antithesis of the resistance so touted by current criticism as essential for personal expression and self-identity. Reflection is deeply personal yet directed outward; thus, it gives us the capacity to express ourselves while speaking truthfully about the external world. While engaging in phenomenological reflection, we stand not like Narcissus trapped at the edge of the pool, imprisoned by the overwhelming image of himself, but rather we gaze at the world like the sun, burning with intensity so as to animate the world with our gaze. Our meaning as living beings is enmeshed in this activity of gazing that brings to life ourselves in the world about us. This kind of reflection is not aesthetic, longing for the purity of an ideal, but rather it is spiritual, striving for the envelopment of universal connection.

As I noted in chapter 3, Husserl technically defined reflection to uncover truth as the "phenomenological reduction," and in his later writings he referred to engagement in reflection more expansively as a spiritual condition of shared consciousness or shared participation in the quest for increased understanding about the meaning of the world. Phenomenological reflection is the process through which we experience the world as meaningful. Reflection both articulates truth within subjective experience and defines us as agents who intend to know. Through reflection we create an ongoing and persistent intentional contact with the world that makes it and ourselves mutually present to one another. In addition, through reflection we take on the world as part of ourselves rather than resist it as a threat to our individual integrity.

Thus, reflection is fundamentally social; it develops meaning not through detachment but through the connection of ego to ego.

In the next few pages I shall describe in greater detail the act of reflection both as a conscious process and as a concrete rhetorical practice; in doing so, I shall refer to several philosophers' interpretations of conscious reflection, but I shall rely most heavily on Husserl's conception of this process and also that of Pierre Teilhard de Chardin, a philosopher and paleontologist who employed the phenomenological perspective to articulate Christian teleology and theology. Teilhard's writing *is* reflection in action. In its expansiveness and imagery it is pure poetry, but it shows, too, what rhetoric can be when it aims to profess rather than resist.

Reflection is more than a studied assessment that our experience adds up to some conclusion providing a general rule that defines it. Analysis that leads to generalizations about experience can ignore variety in the natural world and the continuing diversity of our life within it. Unlike empirical reasoning, which segments the experienced world into discrete observations that individually add up, reflection is an active attempt to touch, contact, and experience others as we do ourselves in a more fundamental quest for unity leading to mutual understanding. In essence, reflection is first and foremost a perpetual and persistent state of attention that is not deflected by perceptions that are inconsistent with or divergent from an expected or proven way of seeing things. Reflection accommodates all.

The most important difference between knowledge gained through reflection and that resulting from empirical observation is the way in which each activity assimilates divergence. The empiricist or scientist seeks to locate in what is observed some universal principle, some way of identifying characteristics that classify events, persons, or objects as belonging together. Although this process can lead to a kind of connection with others, it does so, notes Teilhard de Chardin, "by suppression of all internal and external determinants" (*Toward the Future* 209). The ultimate effect of such inductive generalization is a kind of "common ground— . . . an ineffable of de-differentiation and de-personalization" (*Toward the Future* 209). Generalization freezes experience, making of it an impersonal object. In other words, generalization seeks to obliterate difference as meaningful and sets up some ideal basis for unity that ignores the idiosyncrasy of the personal, the diversity of individual consciousness of reality.

But to deny some shared ground to the meaning of experience is equally misguided. Taking the phenomenological view, the effect of declaring that no common meaning can unite the various experiences of individuals is to deny personal agency. The antifoundational perspectives of relativism and deconstructionism not only assert the unknowability of the natural and spiritual world, but they also undermine the role of personal difference in creating possibilities for shared meaning. For the relativist, difference simply verifies the incommensurability of different individuals' thoughts and actions; because we are so different, we cannot all share common values. For the deconstructionist, difference simply denies a foundation for conscious perceptions of reality; because difference reveals perpetually changing views of reality, there can be no foundational meaning that absolutely accommodates it. For the phenomenologist, in contrast, difference is the effect of independent consciousnesses recognizing one another as joined necessarily in the act of making meaning, an act that only can take place through the attentive effort of every ego contributing to the process. Meaning comes about only through the perpetual, persistent, and mutual conscious reflection of individual agents; meaning is the result of our shared yet different attention to a common experience.

Shared attention leads to common knowledge. As Teilhard de Chardin would put it, knowledge is attained "no longer by 'dissolution,' " that is, by dissolving differences through generalization or dismissing them as signs of relative value, but rather knowledge comes about through concentrated and shared attention to difference and diversity, through intense mutual reflection, leading to a "peak of intensity arrived at by what is most incommunicable in each element" (210). Concentration on diversity within our own perceptions and those of others leads us to a realization of the meaning they hold in common. Reflection that leads one to truth revealed in diversity is the "road of tension, not of relaxation" (*Toward the Future* 210). The relativist, by declaring our differences to be separately meaningful and valid, relaxes the tension they create and chooses to recognize only what is best for himself or herself; the deconstructionist, by declaring difference to evoke meaning in itself, aside from the intentions of individuals, relaxes tension because meaning evoked externally is depersonalized, bereft of human value. Regardless of our commitment to the ontology of meaning presupposed by phenomenology, its approach to meaning through reflection provides a more satisfactory ground for rhetoric than these antifoundationalist views. Reflection initiates with the rhetor who both accepts—rather than falls subject to—external influences and accommodates information that appears irreconcilable with internal beliefs. Reflection is persistent attention to one's interacting with the world to grow in understanding of it.

Reflection, in its persistence, then, is also fully open and wholly inclusive, that is, it takes in all that the world "is" to us and to others. My conception of reflection incorporates Husserl's view of intentionality, that feature of consciousness through which we are both ever attentive and ever open to the world around us as it is "given" or "is" to our consciousness. I find particularly helpful here Emmanuel Levinas's gloss on intentionality as it instantiates Husserl's call that we return our attention to the things in themselves, prior to our rationalizations about them. Levinas artfully describes the open movement between subjective thought and objective presence that is intentionality:

> Intentionality—from thought to thought-of, from subjective to objective—
> is not the equivalent of any of those relations that can be read off the object
> or between objects. Openness of thought onto the thought-of. "Openness
> onto": a thinking that is not, however, a blind shiver [*frisson*] of the mental,
> but that, precisely as intention is a project: "project" of a thought-of, which,
> though not cut out from the mental fabric of thought, is "unreally" inherent
> in it, and presents itself in thought as in-itself. ("Outside the Subject" 152)

I particularly like here Levinas's interactive depiction of intentionality. It is not like a "blind shiver of the mental," but rather a "project," an interactive activity of the mind constructing, shaping, while being ever open to the input of the "in-itself" that is becoming a "thought-of."

In a recent interpretation of Husserl's conceptualization of intentionality as applied to psychoanalytic study, Maurice Apprey observes that Husserl perceived our consciousness as developing a continual, constructive sense of what "is" both through interpreting fragmentary impressions of the past as they contribute to our own present sense, and through comparing our own present sense with what we perceive to be the present and past sense of others. Our perception of past experiences persists within our interpretation of new experience, and thus "here-and-now experiences are . . . continuous with those that vanished moments ago" (Apprey 10). Similarly, the memories and perceptions of others compared to our own are made sense of as a continuous impression of what the world is for us (Apprey 10). This interactive character of intentionality—mediating both our own past and present intentions and our own and other's intentions—is experienced by all conscious beings; thus, we can think of intentionality or reflection as connecting each to the other persistently. Reflection is a function of all consciousnesses that instantiates the interactive spirituality of all conscious beings.

In a more structured view of the "project" of intentionality as Levinas and Husserl have depicted it, Teilhard de Chardin explains reflection as *the* essential phenomenon of "man," who in turn is the essential phenomenon of the living world because of his or her capacity to reflect, that is, to be conscious of what is:

a. The essential phenomenon in the material world is life (because life is interiorized).
b. The essential phenomenon in the living world is man (because man is reflective). . . .
c. The essential phenomenon in the world of man is the gradual totalization of mankind (in which individuals superreflect upon themselves). (*Toward the Future* 175)

Teilhard de Chardin designates superreflection as that conscious process through which humankind collectively determines the meaning of the world and our existence in it as a totalizing, unifying phenomenon. Although this process is collective, it begins with the individual; superreflection requires an individual commitment to truth seeking, which for Teilhard de Chardin is an infinite task: "There is no exhaustive presentation of truth; there are simply lines of penetration through which we can see a still unexplored immensity of the real opening up for us" (*Toward the Future* 164). Yet within the "opening up" that Teilhard de Chardin projects as the end point of truth seeking, he sees not emptiness or endless lack of direction, but rather the opportunity for us collectively to carry on constructively toward developing a more complete understanding of ourselves in our world—an understanding through which we progressively make the world more livable for all within it. In this respect, he echoes the predictions of Husserl and Merleau-Ponty, who project a world where spiritual connection is cultivated for the purpose of reaching truth together, that is, mutual knowledge by which we better ourselves and the world we share with others (see chapter 3). For Teilhard de Chardin, reflective consciousness is a positive and productive force that does not uncover preexisting truths, but rather both produces the world and openly reveals its truth. Thought is viewed as evolutionary, progressing in complexity and function just as the creatures of the biological world have evolved to better support the enterprise of living. Life, in essence, is a dynamic yet reflective process; it is ever-emerging, and it is increasingly progressing toward constructive interiorization, a movement that unites the reflections of all conscious beings:

> At every point in space-time, whatever its curvature and confines may be, we have to see life—and therefore thought itself—as a force which is everywhere and at all times contained under pressure—and which, accordingly, is only waiting for a favourable opportunity to emerge; and once emerged, to carry its constructive processes (and, with them, its interiorization) right through to the end. (Teilhard, *Toward the Future* 170)

Like Levinas, Teilhard de Chardin sees consciousness, which he interprets as "life" or "thought itself," as continuously emerging to carry on "its constructive processes," its "projects," if you will, of persistently making sense of the world, a sense that evolves through individuals' reflecting on the world's diversity and culminates in spiritual connection. The constructiveness of thought as an interiorized process of coming to meaning serves both to "hominize" humankind, that is, increase the capacity of humans to enfold and join the consciousness of all living things through a shared and fully human spirituality (*Toward the Future* 191 et passim) and to "personalize" individuals, that is, define them as "centred" on the goal of finding more "order" and "unity" within their ideas and "de-centred" in the process of "uniting [themselves] with others" to achieve an "added measure of consciousness" (*Toward the Future* 117, 118). Teilhard denies that personalization involves either identifying with social institutions in order to continue a collective order or resisting the social order so that one may maintain some integrity of individual identity. Rather, he views personalization as the process by which individuals realize the progressive necessity of converging their consciousnesses with others in order to know and understand the living world and of asserting their independent ability to shape that convergence by virtue of their unique participation in it.

For Teilhard de Chardin, whose philosophy is directed toward defending Christian theology, "personalization" eventually results in unity with the ultimate Other, God himself. As I have interpreted this concept, personalization is both an objective and a consequence of reflection. To personalize is the process of interpreting experience as one who recognizes in his or her discrete recollections a unity in their meaning and a profound commonality with the experiences of other persons. Emphasis upon the commonality of personal experience, as opposed to dissimilarity among individual interpretations, is at the core of Husserl's phenomenological perspective. The objects we experience transcend our own consciousness, Husserl asserts, when they are demonstrated to exist for others who also have the power to relate them to themselves. As Kathleen M. Haney explains this view, objects have no meaning for us as real objects until our individual consciousness begins to recognize its separateness from others through presenting "the body of the other to itself as determining parts of its own constituting consciousness itself" (36). The process by which the ego comes to determine the meaning of objects that it has found to be independent of itself involves pairing one's experiences of objects with another's. We perceive both sameness and difference in comparing our observations with those of someone else and conclude that both perceptions contribute to the common meaning we attribute to objects we mutually observe. It is the phenomenon of two egos' "overreachings of the meaning each bestows" (Haney 55) that "begins to move the originary ego to another level of consciousness" (Haney 55). An individual's reflective process of pairing his or her personal experiences with those of another "leads to a recognition of difference, but only against a background of commonality, primarily the commonality of possessing a single psychophysical nature in temporal instantiations" (Haney 72). In other words, although we may see things differently, our experience of interpreting the world is essentially the same.

Husserl does not go so far as to say that our consciousnesses unite in a single spirituality through pairing our conscious impressions with those of others—the telos suggested by Teilhard de Chardin—but he does hold that our common psychophysical nature makes shared meaning possible. He emphasizes that sameness is the key quality that allows us to see and understand difference (Haney 72); similarly, Teilhard de Chardin claims that the ultimate aim of reflection is to achieve a unity with others—indeed, with all living things and with God—through recognizing their diversity. Our natures are united inextricably as reciprocally intending conscious beings. Husserl suggests that this very "unity in diversity" accounts for the fact that the world we share is experienced as one and the same; it is only when we try to reason through this experience, developing a shell after we have experienced "pairing" with others, that we have difficulty "accounting for the single identity of the products of two constituting consciousnesses" (Haney 71). Reason detaches us from what we experience as a shared world and allows us to fathom a separateness from others and from the world as it appears to them.

The capacity to fathom a separateness, a distinction, or a difference, of course, is also a linguistic phenomenon. Before I attempt to describe rhetorical practices that enact persistent, open, and personal reflection as a phenomenological approach might inscribe it, I wish to briefly discuss "difference" as it is fathomed in consciousness and as it is reflected in language. In particular, I wish to distinguish the notions of "discrete difference," such as the difference we assume between an apple and an orange, and "dynamic difference," such as the difference we sense between our finite selves and the infinite world outside of us. Discrete difference is categorical; dynamic difference is relational. Dynamic difference animates the relationship between consciousness and language that is behind the process of reflection.

In a work subtitled "An Essay on Overcoming Metaphysics," John D. Caputo provides a lucid and helpful description of the metaphysical problem of providing a linguistic account of dynamic difference, as I am calling it. His task is to describe the relationship among Being, individual beings, and the cause of being or consciousness. The metaphysical problem in attempting this description is this: How do we express in language—which when it is "set down" becomes a finite object of sorts—the continuous dynamic that is being as we actually experience our conscious existence? Caputo's main interest in addressing this question is to reconcile Thomas Aquinas's and Martin Heidegger's account of Being, a reconciliation that I revisit in chapter 5. My purpose in introducing Caputo's argument here is to offer the perspective it provides on conscious reflection as it relates to linguistic practices through the phenomenon of "difference."

The specific metaphysical/linguistic problem Caputo introduces is the problem of describing in language a cause of Being without obliterating the distinction between beings themselves and what it is to be or what gives Being. As Caputo points out, Heidegger's contribution to metaphysics was to demonstrate that it is not sufficient to hold that beings in themselves, which are finite, and the quality of Being, which is infinite, are distinct; rather, we must account for the nature of that difference, we must open up the space where Being operates as that difference. In opening up this space, the relationship between Being and beings is realized as an infinite reciprocal process rather than as the finite and unreciprocal event of cause to effect, which is the way it has traditionally been represented in metaphysical philosophy. Rather than beings receiving Being from a being that is its own first cause, beings and Being are dynamically related, different and yet held together, in effect, circling and mutually determining one another. Interpreting both Heidegger and Hegel, Caputo summarizes this complex process thus:

> Being comes over into beings as the ground, and beings arrive in Being as the grounded. Beings in turn—and this is the completion of the circle—are themselves grounds and causes. The dif-ference not only holds Being and beings apart as ground and grounded; it also holds them together so that, while Being grounds being, beings in turn ground Being. (Caputo 153)

The encircling of Being described above is an attempt to characterize not the difference between beings and Being, but rather the "dif-ference," Caputo's translation of Heidegger's *Austrag*, which is the differing that makes this difference possible. The distinction between finite beings and infinite Being must be expressed as a "dif-ference," instead of as a "difference," lest we lose sight of how the continuance that belongs to infinite Being is effected in ourselves who participate in it, although limitedly, as living beings. In Husserl's phenomenology, this sense of the differing involved in Being is realized in the conscious process of intentionality in which one compares past impressions of experience with current experience and one's personal impressions of reality with those of other conscious beings, thus developing a sense both of the distinctness of these impressions and of their contribution to a single, yet developing and continuous, sense over time. To develop true meaning, he maintains, we must remain ever open to the sense of things as they are. But how can we, finite beings, understand this infinite, unclosable sense of how things "are"? And how do we express it?

Heidegger argues that our knowledge of the relationship between our finite existence and continuous Being, which we both participate in and yet differ from, is effected by language and its use. As Caputo points out, Heidegger radically reconceptualized the role of language in consciousness, claiming that it not only instantiates consciousness but also essentially brings us into Being. The relationship of "differing" between beings and Being is effected concretely through the medium of language, which is "the doing of Being in man, in human speech" (Caputo 159). Language, in effect, "calls up" or summons up the presence of things (Caputo 159) and in the process allows us to see both "things" and "world," that is, both the way in which things give to the world and "the way in which the world makes it possible for things to be things" (Caputo 168); in parallel, language reveals the way in which beings give to Being, and Being gives to beings. As Heidegger explains:

> The intimacy of world and thing is present in the separation of the between; it is present in the dif-ference. . . . The dif-ference carries out world in its worlding, carries out things in their thinging. Thus carrying them out, it carries them toward one another. The dif-ference does not mediate after the fact by connecting world and thing through a middle added on to them. Being the middle, it first determines world and things in their presence, i.e., in their being toward one another, whose unity it carries out. (Heidegger, "Language" 202)

Language and individuals interact to create the dif-ference that leads us to understand and experience the continuance of Being, which is bound up in the relationship of "thing" and "world," beings and Being.

The fact that we speak is a response to our noting the dif-ference that marks our limited being as a participation in unlimited Being (Caputo 162), or as Husserl might put it, an intentional response to noting the past as it participates in a present, and the experiences of others as they contribute to our sense of the world and ourselves. Thus language, in its external instantiation of our intentionality or reflection, does not represent our consciousness but rather manifests it. And this "manifestation" is a ceaseless participatory phenomenon carried out by individual, finite beings whose limited existence together in the world instantiates the phenomenon of perpetual Being, the relationship between thing and world (see Caputo 159).

Dif-ference figures in both Husserl's and Teilhard de Chardin's dynamic descriptions of how our consciousness assimilates past and present perceptions and those of other persons to derive a persistent, open, and personal interpretation of the world. The gap that separates our lived experience of Being from our discrete perceptions of its meaning (or our discrete expressions of those impressions) motivates us to seek a fuller understanding of Being through attending more openly and purposefully to these perceptions and expressions. But beyond acknowledging this essential motivation, Husserl and Teilhard de Chardin suggest that we consciously choose to direct this process to a purposeful end, the end of reaching a true and mutual understanding of the world we share with others.

In a recent inspirational work that calls us to consider reflection as an interpersonal act that both enhances our creativity and binds our separate destinies, Sunnie D. Kidd and James W. Kidd describe reflection as a purposeful activity originating in the self that occurs only when the self aspires to be open to others, to the possibility of both inspiring and being inspired, a possibility realized in what they call an authentic moment:

> Authentic moments arise in the inspired person's life when that person is open to meaning which approaches from beyond that person's own self. This meaning approaches the inspired person through the call to Self issued by

the meaning of the inspiring other. *The appeal to return to the Self in reflection arises not only from the dynamic field of inbetweenness shared with the inspiring other but from within the inspired person's own aspiring nature.* (Kidd and Kidd 58)

This depiction of reflection captures the sense of dynamic difference that results, I would suggest, both from sensing the differing of Being and beings, and from pairing our impressions with those of others. Kidd and Kidd describe this process as a dynamic inspired by dif-ference, yet motivated purposefully by aspiring beings. In chapters 5 and 6, I defend the purposeful directing of reflection toward shared understanding as a necessary constituent of human existence, but for my purposes here I wish to go on now to relate the phenomenological descriptions of purposeful reflection that I have offered to the practice of rhetoric.

Rhetoric, like phenomenological reflection, responds to perceived differences, both between a present and a past stance and between our own stated views and those of others. Rhetoric also serves a purposeful end, the purpose of persuading others to believe a stated view is true. If we are to incorporate reflection as a component of rhetorical practice, we must in turn regard rhetoric as purposefully aimed toward expressing what we commonly share as truth. Reflection begins in individual consciousness as persistent, open, and personal attention to the world we live in and culminates ideally in a shared consciousness with others of its objective meaning, that is, the meaning all hold to be true. The expectation behind both Husserl's and Teilhard de Chardin's depiction of intentionality or reflection, I would submit, is that in reflecting we both are inspired by and inspire others in a common aspiring toward truth. The call to respond expressively to the dif-ference of Being may indeed be one that we cannot fail to heed, but if it is to result in the kind of shared understanding for our mutual benefit that Husserl and Teilhard de Chardin describe, it must be a task to which we dedicate ourselves purposefully.

To reflect in rhetorical practice is, in effect, an act of profession. Unlike Derrida's "Profession of Faith," which is entirely interior and dedicated to confirming a holy and stable ideal, rhetorical reflection is a willful, purposeful exterior expression, a "professing" through which one declares and affirms openly a knowing relationship to the world through engaging in persistent attention, openly construing all that is perceived about the world to be part of what it means, and personally investing oneself in interpreting the truth of one's particular experience. Rhetorical reflection is not self-centered; it is not an invitation to wade "in the morass of our own positionings," a tendency that Daphne Patai has lamented characterizes much of recent scholarship; regrettably, we "have reached new heights," she claims, "in the self-important pretense that the world's ills can be set right merely by making personal disclosures." To profess an attentive, open, and personal relationship to the world, I believe, is not to indulge in such "nouveau solipsism" (Patai); rather, it is to take seriously the claim that all knowledge originates from the self's sense of relating what it knows to itself. To ignore this reality is to find one's felt experience of the world to be irrelevant to its truth. Our current tradition of rhetorical argument, which advocates the separation of empirical observation from personal opinion, runs this risk, a risk we are obligated to acknowledge when evaluating the truth value of conclusions reached when using this genre. As the phenomenological view teaches us, all experience is personal; hence, a categorical separation of observation from opinion is not possible. Furthermore, all experiential evidence contributes to meaning; hence, to reject contradictory or disparate evidence in order to achieve a unified position is to give an inadequate presentation of what something truly means. Our ultimate objective must be to acknowledge plurality as it contributes to an ever richer sense of the world about us.

But can the pluralistic aims of phenomenological reflection indeed work within the rhetorical traditions we have developed thus far, in particular, the tradition of defending a position through argument? Should we aspire always to reveal *all* to which we have attended in garnering evidence for a point of view? Must we avoid rejecting anything we observe for fear of overlooking a new source of knowledge? Should we aim to express ourselves so that the sense of "inbetweenness," of "dif-ference," that truly characterizes our daily existence is represented in our writing and speaking? The answer to all of these questions is both "yes" and "no." We can learn to argue without overlooking the diversity and personal bias informing our view. Yet to do so is not to abandon or dismiss the rhetorical tradition that has thus far defined the way we explain and discover knowledge through speaking and writing. We need not struggle to represent dif-ference in argument, a task for which poetry is perhaps better suited. Rather, we need to assess and respond to the argumentative tradition as it develops through our multiple and separate participation within it, contributing to our mutual quest for a common understanding.

Argument can indeed provide a base from which we can begin the practice of persistent and inclusive reflection. Although we believe that effective argument has the ultimate goal of closing discussion through offering a counter to all opposing views and the most convincing evidence to support a favored position, inevitably argument is never closed; another reader or listener will offer yet another perspective that refutes the position taken, alters its focus, or expands its scope. Similarly, although we judge an argument's effectiveness by its capacity to end debate, we use argument to keep discussion going. Our commitment to argument derives from its natural perpetuity. But argument in itself falls short as a path to reflective knowledge. Argument provides a technology for evaluating, refuting, and reassessing our observations of the world we inhabit, but it does not teach us how to accumulate, build, and synthesize a worldview from the particular positions that it encourages us to hone and defend. To profess what we reflect upon demands that we make a constant effort to express the meaning of what we observe, regardless of its efficacy in solidifying a single position or supporting its defense. Professed reflection aims to keep conversation going through recognizing all discovered within its scope. To adjust argumentative strategy to include disparate and disjunctive observations is easier said than done. Traditional argument leans on the concept of valid evidence, which is most often associated with factual content. This notion of validity is considered sufficient to render some forms of evidence as dismissable from the start.

The concept of factual evidence is grounded in the epistemology of science; thus, argument based on factual evidence is a highly resistant, preferred technique for declaring knowledge. Michael Mulkay, in his well-known and extensive sociological studies of science as knowledge making, has noted how our conceptions of "fact," bolstered by scientific epistemology, have resisted scholarly scrutiny. He notes that few philosophers who are willing to acknowledge that knowledge in science may be socially determined are also willing to see scientific "facts" as anything other than discoveries about order that truly exists in the physical world (Mulkay 19). Argument without facts in science is regarded as theory, whereas facts are held to be certifiable in the natural world. This distinction allows us to easily believe that

> if the conclusions of science *are* simply statements of observable regularities, accurate within the technical limits of the time, then it seems to follow necessarily that the particular personal or social characteristics of those proposing such statements are irrelevant to scientists' judgement of their validity. (Mulkay 24)

The belief that observed "facts" are distinguishable from theory is simply false, asserts Mulkay; facts are nothing more than theories whose belief is taken for truth:

> We have concluded that the factual claims of science are neither independent of theory nor stable in meaning. Even when the symbols on the page of a scientific textbook remain unchanged over a fairly long period, their meaning in the eyes of the research community may well be in continual flux, as the interpretive context of research evolves. In addition, it follows that the meaning of given factual statements will often differ for different sections of the scientific community. (34–35)

Certain individuals or groups may be interested in seeing the world in a particular way, an investment that is often unconscious. Mulkay notes how Darwin, in his natural observation of inherited traits, was unable to reveal the "facts" about dominance of genes as did Mendel. This is because he failed to discern regularity in his results, even though his results were quantitatively quite similar to Mendel's. Mendel, in contrast, had "clear expectations in mind" when he saw the quantities he observed, relating them to specific theoretical values (Mulkay 36). Scientific facts are statements about particular cases that in turn have implications for particular contexts in which these statements are believed to have meaning.

Statements of fact in science and evidence in rhetorical argument share an assumed relationship to a particular context in which a generalization is taken to tell the truth about a particular case. What both statements of fact and evidence fail to reveal is a commitment to their meaning in a particular context by the individual or group making such statements, and the value of knowing that context to our shared acceptance of the generalizations they support. Generalization from facts conceals the differing of both particular experiences and particular contexts. Through reflection, as opposed to the practice of arguing solely from factual evidence and scientific observation to develop generalizations, we find within the particular the opportunity to create new contexts for shared understanding.

Reflection in its attention to the diversity of particulars instantiates an epistemological tradition that literary theorists have recently given significant attention. In summarizing the origins of a conference on particularism in 1989, Irving Massey notes that observation of what is particular and unique about personal perceptions, that is, undefinable by an overriding rule or convention, need not lead us to despair that no universal exists. What joins one person's experience to that of another is the fact that "every experience is real" (Massey 276), grounded in some individual's actual existence. Scholars in a variety of fields have reached this conclusion and have come to explore what universally can "be learned from situations characterized by singularity, discontinuity, or uniqueness" (Massey 277).

What is most surprising about someone's personal experience, as opposed to a general observation designed to include some singularities and exclude others, is that the individual example is often the means by which we discover some shared ground with another. The particular, personal experience has within it always an element of the new, provided—some phenomenologists would argue—by the dynamic of the consciousness that relates it. The novelty of personal experience is what allows it to be shared. As Massey observes:

> The particularity, the uniqueness of the new experience is the guarantee of its universality. We all recognize each other at the point of sharing in an act of the imagination, the point at which someone else's imagination also becomes the focus of our imagination. Such an event may take place in our

encounter with the artist through works of art or literature, but it may also occur in much more ordinary circumstances: for instance, in recognizing shapes in clouds: "Very like a whale. Or is it perhaps more like a camel?" (283)

Behind the particular experience shared is an act of consciousness reaching out to the world it both constructs and has a stake in, an act that entails professing one's personal experience so as to be included in the imagination of another.

There are various ways in which one's personal view enhances a shared understanding of the world. Traditionally in the practice of rhetoric, we have acknowledged the danger of adopting an overly idiosyncratic or personal perspective, conceding its blindness to some larger truth. Yet recently, scholars and critics have urged that we must acknowledge how personal perspectives animate and motivate our theories about what is generally true. Reed Way Dasenbrock, for instance, in a critique of Derrida's personal investment in his own writing, notes that Derrida has argued persistently throughout his career for a perspective on language that diminishes the author's control or authority over textual meaning, yet now he conducts intense personal defenses of that argument, investing his identity in its particular truth, if you will. Derrida's failure to be consistent—belittling the significance of personal authorship in early life and defending his own works as " 'my text' " in his later years (Dasenbrock 274)—actually helps us understand the significance of his theoretical claims. Dasenbrock explains: "The actions of the older Derrida remind us that being an author means to fight against that loss of control, to fight to stay alive" (276). In short, Derrida's personal struggle with authorial control gives validity to the meaning of his textual theory. Dasenbrock concludes: "It is precisely because authors must struggle to assert control over the meaning of their texts that theories of writing must leave an important role for authors and their intentional attitudes toward their texts" (276).

The particular position of the author, the stance that makes every observation a personal case, is crucial to defining the ground we share with someone else when a text is read. The rhetorical tradition of establishing ethos gives us room to explore how rhetoric might best reveal the personal and particular as this leads to shared understanding. In a recent reconsideration of ethos as it locates the self, Nedra Reynolds argues that all too often we limit ethos to the notion of ethical proof, rather than consider its broader reference to individual character and, broader still, the relationship between individuals and the community that shapes character. To reflect on the meaning of personal experience as it may touch the imagination of another entails an acknowledgment of how our consciousness has been shaped by a community of others. To appeal to that community on the basis of an individual's moral character, then, is to reveal that character as a complex of habits learned "by looking to the community" (Reynolds 329). This revelation, however, aims not only to find commonality, but also to admit the differences and our inability to *see* them all. What aids us in discovering differences is ceding to our particular positionality in professing a view of the world we share.

Acknowledged positionality allows for the possibility of change as we struggle together to find space for all and meaning for each. Claims to location help us fashion new ways of defining our shared world as well. Reynolds notes that "claiming marginality has become a potent declaration of authority for those writers who have not historically occupied the centers of power" (332). One can claim to be heard through asserting that one exists in a place that is different from where others reside; difference provides that contrast through which meaning is developed. Positionality that allows us to see difference is not stifling and not wedded to ideology and its rhetoric, nor is it a mere taking up of a subject position for rhetorical effect. Rather, positionality is an awareness of perspective, of one's personal opportunity to see the world as no one else sees it and thus to help others to see it differently.

To briefly recapitulate, reflection interpreted as a rhetorical act expresses a persistent, open, and personal perspective on the world that leads to shared knowledge. To conduct argument with reflection, authors would aim to maintain a perpetual state of attention both to their particular experience of the world and to their process of interacting with others in order to accommodate others' perspectives on shared phenomena. In reflectively moving others to see what they see, authors would aim to create a totalizing experience, one that unites them and their audiences in a common field, one to which their potentially divergent perspectives openly and reciprocally contribute. And furthermore, through recognizing their expression of the world as personal and positioned, authors who argue with reflection would reconstruct their own particular experience as it connects to and transforms the particular experiences of others and becomes included in a shared imagining of the world as it is or can be.

I have described rhetorical reflection as it involves three activities: persistent attention to unfolding experience, openness to diversity of perception as it contributes to total meaning, and engagement in the personal meaning of particular experience. These processes are fully integral in consciousness and human action. To practice reflection in the way I have described, we personally invest ourselves in interpreting experience through attending persistently and openly to all it encompasses, striving to include, not exclude, the disparate and the disjunctive. In its boundless inclusivity, reflection requires us to adjust our traditional notion of what constitutes effective reasoning in rhetoric. We need to admit that reasoning is an intersubjective activity, one that is receptive to the role of personal interaction in creating valid meaning. In short, reflection in rhetoric requires reasoning that moves beyond rules for conditional necessity to accommodate unconditional receptivity.

Receptivity

Rhetoric has long been the technology by which we communicate our reasoning to others, but as such, its primary function to present and give reasons readily has been assumed to be the basis of reasoning itself. Phenomenology calls this assumption into question, not only in its location of reasoning in consciousness, but also in its depiction of reasoning as the interactive process of remaining open to experience rather than inscribing and delimiting experience. In a series of twelve published essays on the "principle of reason," Heidegger offers an illuminating account of this difference. He calls us here to reconceptualize reason through focusing on its seventeenth-century roots in Leibniz's statement of the "principle of reason," which reads in Latin "nihil est sine ratione" or "nothing is without reason" (Heidegger, *Principle* 3). Heidegger argues that in our modern, technical age we have interpreted this principle as it states the need for a cause for every effect and an explanation for every observation, an interpretation that obscures the call to practice "reasoning" within the "principle of reason." Our attention has been given over to the words *nothing* and *without,* interpreting "nothing is without reason" to mean "no effect is without a cause" (Heidegger, *Principle* 21). We have forgotten to converse, as it were, with the principle in itself, consigning "our speaking to electronic thinking and calculating machines, an occurence that will lead modern technology and science," says Heidegger, "to completely new procedures and unforseeable results that probably will push reflective thinking aside as something useless and hence superfluous" (*Principle* 15). Such is the possible end of a reasoning that focuses only on defining causes for effects, explanations for perceptions. Reason in this interpretation is about representing what is already known to us, putting it into words. Heidegger asks us to reconsider the principle of reason, putting emphasis on "reason" and the copula "is": "nothing *is* without *reason*" (*Principle* 50). Our interpretation of reason as representative, he claims, has suppressed reason itself as *the* means by which things come into being. Thus in limiting reason to representation, we have forgotten that while beings are representable, Being itself is not. As Heidegger explains: "Only a being 'is'; the 'is' itself—being—'is' not" (*Principle* 51).

The focus on the "is" of the principle of reason retrieves reason's sense as determining the "why" of being, whereas the focus on "nothing" and "without" limits reason to explanation or representation. Being—as Heidegger claims, returning to Aristotle's views on the matter—"is what of itself is more overt" than the objects—persons and things—that reason brings about (*Principle* 64). Heidegger ponders a striking example of this quality:

> If, for example, the meadows turn green in the spring, then in the appearing of the greening meadows, that is, in the appearing of this being, there comes to shine the prowess and rule of nature. . . . And even if we thereby have an inkling of the essence of nature and grasp what we have inkling of in the definitive representation or even as a concept proper, then the essence of nature still keeps itself concealed, as does being. Yet the self-concealing of the essence of being at the same time is precisely the manner that being bestows itself, proffers itself to us in beings. (*Principle* 54)

In short, what we can represent about nature in its "beingness," as it were, can never fully capture Being. Yet at the same time our very capacity to reason allows us to participate in the Being that exists *more overtly* as nature itself. Our capacity to reason, Heidegger thus reminds us, is not the same as reason represented in language, in the reasoning of rhetoric. Our rhetorical practices are representative; we create objects in language that stand as things and explanations of things without explicitly acknowledging that reason is that which brings things into being for us.

We bypass the capacity of rhetorical reasoning to make things of things, I would argue, when we draw a categorical distinction between facts, which we take to truly represent physical things, and theories, which we take to be speculations about things. Yet this distinction is at the basis of our determination of the validity of reasoning in rhetorical argument, a distinction that is blind to both the creative power of reasoning and the Being that reason fails to capture. As I noted in the last section, our most widely accepted practice of reasoning through rhetoric leads us to make knowledge claims on the basis of clearly distinguishing fact from theory. This form of reasoning defines validity through exclusion: those claims not supported by factual evidence are dismissed as untrue or, at the very least, as unproven theory about what may be true. As Mulkay has argued, reasoning in the rhetoric of science depends on our distinguishing claims of fact and those of theory, even though what we establish as "fact" is but theory that has not been refuted (36). Reasoning that maintains this distinction is generally considered rational, and the scientist in practicing it is assumed to be the "moral exemplar" of rational thinking, as philosopher Richard Rorty has noted, because he "selflessly exposes himself again and again to the hardness of fact" ("Science" 38).

Scientific rhetoric, interpreted as objective reasoning, is designed to demonstrate how the subjective bias of the observer has been removed through holding him or her to some strict criteria for what can be taken as a verifiable statement, a statement truly representing the world of things. As Rorty points out, the important distinction between arguments made in science as opposed to other fields or endeavors is that scientific argument predicts outcomes through laying down stable criteria "in advance" ("Science" 39–40), criteria that establish certain observations as facts that support or refute a theory. Studies in the humanities do not evaluate discrete observations against immutable, predetermined criteria for validity; often they assess observations as they reflect the character of the one who observes. In taking such personal information into account, humanistic assessments of reality often say much more about what the things of the world mean to those who consciously interact with it.

We can draw an analogy between Heidegger's distinction of how we experience Being and beings and Rorty's distinction of how we argue in the humanities and in the sciences. The personal, intersubjective commentary on human affairs that marks humanistic study attempts to capture how we experience Being, in Heidegger's sense, an experience that is not represented adequately by rhetoric that submits to criteria for argumentative logic or empirical reasoning. The latter works to make objects of what we experience, defining objectively discrete beings as opposed to representing Being as a dynamic event, lived personally. Both ways of depicting the world—the impersonal and discrete as well as the personal and dynamic—are valid forms of representation reflecting valid forms of reasoning. Yet in order to include personal interpretations of the world under the umbrella of "valid reasoning," we must reconstrue our current notion of rationality and with it, our notion of how rationality is communicated rhetorically. A reconstrual of rationality as reflecting human character would accomplish two aims, I believe. First, it would acknowledge that rationality in language is a purely human notion, rather than a disembodied technical criterion applied to statements from without; and second, it would allow us to validate more readily the diverse ways in which beings express and understand their being in this world. This reconstrual of reasoning in rhetoric would thus acknowledge the distinction between "giving reasons," that is, declaring that nature conforms to criteria that define its aspects as graspable objects, and "reasoning," that is, attempting to fully participate in the infinitely changing continuance that nature truly is. It would allow us to think of giving reasons as but a way of *accounting for* verbally and categorically what we all *live through* overtly and diversely.

Rational rhetoric that accounts for the diverse ways individuals experience the world must be receptive to a variety of ways of interpreting experience; at the same time, it need not embrace relativism, at least not in the sense of holding that "every belief is as good as every other" or that " 'true' is an equivocal term, having as many meanings as there are contexts of justification" (Rorty, "Science" 42). Rorty proposes a *new* way of reasoning through language that accommodates "the familiar procedures of justification which a given society—*ours*—uses in one or another area of inquiry" ("Science" 42). He contends that we need not give up a search for what is true in accepting as valid the contingent criteria for belief established by a specific community; rather, we must give up the thought that there must be a direct correspondence between our expressed thoughts, our rhetoric, if you will, and the real world: "From a pragmatist point of view, to say that what is rational for us now to believe may not be *true* is simply to say that somebody else may come up with a better idea" (Rorty, "Science" 43–44).

Rationality, in Rorty's sense, obligates us not to be limited by certain criteria for validity, but rather to acknowledge our fixation with those criteria and the insights they both encourage and deflect. Pragmatic rationality admits that criteria for validity establish a common ground for understanding, but at the same time concedes that such criteria are fixed things we have created in language, things that in their fixity cannot help us capture all that it means to be. Understanding this point fully leads us to pragmatically approach rhetorical argument not with the object of reaching a definitive end point to discussion and inquiry, but rather of encouraging better discussion and more productive inquiry: "The end of human activity is not rest, but rather richer and better human activity" (Rorty, "Science" 45). Fundamental to a commitment to this new sense of rationality is letting go of the idea that inference from observation is somehow different from imagination or belief, and being receptive to the idea that belief speaks truth.

Although we may easily disabuse ourselves of the notion that scientific or empirical methodology is the only kind of reasoning that validates our beliefs, it is more difficult, says Rorty, to reject the realist view "that inquiry is a matter of finding out the nature of something that lies outside the web of beliefs and desires." Our illusion that some stable reality exists waiting to be observed presupposes that objects have a context of their own, one "that is privileged by virtue of being the object's rather than the inquirer's" (Rorty, "Inquiry" 63). The pragmatist's view of this illusion is simply to recognize that "relations of *justification* [and] *causation*" hold "between beliefs and desires" and other entities without positing that beliefs represent reality (Rorty, "Inquiry" 64). Rorty asks us to admit that in attempting to determine facts about the world, we are not representing objective reality, but rather, we are " 'recontextualizing beliefs.' " Our constant efforts to validate expressed beliefs result in reweaving the web of beliefs and desires we have created "so as to accommodate new beliefs and desires" (Rorty, "Inquiry" 69). This process accommodates our constant "desire to know the truth," which Rorty declares is "characteristically human," redefining it in pragmatic terms as the "desire to recontextualize." Although he attributes this desire to all human beings, Rorty finds it to be heightened in "the well-read, tolerant, conversable inhabitant of a free society" in which ambition is "to dream up as many new contexts as possible" (Rorty, "Inquiry" 80). Far from our being limited to finding truth within the parameters of inductive reason, through tolerance we become increasingly more receptive to a variety of ways of experiencing our world, finding meaning—and connection to one another, I might add—in a diversity of contextualizing contexts.

The pragmatist perspective on rationality in rhetoric assumes that our consciousness is interactive with its environment, reconstructing new beliefs and ways of constructing belief in response to our personal experiences and the perceptions of others. Reasoning and nature affect one another. We "reason" a world to be like ourselves and the world is likewise shaped by our beliefs about it; we affect the way others recontextualize their beliefs as they do ours, and we order the things of the natural world to conform to these changing beliefs. This process as described by Rorty echoes the dynamic process of bringing world to things and things to world that Heidegger attributes to language. Yet Rorty's depiction of the process implicates more directly the willful and purposeful activity of humankind as the source of this dynamic. Husserl and Teilhard de Chardin also find a concrete ontological basis for the reciprocal "reasoning" relationship between the person and nature in human consciousness. For them, our progressive and continual shaping of beliefs to reflect our context, and likewise our recontextualizing of belief as our life experience changes *is* the purpose of our conscious existence. Husserl, as we have discussed before, defines consciousness as "consciousness of." The meaning we have for the world, whether we call it objective, subjective, or fantastic, is always a product of the relationship between consciousness and what it is conscious of—there is no meaning beyond this relationship. Our ability to conceive that a reality exists that is independent of our subjective relation to the world is a function of our ability to rationalize and not of the way we actually experience or live in the world.

To be conscious is to continue to carry on the process of making meaning through relating to the things we are conscious of, thus "recontextualizing" our beliefs to accommodate new experience. Husserl also says the process of accommodating our conscious perceptions to those of others in order to reason about the world is part and parcel of the development of a personal life:

> There is an inseparable correlation here between individual persons and communities by virtue of their inner immediate and mediate interrelatedness in all their interests—interrelated in both harmony and conflict—and also in the necessity of allowing individual-person reason to come to ever more perfect realization only as communal-person reason and vice versa. (*The Crisis of European Sciences* 338)

Our personal life *is* our continual reasoning to accommodate belief, both ours to a community and a community to ours. Like Husserl, Teilhard de Chardin also emphasizes the organic and dynamic nature of such receptive reasoning; however, he finds our effort to recontextualize belief to be rooted in our evolutionary process of becoming more closely related to others through consciousness. Teilhard de Chardin suggests that just as our brains have developed into their present state of sophistication from a more primitive form, so our thought processes, which are limited to independent reasoning at present, will evolve to embrace mysticism, a kind of conscious awareness that is dependent upon our spiritual connections to one another. Both truth and personal development are found, he claims, at the juncture of rational thought and mysticism:

> In the mutual reinforcement of these two still opposed powers, in the conjunction of reason and mysticism, the human spirit is destined, by the very nature of its development, to find the uttermost degree of its penetration with the maximum of its vital force. (Teilhard de Chardin, *The Phenomenon of Man* 285)

Along with Husserl and Rorty, Teilhard de Chardin forecasts a progressive development of our consciousness. Where Husserl and Rorty explain the progressive elaboration of our beliefs in terms of continuous receptivity to experience, Teilhard de Chardin attributes progress in understanding to the evolutionary development of our consciousness to be more open to the consciousness of others. This natural evolution of consciousness, as well as our willful desire to be more connected with one another, together will increase each individual's receptivity to all that is humanly experienced and hence all human beings' capacity to shape shared experiences to their mutual benefit.

There is a vitality to the very open, receptive, and yet directed intersubjective activity that Husserl, Teilhard de Chardin, and Rorty call reason, concretely palpable as motivated human action. Although many of us may not ascribe to Teilhard's biological imperative that asserts that our consciousness is evolving toward a collective mysticism or to Husserl's insistence that our personal reason is perfected through communal reason, most of us would be inclined to accept Rorty's pragmatic assertion that we define our beliefs through intersecting them with the beliefs of others. I would suggest further that this process, precisely because it involves our relations with others, is not an abstract, technical procedure, divested of human engagement. Receptive reasoning, as we have been elaborating it here, is not the cold experience of mechanically assessing one belief or another as it fits or fails to fit with a set of predetermined scientific criteria; it is rather the hot anticipation of creating new knowledge from the infusion of a new context within which to reformulate our beliefs. The psychologist Alice G. Brand finds a parallel for this discovery process in the creative act of writing, a task that she declares is not a cognitive process but rather an emotional experience. The writer experiences in the creative act the tension of conflicting commitments that inspire new alternatives:

> What may be the most apt description of writers' emotional experiences is not one negative emotion eclipsing another or one positive emotion eclipsing another or even one set of emotions eclipsing some other but a strength drawn from emotional antitheses. There seems to be a tension, a collision that arises when positive and negative feelings are juxtaposed. (Brand 9)

Emotion, says Brand, is just one of the components of personal mental life that enrich the composing experience, that is, the experience of creating knowledge through writing. Emotion is the key to how subjective experience means for both writers and readers. Brand concedes that "it is certainly too early to construct a model of the various ways affect interacts with cold cognition" (10), but it is nevertheless clear that emotion is essential to the creative process, whether that be expressed in the process of revealing a new internal understanding or of speaking or writing one's mind. Emotion is requisite for engagement; it is fundamentally personal and unique for each subject. Individual engagement and abstract cognition intersect and contribute to the "new rationality" that I am trying to define here as a ground for phenomenological rhetoric, one that defines reason in terms of personal receptivity to experience. Clues to the nature of this interconnection lie within our everyday experience of the intersection of science with personal knowledge. Let me illustrate.

The practice of medical diagnosis as a mode of inquiry involves a delicate balance between observations of individuals who evaluate their personal experience of illness and the judgments of those who assess these interpretations against general descriptions associated with known diseases. Generally, patients perform the first task and doctors the second, yet attention to the gaps that exist between the facts of the particular patient case and the general or abstract diagnosis that defines it is crucial to determining accurate knowledge. As Laurence B. McCullough has noted in assessing the dynamics of medical diagnosis, the tension between the particular and the abstract is transformative: Particular cases change the meaning of abstract characterizations of disease, and the latter change our understanding of a particular instance, or at least the potential for this transformation exists. The abstract language of medicine can impose a paternalist, hegemonic hold on the patient's experience, transforming one's experience of disease into an impersonal instance of a particular medical phenomenon; the patient's story of his individual experience, in contrast, has little impact on the meaning of the medical language that defines it. This lack of reciprocity may account for "the systematic mismatch between what physicians think about and say to patients and what patients experience in response to what is thought about what is said to them" (McCullough 368).

Medical diagnosis would improve if changes were made in the language transactions between doctors and patients so that the experiences of individual patients would impact upon the abstract language of diagnosis, in other words, if the system of medical diagnosis were receptive to the input of individual patient experience. At present, the abstract language of medicine alone has an impact on both the patient and the process of diagnosis. In order for the patient's story to affect medical knowledge formation, attention would need to be paid not only to the patient's narrative of his or her experience but also to the patient's engaged interpretation of that story. McCullough's point is that in order for medicine to be truly transformative, affecting individuals' lives in a positive way, not only must it transform the patient, inscribing his or her particular experience as an instance of disease, but it must also respond to the patient's personal interpretation of that experience as it changes a knowledge base.

The new rationality called for by the phenomenological perspective involves the reciprocity between abstract and particular conceptions that McCullough declares a necessary component of knowledge making in medicine. This new rationality equates reasons with beliefs and at the same time denies that such beliefs form relative truths. The process of reflection, through which the self perpetually looks toward the world and others in it with openness, and of reasoned receptivity, through which the self develops and resolves the tension between abstract principles and particular experience, are together transformative. Reasoned receptivity assumes an interdependence between consciousness and the given world and between individual consciousnesses. Such interdependence dismisses relativism as a threat to truth. Because interpretation derives from the interdependence of human consciousness with its environment, it cannot be relative, for by definition no interpretive statement can be excluded from the condition of interdependency—all interpretation relates. This condition is not a contingency; it is, rather, essential.

Through the act of reasoned receptivity, my observations are transformed by others as theirs are transformed by mine. I will, of course, generalize from my experience and reduce it to a verbal abstraction; this technique allows me to communicate my perceived sameness with others. But at the same time, I must acknowledge those qualities of my particular experience that are not captured by an abstract verbalization, and concede that my conception of personal experience is continually changing, growing, and complexifying as a result of many individuals' engagement with me. In other words, I must view myself as knowing about the world because I am affected, engaged, emotionally invested in the meaning of my experience as it defines my future actions; this can never be reduced satisfactorily to words. Nevertheless, my emotional investment in understanding my experience so that I might act drives me to strive to continually reconcile particular perceptions with general beliefs about my experience, shaped through comparing my beliefs to the beliefs of others about theirs.

In an essay on the relationship between abstract concepts and individual experience, René Thom notes that no ideal exists that we can hope to reach and declare unchangeable in our process of reconciling general claims with particular experience. Our descriptions of ideal types (the perfect conception of a person, the most complete depiction of a flower) always fail; a claimed ideal even "having remained unchanged for a long time, gives way all of a sudden (catastrophically) to a new ideal, and the real, in its continuity, tries to attain it" (Thom 389). Reality will never match our idealized conceptualizations because communication, interaction, and our very intersubjective nature make reality continuously transformative. What our attempts to generalize and idealize do accomplish is a connection to one another as participants in a common experience. Idealizations, generalizations, and theories direct our experience so that we can see together "the totality of what is true" (Thom 389).

To practice reasoned receptivity, as I am attempting to define it here, is not to deny experience that is incommensurate with some general or ideal type that is validated by empirical observation or some communal belief standard. Rather, it is to be fully receptive to my own experiences and to those of others, and to see in apparent differences a new opportunity to discover what may be the same once again. The implications of this kind of reasoning for rhetoric are profound. The goal of our communication becomes not to disconnect, dismiss, or discredit all that is not consistent with an established or proven perspective, but rather to assist the transformation of another's experience as well as my own in reaching a new level of understanding about where we are together. Attending to and developing narratives of experience may very well be the key to this way of knowing and its power to engender perceptivity and to stimulate the growth of ideas. Personal narrative has the potential to show not only how experience has changed me, but also how my telling of it is changing me in my relation to you. This kind of narrative is not designed to fix belief, like the stories of legend or myth. Rather it is a revelation of my consciousness in the process of bestowing and discovering meaning. Transformative personal narrative is but one communicative outcome of reasoned receptivity; another is acknowledgement of the role of personal histories in our judgment of the validity of any argument—from the most personal, overtly self-revelatory statement to the least personal, overtly objective report of empirical research.

We are accustomed to layering onto judgments of personal affairs an assessment of the state of mind of the participants, of events and attitudes that may account for how they behave and what they choose to say about behavior. In a divorce, a dispute over property, or a conflict over appropriate social protocols, we are not hesitant to include some mention of the history of the participants involved, particularly as this history has transformed them and made them see the world as they do today, a history that must be taken into account if an agreement is ever to be reached. The law or social convention may prescribe a path for settling such matters, but the outcome in which participants see "eye to eye," that is, perceive theirs to be a shared truth, requires their having felt similarly transformed so that their disparate views have in some way become part of each other. (We do not generally apply this same criterion in matters in which institutional truths are perceived to take precedence over personal history.) The rhetorical focus for such an experiential narrative is not upon telling or elaborating a story, but rather upon regenerating at will the newfound sense that has come to me as a result of interpreting my life as a life among others making sense of their lives. I shall explore this possibility in some detail next as I introduce the task of regeneration, the third process, in combination with reflection and receptivity, that grounds the rhetorical practice of profession.

Regeneration

The practice of profession incorporates persistent, open, and personal reflection on experience as well as reasoned receptivity that responds to the difference between particular experience and generalizations about it, acknowledging the dif-ference between experience lived and experience writ, as it were. The goal of profession is regeneration, the creation of ideas that animate and elaborate what appears to exist for ourselves and others. Regeneration is not the purposeful end of argumentative rhetoric as we have traditionally described it. The latter aims to effect a change in someone else in order to accommodate me. This kind of transformation is valued in the critical stance that advocates resistance as a means to knowledge; although it is potentially transformative, resistance responds to what is perceived as the tyranny of culture with the limited goal of changing its influence through exercising opposition. Transformation achieved only through resistance is limited because resistance presumes from the start that little or nothing exists in what I stand against that can add to my experience of what is true. What resistance fails to see in opposition is the opportunity to cross the boundary that keeps my belief separate from others and to move what I know beyond its current state.

Resistance, although considered a tactic to maintain the integrity of one's personal growth, ironically is motivated by a rigid absolutism: I resist because I cannot exist as I am now except to resist. Phenomenology offers a much richer depiction of human agency, defining individual spirit or motivation to act not as a function of negativity (that is, I aim to resist what ideology or biology inscribes me to be), but rather as the positive outcome of assessing past experience against present, one memory against another, prior motivation against future desires. Phenomenology claims that consciousness can move forward; it can anticipate possible action beyond the spontaneous activity of my body responding to biological, cultural, or physical forces. Regeneration is the product of the tension that exists between what I experience in the present and my potential to reflect on that experience with reason to guide future action. Regeneration is actuated by individual will and a belief in progress.

Phenomenology articulates the role of will in the construction of meaning and, consequently, the possibility of agency. If nothing else, agency is the pragmatic assumption that we *can* declare what something means to us, an assumption that stands behind all our efforts to reach out in speech toward others. In order to elaborate the relationship between will and agency, I wish to discuss briefly the phenomenological perspective on will as it relates to meaning formation. Phenomenological philosophy both defends the possibility of will and finds that with our capacity to will, a search for truth is within our grasp.

In a discussion of our modern conception of personhood as it relates to truth and value, Frederick A. Olafson notes that Husserl's location of meaning in human consciousness effectively launched the development of existentialist conceptions of will. Husserl also provided the basis for Heidegger's conception that the human individual is a being concerned with his or her own being and for Nietzsche's insistence that the human individual asserts a "will to power" over the meaning of his or her environment. All three philosophers struggled against the Cartesian position that we can validate the truth of our conception of the world against an external reality. Husserl described our knowledge of the world as fully a function of consciousness; in short, meaning outside of consciousness does not exist. Although Nietzsche rejected Husserl's advocacy of essential meaning, he clearly sited the origin of meaning in consciousness, as Olafson puts it, positing that "all of our knowledge and our modes of conceptualizing experience involve an evaluative component and represent a decision to construe the world in a certain way" (48).

Existentialist philosophers likewise believe that nothing external or in our nature dictates our moral behavior: "In place of the intellectualistic ontology of moral determinacy, the existentialists have attempted to construct an ontology of moral freedom" (Olafson 59). The primary basis for their belief in freedom of choice rests upon the individual's existence as a conscious being, able to invent or imagine a reality that he or she does not physically experience. In short, a person can conceive of nonbeing, and can construct mentally situations that have no physical correlate. The sphere of our intention goes beyond "being in itself," and our ability to choose a mental mode of existence is evidence of our ability to go beyond ourselves, to create meaning on our own terms. In our mental mode of being, we are not subjugated by the external constraint of a moral law or even a God—we have the freedom to choose (Olafson 69–73). For the existentialists, being, in effect, involves a "continuous reading of the world in terms of the concepts of contingent being [or what we experience as factual in the world] and possibility [that is, the alternatives that a contingent situation suggests]" (Olafson 100). The constant tension between these two "realities" puts before us always the possibility of choice and evaluation; hence, our very day-to-day existence is a matter of willing to act a certain way amidst a host of possible actions. What we do each minute, each hour, is always preceded by a conscious choice: We constantly assess what we want to do and become, and we "will" to choose according to that assessment.

Husserl does not explain the relationship between will and language other than to note that willing and doing have significatory correlates that differ; in other words, willed desires and willed actions each bear a different relationship to language. Paul Ricoeur in elaborating upon Husserl's work, however, explains will more specifically as a conscious phenomenon related to signification. Ricoeur argues that the tension created between the body's involuntary responses and consciousness's voluntary intentions creates the motivation for individual constitutions of the world; in other words, this natural tension stimulates our continued, willful reinterpretation of reality. He describes the "mediations between the body and the will" as activities that perpetuate the responsiveness of both. Although my body may respond involuntarily to environmental pressures, my will decides whatever "projects" I shall take on. Willing and doing are inextricably related: "The 'to be done' is on the way toward the doing" (Ricoeur 217). At the same time, however, willing is essential to doing. Even when I am denied the choice to decide, the possibility of decision is still there; this is a function of being human (Ricoeur 218–19). Hence, my being human means that for me to desire or to suffer involves my "already having begun to assume a position in relation to desiring or suffering" (Ricoeur 219). I do not experience feeling without some view toward its coming about. Likewise my body affects my willed experience of certain feelings, such as hunger, for instance. Ricoeur explains:

> The body in one way or another nourishes motivation so that it can be balanced by a non-corporeal value. Thus, only man can go on a hunger strike; the sacrifice of need attests to the fact that need is ready to submit to a general evaluation. . . . An affection [such as the anticipation of future pleasure] transfigured by an evaluating intention brings the body to the level of a field of motivation and makes it a human body. (224–25)

Will, in other words, allows us to signify through the body, to be in our very corporeal beings the conveyors of meaning. We do not through will and body "create" in the sense of inventing the world to be experienced; rather, we constitute the world as it means to us through the dynamic interplay of experience felt in the body and intention willed in the mind. We are free to constitute the world at will, but that freedom has limits. Ricoeur explains further: "The reciprocity of the voluntary and the involuntary illustrates the specifically human modality of freedom. Human freedom is a dependent independence, a receptive initiative" (228). Important for our purposes is phenomenology's claim that will is primary: I experience the world through the filter of my will, which assigns meaning to what I say and do. Will is thus the foundation for what I am designating as the function of regeneration—the act of creating ideas that animate and elaborate the world as it exists for ourselves and others. Central to my conception of willful regeneration are individual agency and judgment, which I regard as positive creative forces, reflecting not only individual development of character but also contribution to a collective human destiny.

Will, in the context of our signifying processes, is the individual's choice to locate himself or herself within a discursive context, choosing the role that he or she will play within it. Individuals can choose to create a location for themselves within a discursive construction of reality, selecting characteristics that they then attribute to themselves. In *The Discursive Mind*, Rom Harré and Grant Gillett effectively describe how such willful agency is realized in discursive processes. They define individuality as a unique relational function characterized by the circumstance that "each human individual stands at a unique intersection point of human discourses and relationships" (Harré and Gillett 133). Human beings continually integrate their experience into discursive contexts that conform to an individual "overall life project" (Harré and Gillett 141) that they enact with some consistency. At any point in time, individuals are free to act in conformance with this personal construction, to act contrary to it, and to adjust and modify it. It is this very ability to will a place for oneself within a discourse, I would posit, that makes our rhetorical practices uniquely suited to providing the occasion for shared belief. As reflected in authorial intention, will is revealed in the commitment an author makes to stating a belief, in giving a meaning to his or her experience that is intended to be shared with others. Will also is figured in the attempt an author makes to close the gap between individual experience and general interpretations of his or her life as lived that are shared by the community he or she addresses. I wish to speak briefly here about each of these points.

As Ricoeur has explained, our will allows us to signify through the body: He gives the example of the hunger strike, of choosing not to eat, even though it is necessary to do so, because this choice *means* something. Our will also directs how we signify through language, that is, how we declare something to have meaning in those social situations in which we put language to use. To make a willful declaration is to do more than respond in kind to the simple exigency of a situation, to match what one says to the actions of others as one would match the choice to eat with the need to do so. To declare willfully is also to exceed the desire to simply record experience as a way of capturing it for future reference should one encounter such a situation again or to assign a meaning to an experience in order to test whether that meaning is shared with others. To willfully declare is a rhetorical act; it is a choice to persuade someone, if only oneself, that a belief is true through associating that belief with the internal commitment of its author to its posited truth. In making this point, I am expanding upon a metaphor posed by Jeremy Smith, who theorizes that rhetoric, as opposed to literary communication, functions similarly to religious commitment. He notes: "Religious commitment means the direct concern of my own actual being. Moving beyond simply perceiving the world, toward a decision about how I will involve myself in the world, is the meaning of that direct concern" (72). For Smith, the evocative literary work aims to record a perception as a possible rendering of the truth of experience; it does not entail the author's commitment to the truth of that perception. Rhetoric, however, is a declaration with commitment; rhetoric conveys the sense that the point of view that we declare is "a cause to which we pledge our loyalty and in which we trust to bestow worth and meaning on our existence" (Smith 70).

Commitment to an idea is generally approached in practical rhetoric as a problem of generating sufficient valid evidence and substantiating authorial credibility, not a problem of demonstrating one's faith in an idea. To approach rhetoric in this latter way requires authors to engage in a far more substantial investigation of their own personal motives, knowledge, conditions for belief, and feelings toward others. Likewise, to take communication this seriously is to assign a far richer objective for rhetoric than harnessing the power to persuade. Smith interprets this greater aim like this: "The unifying purpose of a rhetorical work is to open up a new possibility to others, and in avowing a commitment, to confront them with the real possibility of commitment" (75). In other words, as I express what I will to believe, I am asking others to commit to this stance, not only because of what evidence I provide to support it, but also because this is where I have placed my faith.

Rhetoric that effects willing, as I've described it, addresses the gaps between culturally powerful ideas and the contingency of individual experience. Each time we make a choice to act in a situation in which the rightness of a decision is ambiguous, we must weigh the exigency of our personally felt experience against the advice or experience of others, and in so doing we take the opportunity to evaluate the collective experience of those who have gone before us and to assess whether that collective experience points to a larger principle; one that defines our common humanity. But such evaluation does not assure commitment to this larger principle, it may merely reflect one's having found in a particular experience some general meaning. Such a willful evaluation, for instance, allows the artist to depict experience in such a way that the depiction captures in its meaning the effect of the actual experience without declaring it as a general principle or theme. In presenting a theory of how we interpret the effects of art, Leo Bersani claims that our perception that a work of art is beautiful comes from its effect of revealing a truth about something represented that is in fact not represented:

> *The beautiful is the effect of our discovering the nonrepresented in the represented.* . . . The relation of the ideal to the particular is analogous to that of the eternal to the transitory. The ideal and the eternal are the veiled presence of what the particular or the transitory lacks; they are the form the circumstantial takes in aspiring to be different from itself. (67)

Smith makes a similar claim about the ability of a literary work to present some idealized depiction of experience that correspondingly can be shared without regard to one's interpretation of its truth. He claims that literary art invites the audience to share the larger meaning of a particular experience as envisioned by the author without overtly adopting that meaning as a belief, and he distinguishes literary art from rhetoric in this regard. The former presents "the truth of the human condition" (Smith 61) without declaring the author's version of or belief in it; the latter, however, is a public commitment to belief in the truth of its statement about the human condition. Rhetoric, hence, declares a commitment of will in the interpretive process. Pressing beyond Smith's distinction, I wish to assert that rhetorical practice approached from the phenomenological perspective demands of us even more than an individual willed commitment to a belief; it demands that we substantiate belief as a truth to be shared by others, one that inscribes an essential human experience, interpreted as such through attention to one's own and others' histories.

For some, as I noted in chapter 3, it would seem that attention to history is antithetical to the phenomenological quest for essential meaning. History in one sense is the record of contextual contingency as it impinges upon human action, showing a decision to be regarded as perhaps true and right in one instance and perhaps wrong and unethical in another. Attention to history, nevertheless, is compatible with the phenomenological construction of truth as an accumulative sense; it constantly becomes elaborated as individuals integrate and evaluate new experience, and clarify the meaning of past experience in the light of new insights.

Husserl was inspired to reflect upon the historical dimension of truth during the late 1930s, when his phenomenological project was threatened by the Nazis, who directed scholarly projects to locate humans' essential nature in physical biology as opposed to conscious reason. Through this happenstance, notes Ricoeur, Husserl, "the most non-historic of professors" working on philosophical projects at the time, "was summoned by history to interpret himself historically" (144). National Socialism led Husserl not only to reflect upon how the spirit can become ill, but also to take on, "out of respect for rationalism," the responsibility of saying "who was ill and hence to point to the sense and senselessness of man" (Ricoeur 144). Ricoeur suggests that Husserl's response to his own situation inspired his conclusion that philosophy is historical, despite his earlier claim that the phenomenological reduction achieved a sense that is ahistorical, having no reference to a particular moment, no response to a specific cultural or biological imperative. History is incorporated in the phenomenological perspective because the ego that engages in reflection is a historical entity; as Ricoeur explains: "Because history is our history, the sense of history is our sense" (155). The ego's fulfillment of its potential to derive sense phenomenologically depends on its attending to its history and, furthermore, to the history of others' egos efforts to attain sense.

With the concept of history, Husserl posits a path for reason that is naturally progressive. Reason involves more than reflecting on what I know; it involves unifying all of my perceptions, "speculative, ethical, aesthetic" and other (Ricoeur 157). To reason, thus, is to incorporate all that is conscious human existence. But it is still more than this. Reason makes me receptive to all experiences as I *choose* to see myself in relation to whom I understand I am to become. Through reason I reflect on the idea of becoming human, of understanding my identity in a world of others like me now, in the past and in the future yet to come. Ricoeur interprets this notion so: "Man is the image of his Ideas, and Ideas are like the paradigm for existence" (159). This person who is the "image of his Ideas" is continually becoming, an act for which all egos that occupy a temporal space ultimately are responsible (Ricoeur 158–59). The paradigm which defines human existence is a structure in progress, built and elaborated upon through our interactions with one another. No single aspect of our existence—biology, culture, appearance—dictates its shape; rather, it is being shaped as we continue our collective historical enterprise of urging on humanity's becoming. Hence, we live both with the sense of having been generated, constructed, and influenced by all that is physically and consciously experienced in life, and with the sense of regenerating continuously, that is, of rebuilding what is into what it shall become. This willful act of "regeneration" has a corollary in the practice of rhetoric.

As practical communication, rhetoric aims to make explicit general themes and principles that direct the course of human action, whether these themes be stated overtly in language or become enacted as a result of readers' or listeners' exposure to rhetoric. In the task of persuading, will is paramount—the will of the author to urge others to "believe what I say." Progress is also requisite: In aiming to move another to accept my position, I interpret such a move as progressive, resulting in action that improves upon what was done or existed before. "Will" and the potential for "progress" have girded the most persuasive political speeches of our time—Kennedy's "ask not what you can do for your country" comes to mind, as does Churchill's "there is nothing to fear but fear itself." Each theme was stated explicitly, urged the recipients' commitment to belief, and carried the promise that things would indeed be better because of that commitment.

For rhetoric to accomplish regeneration, as I have been describing this phenomenological principle, it must engage both author and recipient in a willful commitment to rebuilding, reforming the world they share together. It must instantiate faith in an idea and its power to change and be changed as it is expressed, interpreted, reexpressed, and reinterpreted. This continuous cycle, of course, is what has made statements such as those of Kennedy and Churchill so powerful, so deeply felt even today. It is an effect that can be experienced on a much smaller scale as well, in boardrooms, classrooms, and living rooms. The board chair's success in committing a corporation to quality of service, the professor's success in getting term papers on time, the parent's success in quieting the screams of a small child all require a commitment on both sides of the exchange to a common belief. The progressive power of regenerative rhetoric ultimately comes from its objective to bring us together in professing our common aspirations. Our choice to commit to what we profess is tantamount to the possibility of declaring its truth.

Profession: A Rhetorical Practice

The phenomenological acts of reflection, receptivity, and regeneration comprise what I have chosen to call the rhetorical practice of profession. This practice is reflective, attending to experience as it changes us, rather than solely as it has the potential to change others. It is rational, not in the sense of being methodologically subject to valued methods of reasoning, but rather in the sense of being receptive to the reciprocal relationship between general ideas and the particular and personal experiences that continually inform them. And profession is regenerative, expressing the willful progress of authors beyond the constraints of their or their reader's disparate social histories to establish new ground for shared understanding.

To practice profession is not to be a professional, a form of agency that defines many twentieth-century rhetorical behaviors, either in the sense of representing the interests of occupational groups rhetorically or of delivering a message with the express aim of transforming the beliefs of those who hear to match expert criteria. Both of these perspectives are too narrow to encompass the level of an agent's responsibility, initiative, and engagement implied by profession within a phenomenological rhetoric. Profession is inflected, of course, by some of the more common notions of professionalism that have pervaded modern industrial society with the rise of the professional middle class. Profession, like professionalism, respects our link with the past. As Frank Hayward argued so readily a century ago, professionalism supports "traditions handed down through speech, books, institution, and professions"; it is "one of the chief agents by which social heredity is handed down" (4). Yet at the same time profession does not necessarily imply, as does professionalism, the application of specialized training, adherence to standards, and evaluation of merit based on those standards (Hayward 5–7). Profession does imply, however, an obligation to contribute to some collective enterprise to discover common values, and to assess our quality of life in the light of those discoveries.

To practice profession is also not to subscribe to methodological activism, regardless of whether this is inspired by identity with a social group or a passionate commitment to one's particular beliefs. Hence, to practice profession is not to aspire to become a *"transformative professional"* as has been advocated by Paul Jude Beauvais and, in principle, by a number of other theorists who link political activism with writing instruction. Beauvais sees the transformative professional as one who assists "students in developing not only technical skills [as writers] but also critical consciousness and social commitment, [so that] they may participate in the broad project of social transformation to which we ourselves are committed" (26). Beauvais's prescription doubly determines "professional" to refer both to individuals who identify themselves with the "broad project" of transforming society and to those who speak with the aim of transforming individuals. Underlying this notion of the professional and the rhetoric that communicates this identity is an assumption that the goal of transformation precludes a change in the perspective of the speaker. In this construction of professional behavior, the political agenda to change others ignores the phenomenology of human consciousness that roots profession, as I have defined it, in inclusive reflection, intersubjective reasoning, and the acceptance of a will toward collective progress that I have called regeneration. Profession enacted in a phenomenological rhetoric foregrounds the rhetor's ambition to both find and be changed by truth. This is not to say that identifying with a profession or a political cause denies this, but rather to say that neither constraint must fully determine the practice of profession. Defined proactively, rhetorical profession aims to negotiate the relationship between abstract ideals and our particular experiences, animating the former with individual engagement and emotional meaning.

Profession, as I have described it, calls into question several rhetorical strategies currently assumed to be effective. For instance, narrowing one's focus to a single argument delivered for a specific purpose can be construed as a misdirected effort to favor a specific view and control the dynamism of the discursive context. Revising to eliminate irrelevancies can be construed as reasoning to accommodate method rather than writing to give meaning to experience. And finally, altering expression specifically to meet the anticipated needs of a listening or reading audience may prohibit one from interpreting experience as it truly has meaning for oneself, and thus limit one's potential to share that experience with others. Yet our common experience as discoursing subjects suggests that all of these practices are straightforward and practical means of assuring that our communications help us get on with our daily lives. How might the concept of profession, as I have described it here, direct these practices toward the phenomenological goal of committed progress toward a common belief? Certainly the particulars of this transformation would require a much longer discussion to articulate, but I can present its focus in outline with a brief illustration of how rhetorical tasks would be concluded more satisfactorily should their authors approach them from the standpoint of profession.

Consider a myriad of ordinary communication problems: arguing for pollution control in one's neighborhood, reporting a test result on an automobile brake system, completing an employee evaluation, proposing a new graduate program. How would the approach to these issues be changed? In reflecting on such rhetorical tasks, writers would not strive to separate themselves as conscious observers from the situations they address; rather, they would obligate themselves to continue ongoing intentional contact with all aspects of their environment, accommodating all forms of information as potentially significant. They would view the situation under study as part of what makes up their very selves and not distance themselves from it dispassionately. They would see necessarily that diverse perspectives contribute to an evolving sense of what truly is and therefore should not be considered competitive, but rather constitutive of the truth they are trying to tell—the city incinerator leaves ash in the night air *and* reduces disposal costs for local citizens; the brake system meets all crash test results *and* increases tire wear; the employee never arrives on time *and* has a child who requires constant care; the computer science student cannot meet the entrance requirements to a graduate program *and* is typical of most of the students who would benefit from it. Most important, they would see their own position in relation to the situation to provide a unique vantage point from which to convey its meaning to others, rather than to pose an obstacle to an ideal objective evaluation.

In reasoning about the kind of evidence they wish to forward to make their arguments, or to depict the worlds they see, writers would understand more fully the relationship between reasoning and emotional involvement. They would understand that out of the particular comes a greater understanding of the whole. They would know that to generalize from their experience is to reduce and eliminate detail; and they would also know that not to generalize is to forfeit their right and responsibility to interpret the world as it has meaning for themselves to others. And they would write about that very problem and its implications for the situation at hand.

Finally, writers who equated their task with profession would understand that their goal is not only to transform the world as it is seen by others but also to transform themselves in the process. They would see their task to be one of committing themselves to a belief and standing behind it as if it defined in some way, however small, their very being. The ground for persuading others of this idea would then be the ground for persuading others of their own commitment to its truth. They would understand their choice to interpret a situation as meaningful to others as an act of will, of imposing their agency on the shape of the world that others share. And so the argument against the incinerator becomes its author's commitment to a safer community, the test report on the brake system a reflection of the engineer's commitment to produce a reliable product, the employee evaluation the evaluator's commitment to mentoring another, and the proposal for a new graduate program the faculty's commitment to both their students and their discipline. In short, to approach rhetoric as the practice of profession is to embody truth in self-expression, that is, to understand truth telling as a personal commitment to interpret the world meaningfully to both oneself and others. As a lab technician reporting the results of an experiment, I express my commitment to a methodology for observing the natural world and stand behind the integrity of my enactment of it; as a scholar reviewing the manuscript of a colleague, I express my personal commitment to the respected epistemologies of my field and my particular balance of the value of innovation against allegiance to method; as a father advising my son about his future, I express my personal response to fortunes that have directed my life as I honestly understand these to suggest a direction for him. Approached from the standpoint of profession, none of these activities, from the overtly public and material to the intimately private and spiritual, are divorced from the commitment of self.

Most important, the investment of self implied by profession is equally an investment in that to which the self looks, to the world and others in it. And so profession, the very ultimate commitment to interpretation, has an important corollary in altruism, the very ultimate commitment to others, and it is this function in a phenomenological rhetoric that we shall explore in some detail next.

5

Altruism

Embracing Truth Through Interaction

Love is the most universal, the most tremendous and the most mysterious
of the cosmic forces. After centuries of tentative effort, social institutions
have externally diked and canalized it. Taking advantage of this situation, the
moralists have tried to submit it to rules. But in constructing their theories
they have never got beyond the level of an elementary empiricism influenced
by out-of-date conceptions of matter and the relics of old taboos. Socially, in
science, business and public affairs, men pretend not to know it, though under
the surface it is everywhere. Huge, ubiquitous and always unsubdued—this
wild force seems to have defeated all hopes of understanding and governing
it. It is therefore allowed to run everywhere beneath our civilization. We
are conscious of it, but all we ask of it is to amuse us, or not to harm us.
Is it truly possible for humanity to continue to live and grow without
asking itself how much truth and energy it is losing by
neglecting its incredible power of love?

—Pierre Teilhard de Chardin, *On Love and Happiness*

To BEGIN AS I have by invoking the words of Pierre Teilhard de Chardin
on the ubiquity of love may be for the reader a bit of a jolt. Although I
noted earlier that authors must be invested emotionally in rhetoric that has
any claim to truth, this does not immediately suggest that a truthful author
must also love the world and all who are in it. At the same time, my argument
that truth comes to us through our conscious, engaged attention to the lived-
in world, particularly through engaged interaction with the consciousnesses
of others, suggests strongly that the ultimate form of emotionally engaged
attention—love—plays both an essential and a practical role.

In this chapter, I define the nature of engaged attention to others within
a phenomenological rhetoric, through interpreting *altruism* as a rhetorical
practice. In doing so, I revisit the conscious activities that I introduced in
chapter 4 as components of rhetorical profession and show them to be realized
most fruitfully when their goal is altruism, which I define here as the practice
of selflessly seeking truth as a shared good through verbal interaction. I also
develop further the activities that compose profession, that is, reflection, re-

ceptivity, and regeneration, defining their purposeful end: to reach an understanding with others about the truth of our situation that results in a shared
good. My conflation of truth and goodness here is deliberate, for in the course
of my argument, I define truth as a value with good end for human beings.

In the previous chapter, I focused on the practice of rhetoric at its point
of origin, that is, the mind of the rhetor or the writer. Yet this point of origin
is, at the same time, its end, for from the point of view of writers/rhetors,
all that can be known about the meaning of their own words rests with them.
It follows that for this meaning to have external validity, writers/rhetors must
have engaged with others to the point of establishing confidence that their
meaning is shared. We can interrogate the task of profession, in fact, as it
serves this end.

For instance, as writers, our first task in expressing the meaning of experience is to reflect with persistent and open attention on that experience, to
account for diversity in our personal perceptions and those of others, and to
appreciate life experiences from our singular and unique position within them.
Yet to convey that appreciation to others, we must recognize within our experience a thing of common value, something that attunes us to others' concerns for the world we share. This necessarily involves *acknowledgment* that
our reflections refer to a shared reality and further that others' reflections on
experience have the value that we attribute to our own. Similarly, the practice
of reasoned receptivity has as its ultimate end mutual knowledge; it is a process through which we compare our perceptions of the world with those of
others and see their perceptions—and our own—as products of an emotional
engagement with our environment, colored and gradated by the experiences
we have had prior to this moment and the direction in which we choose to
go after this moment. Thus, the validity of our reasoning does not rest on its
adherence to strict criteria for rational judgments made on the basis of logical
or empirical evidence; it rests, rather, on the *authenticity* of our response to
our own and others' experience. This authenticity is measured, I contend, by
the way in which our reasoning respects the persons and perceptions of those
within the community we address by recognizing our mutual obligation to
construct communal solutions. And finally, the act of regeneration, that is, of
expressing beliefs to which we are committed personally, requires a positive investment in our future, and by extension, the future of others. For the future
is shaped by the actions of all the beings we call our own—all of humankind.
Regeneration, as we have said, attends to our personal histories and inscribes
us as "beings in progress" who are continuously being built and rebuilt
through the willed and intended actions of one another. Regeneration is not
a passive act; it is born of *ardor*, a passion for knowing, understanding, and
valuing what is other. Ardor, as I am defining it within a phenomenological
rhetoric, conveys a selfless enthusiasm for relation to others and for the idea

that we are creating together something more valuable than we can fathom individually.

The ideas I have sketched in outline here are simple, yet to find reason to act upon them, or even to believe that we should, renders them exceedingly complex. Within the pages of this chapter and my concluding chapter, I hope to clarify these principles, defending them as specific guidelines for our everyday practice of rhetoric.

Acknowledgment

In chapter 4, I described reflection as the first component of the rhetorical act of profession. Reflection involves: first, persistent attention to the world and one's experience within it; second, an open attitude toward all that one observes, that is, a tendency to include or accept information that conflicts with one's current sense of the meaning of things, rather than to reject disparate detail; and, finally, a personal stance, a recognition that the view one takes toward experience is by nature distinctive because it is embodied in our unique persons. Yet this "unique" perspective need not be alien to others; it may indeed be *the* view through which others better understand their own experience. For reflection to function in this way, however, it must transform the rhetor, moving him or her to acknowledge the relationship of his or her own life to that of others, in other words, to recognize how personal experience implicates one's own survival and prosperity and that of others. But reflection must go further even than this, as I shall show, to acknowledge the intrinsic value of other persons as persons.

Acknowledgment of our relationship to both things and persons other than ourselves is an essential requirement of verbal meaning. Mario J. Valdés amplifies this point, noting that textual meaning is entirely relational; it is dependent upon our drawing connections between bodies of texts as well as bodies of persons. Hence, our understanding of texts reflects our relationship to past meaning that we have gleaned from our interpretation of other texts as well as our relationship to a community of others who read and interpret texts. He writes:

> If we are to understand a written page, we must first situate the page within the body of the writing, then, place the writing within a particular practice of writing . . . and then, in the experience of social interaction, locate our page within the whole network of conventions of writing, of beliefs and commitments to these beliefs, of institutions and the whole configuration of the historical make-up of culture as we understand it. . . . If a text were to be deprived of its history, it would also be deprived of meaning. (Valdés 32)

Not only does textual meaning depend on historical context, that is, meanings developed over time, but it also embodies a totalizing, concrete relationship established between a human author and a reader; this, in effect, is what centers the text as a unified composition:

> The characteristics of a text are that it is written discourse with a discernible unit totality—that is, a composition, a product of a writer's labour that is available only through an immersion in this text-reader relationship—and that the author-text relationship is the event of composition. (Valdés 37–38)

The phenomenological interpretation of textual meaning differs sharply from deconstructive technique in its regard for history and embodied meaning. For the deconstructionist, holding to past meanings and their history is merely nostalgic, for all relevant meaning is always being created anew, but for the phenomenologist, past meaning is part of the lived experience of concrete beings who understand themselves as temporally persistent and as developing meaning over time with other sentient beings. As Valdés has put it, the essential difference between the deconstructionist approach and the phenomenological interpretation is that the former fails to acknowledge that interpretation is a shared experience among a community of beings with history and purpose:

> Phenomenological hermeneutics has postulated its domain as the world of social action and the concept of community. A community is defined by a shared activity. It is the engagement in social action marked by a feeling of a unity but also an activity wherein individual participation is completely willing and not forced or coerced. In short, for there to be a community there must be a consciousness of the collective identity and there must also exist a strong sense of purposive sharing among its members. (55)

The relationship between rhetors/authors and the others with whom they communicate is essential to meaning, to knowledge, and to truth. In order for authors/rhetors to profess their views with the hope of arriving at meaning shared with others, they must first fully acknowledge a relationship to the world and to others in it.

I intend to explore here three stages of acknowledgment as a rhetorical practice: first, to acknowledge that what we know about the world results from relating the world to ourselves; second, to acknowledge that what we know about the world relates to our mental and physical persistence over time; and third, to acknowledge that what we know about the world is validated by the lives and experiences of others. This third stage, I shall explain, involves an emotional admission of the intrinsic worth of persons, both oneself and others.

In order to recognize truthful meaning as an outcome of relating to others, we must first understand ourselves as beings who compose reality through relating what we are conscious of to ourselves. In other words, we must acknowledge that the reality of the world is a matter of the beliefs we have constructed about it in relating to it and others in it. That earthly reality is a matter of conscious belief is evident on the most basic level in our ability to adopt several beliefs about how the world is structured and to suspend them all at will (Haney 4–6). The very fact that our consciousness can, in effect, destroy every conception that we hold about the natural world must illustrate that consciousness has precedence over these conceptions themselves; in other words, that our consciousness is truly fundamental in that we as conscious beings perform the relational act that generates a conception. But given this power of our consciousness, what is to prevent us from continuously constructing and reconstructing conceptions of the world on our own terms; in other words, through what mechanism do we validly recognize the reality of an existing world outside ourselves? Our validation of the world's stable reality is based on our relating to others, on our intersubjectivity. It is intersubjectivity, in the terms of Husserl's phenomenology, "which guarantees that an object can be meant as public and not simply a determining aspect of the originary ego itself" (Haney 15). We begin to understand ourselves as separate beings who are relating things to ourselves when we begin to understand other people as beings for whom it is possible to constitute things consciously, just as we do ourselves, and for whom that constitution is independent from us.

The possibility of constituting objects and beings as existing independently from ourselves is logically derived from what Husserl describes as the act of "appresentation." This is the mental process that occurs when we encounter familiar objects and "fill in" what we do not know about something from our immediate direct experience of it with what we do know about it from our recalled experience (Haney 48). The repetition of this process results in a stable conception of objects in the real world. For instance, in looking at what I judge to be a house from the front, I can fill in what it may look like from the back and sides by comparing this conception with previous experiences of what "I register as house" (Haney 48). Several pairings of present experience with past conceptions result in us discerning that an object has a stable reality separate from ourselves, and this leads to the possibility of acknowledging someone else who is independent of ourselves who also consciously constitutes objects as we do.

Husserl's depiction of the ego's acknowledgment of the other involves two stages. First, one ego recognizes "another body" as "an aspect of its own consciousness" (Haney 55). Second, following this recognition, the original ego experiences the ego of the other to intrude upon its consciousness "through its acts which, insofar as they are the reciprocal complements of the originary ego's meanings, participate with it in a single intention which nevertheless requires two intentionalities to establish that intention as the unity of a single paired meaning" (Haney 55). In other words, individuals experience within consciousness the intrusion of meanings that are derived by other beings; furthermore, individuals treat the meanings that they learn from others as conscious intentions much like their own and pair these meanings with their own to construct a unified meaning for the objects that are constituted by both. As I noted in the last chapter, Haney argues that the intentions of two egos' "overreachings of the meaning each bestows" (55) is the process that "begins to move the originary ego to another level of consciousness" (55). In other words, our individual meanings progress, become more elaborate, and develop new sense when they are paired with the meanings of others.

To summarize, the phenomenological process of acknowledgment as an aspect of determining meaning involves: first, acknowledging the external world as constituted in our consciousness; second, acknowledging the stability of objects in the world through pairing our various apperceptions of them, thus constituting a unified idea about something that persists over time; and third, acknowledging others who are constituting conceptions of the world along with us and contributing to our own conceptions of what we know about the world, for these are formed in part by the conceptions of others paired and unified with ours.

But acknowledgment as a rhetorical feature involves more than the epistemological process I have just described. It also involves an active response to the inherent value of the persons whose lives and experiences I acknowledge. Rhetoric, after all, moves beyond our conscious reasoning to action that affects other persons. There are two aspects to recognizing personhood that I would like to explore here: First, one acknowledges oneself as a person who has had past interests and can formulate future interests in the light of one's existence over time as a single living being; and second, one acknowledges others as persons with past and present interests that must be treated with the same respect that one gives one's own. The move from logically conceiving an external world and others in it to acting within that world necessarily raises the issue of affecting the existence of that world, for my actions do have an effect on the livelihood of myself, others, and the world we share. Our contemplation of this very fact, I wish to argue, suggests that our acknowledgment of others in rhetorical communication must be altruistically motivated. We can, in fact, cite both logical and ethical reasons to acknowledge others' interests and to act altruistically on those interests within our rhetorical practice. My defense of this claim is derived from the work of three philosophers who have linked altruism to rational thinking: Thomas Nagel, Pierre Teilhard de Chardin, and James Kellenberger.

A rationale for acknowledging that others' interests must be treated with the respect I give my own, in other words, for acting altruistically toward them, has been defended by Nagel most notably in *The Possibility of Altruism*. Motivation to act on another's behalf does not arise by necessity, Nagel claims, from an egoistic sentiment such as "sympathy, pity, or benevolence" (*Altruism* 84), nor must it arise from the purely solipsistic desire to help someone else because it is of direct benefit to me. When we act rationally in our own interests, Nagel asserts, we decide to do so on the basis of universal, impersonal principles that stay the same over time (*Altruism* 84–89). Failure to act from universal principles risks our dissociation from the fact that we are persons existing among other persons and living out a singular, fragile existence that is extended over time. We make decisions about the future through applying universal, impersonal principles, judging that it would be good to do something in the future even though we are not in the circumstances that would dictate that it is good to do that very thing right now. As Nagel notes, the "metaphysics of the person," that is, our ontological sense of existing temporally, supports "the objective validity of prudential constraints by interpreting them as the practical expression of an awareness that one persists over time." The fact that we act with prudence and understand our motivation to do so reflects our acknowledgment that we are "temporally persistent being[s] [with] ability to identify with past and future stages of [ourselves] and to regard them as forming a single life" (*Altruism* 58). This understanding of our being leads us to apply rationally our own concerns for survival and prosperity to others.

We not only have reason to act prudentially and altruistically because we and others each live out a single life, extended over time, but we also have reason to think of ourselves as progressing, along with others, moving toward a more integrated and comfortable relationship with the world. Teilhard de Chardin refers to the fact of our temporally extended being to argue that reason evolves over time, both within an individual's personal development and across our species over several generations. His aim is not to demonstrate narrowly, as does Nagel, that a given reason or proposition can apply to different situations universally over time, thus justifying prudential action within the formal procedures of logic. For Teilhard de Chardin, the possibility of rationalizing a future, rather, is evidence of our existence in a collective of conscious beings, moving forward toward greater integration and, consequently, toward more unified understanding; this evolution comprises the phenomenon of human rationality.

Rationality, the power by which humankind develops as a species, corresponds with two other human attributes: conscious knowledge of future existence and awareness of our individual value as conscious beings capable of integration with other conscious beings. Teilhard de Chardin tells us:

> The fact is that three associated factors invade the human phenomenon at the same time as thought: the first is the power of rational invention, by which . . . evolution acts as its own springboard; the second is pre-awareness of the future, which presents life with the double problem of death and action; and finally the third is attribution of value to the individual, who moves from being a mere link in the phyletic chain, to the dignity of an element capable of being integrated in an organic totalization. (*Toward the Future* 174)

Mental reasoning for Teilhard de Chardin directs our bodily existence both as individual human beings and as members of a species with continuity across generations. He defines that directed existence in terms of a mutual telos, or purposeful end. Because we can reason, we can, as Nagel has shown, act prudentially in planning our future. And because we are temporally extended beings, we can think of our actions as they have consequences over time, both for our own survival and the survival of others. But in addition to this, our ability to reason, as Teilhard has suggested, makes us capable of joining with others who reason to determine or realize a mutual purpose through acting together. As I have said earlier, I do not wish to specifically defend Teilhard de Chardin's evolutionary theory; but I believe that we can abstract from his philosophy a view toward humanity's unique capacities that speaks to our agency, will, and common function. The ability to reason together, as Teilhard de Chardin describes it, vindicates the inherent value of the individual person; it makes of each person more than "a mere link in the phyletic chain."

But just what constitutes our individual value as persons? And how does respect for that value as persons affect our process of developing mutual knowledge? Nagel defends the rational possibility of altruism without providing a means to assess how or why I should value a particular person. Nevertheless, he does articulate the rational consequence of believing that each person should be valued as having the same worth as every other. If we believe this, he concludes, then we must regard all persons as having separate lives with equal value over extended time. Hence, we could not make a decision to deprive one person of something simply because the gain is greater and more important for the well-being of some other person or persons; this kind of decision fails to regard each person's life with the significance it has for that person. Rather, in order to behave justly toward all persons, we must weigh good outcomes against bad ones by taking into account all of the lives affected by such outcomes as actual lives that we ourselves might live. Following this guideline, we might work both to improve "the lot of those in the population who are worst off" and to increase "the benefits of those who are better off only if it is not at a cost to those below them" (Nagel, *Altruism* 142). In justifying this kind of judgment, Nagel assumes the inherent value of individual persons without specifically defending it or articulating it.

Interestingly, in a more recent work, *The Last Word*, Nagel comes close to suggesting a rationale for assuring the inherent value of persons but still stops short of it. Nagel's focus in *Last Word* is upon defending the primacy of reason, that is, upon articulating its objective value and presence as a tool we put to use to decide how to act. Reason, he argues, is an objective reality quite independent from psychological motivation, sociological influence, or even biological imperative to behave as reasoning creatures. Nagel defends reason as a reliable tool to make objective judgments in both scientific and moral matters. Scientific beliefs can be proven to be "objectively true," for instance, because we arrive at them by reliable methods (this does not discount, by the way, the possibility of empirical disconfirmation) (*Last Word* 101–02). All reasoning, even about moral matters, Nagel argues, "is not merely a development of a point of view, but objective thought about how things are" (*Last Word* 88). The way we deal with beliefs that are in conflict, whether they are established on scientific or moral grounds, is to apply reasoning that takes into account what he calls "first order" claims. He calls to mind here G. E. Moore's rebuttal of "skepticism about the external world on the ground that he has two hands" (*Last Word* 85). To claim the reality of the world is not to beg the question, Nagel claims, but rather to apply reason to conclude that given the alternatives of there being a real world and there being an imaginary world, my incontrovertible "first order" experience that I have two hands suggests that the real world is the more plausible alternative.

Nagel concludes his discussion of ethics and reasoning by attempting to "reason" why we have objective value, a point, as I have shown, that he also addresses in *The Possibility of Altruism*. We are left with the conclusion that we are "objectively worthless," he suggests, when we accept the subjectivist positions that, first, all that we do we do only for ourselves, and second, all the reasons we have for doing something are valuable only to ourselves and those who care about us. If we have no value other than personal value, we are by default "objectively worthless." Finding this conclusion untenable on the grounds that first-order claims suggest to us both individually and collectively that we have value beyond mere value to ourselves, Nagel goes on to argue for our worth. But he does so, again, only on rational grounds. He finds these grounds within existing utilitarian theory by which one's worth is calculated as a value weighed against other values and within the Kantian categorical imperative by which one's worth among others is shown to stem from "our equality of status" (*Last Word* 123), which accords individuals certain rights (see *Last Word* 122–25). Yet the question of how to choose one rational scheme over the other in judging how we should behave toward others in the face of these opposing philosophies is still unresolved, as is the question of why we have inherent value quite aside from our value in relation to one another.

In my view, Nagel, in reasoning about our objective worth, ignores a first-order assumption in the determination of human value that is just as compelling as the fact of "my two hands." And that first-order assumption is this: We believe that we and others have value because not to believe so is not to have a reason to live. In the face of this reality, it is far more pragmatic to believe that I am inherently worthy than to believe that I am not. And just as the reality of my two hands suggests that I can use them to shape the world about me, the reality of my worthiness suggests that I must act toward myself and others as if we all have essential value.

Although we can argue objectively, as Nagel does, for the rationality of altruistic behavior in terms of its prudence, that is, its contribution to ensuring our mutual survival over time, our choice to act altruistically, in the end, is linked fundamentally to how we regard human persons, that is, to our sense that we are inherently worthy. But given that we have first-order reasons to believe we are worthy, just what attitudes should motivate us to act on that belief? Kellenberger suggests that the possibility of behaving altruistically as opposed to merely having rational reason to do so is, in fact, dependent upon our acknowledging emotionally "the intrinsic worth that persons have as persons, as opposed to their moral worth or merit, or their esthetic worth, or indeed any earned or genetically endowed worth that persons may or may not have" (50). It is respect for the intrinsic worth of persons, including ourselves, Kellenberger believes, that truly allows us to act "for the sake of others" as opposed to "acting for the sake of a principle" (52).

Certain emotional conditions within ourselves must abide if we are to acknowledge the intrinsic worth of persons. For instance, it may be impossible to recognize intrinsic worth if our personal feelings toward others are in the range of hate (Kellenberger 55). Kellenberger reasons that "one who recognizes the value of another would feel the fittingness of respecting, revering, or loving the other"; hence, "an affective attitude in the . . . respect/love . . . range is a part of the recognition of the worth of persons" (55). Recognition of the intrinsic worth of persons, of course, applies to oneself as well as to others, and we could say that it provides the emotional motivation for us to "act" prudentially on our own behalf in addition to having logical reasons to do so. The entire phenomenon of discovering the intrinsic worth of persons, concludes Kellenberger, involves our adopting toward persons a posture of understanding love. He claims that "love that forms the affective dimension of discovering the inherent worth of persons will have a feeling side (in opposition to emotional indifference) and a dispositional side (in opposition to behavioral indifference)" (87). In other words, discovering the worth of persons entails that we both feel and act toward them in a loving way. These feelings and actions are not dependent on the behavior of the persons in question. Kellenberger notes:

> Love of persons as persons accepts human beings as they are, not for the sake of their potential to change. It is concerned for the well-being of persons and will encourage change for the sake of that well-being, but not for the sake of the relief of one's anxiety or out of resentment or from the inspiration of . . . other negative feelings. (91)

Failure to feel love for persons as persons is not a failure in rationality, for we can find reasons to act lovingly out of duty without any emotional investment; rather, a failure to feel love toward persons, that is, a failure to acknowledge their intrinsic worth, is a failure in sensitivity, or as Kellenberger calls it, a failure of "realization-rationality [rather than] a failure of enquiry-rationality" (88). Hence, acknowledgment of the intrinsic worth of persons and the consequent adoption of a loving attitude toward them involves a personal realization, an emotional discovery that is the result of our acknowledging a relationship to them: "Persons are discovered to be persons, are beheld as persons, just when one discovers that one is related to them as person to person" (Kellenberger 130).

Just what is at the basis of this emotional discovery of persons as persons? Certainly this discovery entails developing a respect for human beings, which stems from a wonder at the very potential of their being, their capacity to will and to execute changes in the conditions about themselves and others. W. G. Maclagan, who is among many philosophers whom Kellenberger cites to develop his conception of the intrinsic worth of persons, tells us that the potential for human goodness, stemming from our contemplation of "the mere fact of free rational agency, and altogether without regard to whether it is actualized in good or evil forms" (200), captures our attention, giving us rational reason to respect persons. But this is not enough to account for our acknowledgment of their intrinsic worth. For this, we must experience a kind of "active human sympathy" (213), as Maclagan calls it, fused with a sense of "obligation" (216) based on our rational judgment of the worth of persons. Together these attitudes form the emotional commitment the Greeks termed agape, an uncompromising love of persons simply because that is what they are (Maclagan 213–17). This discovery of the "person to person" relationship through the attitude of agape has practical moral consequences. Moral behavior becomes more than a response to principle; it becomes a consequence of having discovered persons as persons.

Through discovery of the "person to person" relationship, we can adopt an attachment to others that is detached "from egocentric concerns," one that is fully giving, unconditional, spontaneous and "indifferent to [the] accidental value" of others (Kellenberger 113), the attachment implied in the attitude of agape. At the same time, discovery of the intrinsic worth of persons does not suggest that our behavior toward others must always be "agreeable or uncontroversial." To care for others as persons also "may require opposition to another's wishes and entering into controversy" (Kellenberger 114). Yet whether we behave agreeably toward others or engage them in controversy, our reasons and methods for doing so are shaped by a sense of their inherent worth as persons.

I have been talking about acknowledgment of the value of others here in fairly abstract terms, speaking of it as a cognitive and affective process without elaborating its specific consequences for rhetorical practice. If we were to apply the cognitive and affective process of acknowledgment to the phenomenological perspective on interpretation that I am developing, we might sketch its place within that scheme as follows. To begin, we acknowledge that all we claim to know is derived from evaluating our own conceptions of personal experience, both present and past, and from pairing these conceptions with those of others who have the same power to conceive of the world as we do. Hence, we conclude that to truly understand the world and thus improve my place and the place of others within it, I must acknowledge the place and interests of others in that world. Finally, a decision to act altruistically toward others upon this acknowledgment is motivated by my own sense of intrinsic worth as a person, which I extend to those others I perceive to be conscious beings like myself. In giving here a few examples of how the activity of acknowledgment comes into play in rhetorical practice, I only can suggest how rhetorical practices might be conducted were acknowledgment to guide them, without fully elaborating their consequences, that is, without taking into account the range of particular circumstances that affect the ways we engage with others, such as blood relationship, supervisory responsibility, and the complications of various historical obligations developed between individuals and groups.

To begin, acknowledgment as a rhetorical principle demands that when we write and speak to others, we think first about their having intrinsic worth, as we do ourselves, and about the fact that what I know about the world depends upon the circumstance that I am a person who is relating to these other persons. One consideration that such a realization may entail is that I revise my notion of what is an effective rhetorical strategy, including the tactic of assessing the needs of an audience precisely so that I may discover how to persuade them to consider my point of view. If I acknowledge from the "get go" that the reliability of my conception of the world is dependent upon the conceptions of others, I will need first to attempt to see and speak of things on their terms. I will need to seek out those points at which I miss or lose contact with the communications of others because they are not familiar to me or congruent with my own. Such an attempt to accept others' communication practices on their own terms takes some doing, as Mary Louise Pratt has observed; to do so, we need to put aside the prejudice of viewing others' language practices as subnormal or marginal when they differ from widely accepted practices or from our own. But viewing another's language use entirely without prejudice is a rare accomplishment.

Prejudicial beliefs about language invade even linguists' descriptions of how language is used within a given community; in fact, their interpretations at times overtly fail to reflect disinterested observation. Linguists often assume the existence of a kind of "linguistic utopia" in social communities, believing groups of language users to follow coherent rules for interacting with each other consistently. Pratt cites as an example William Labov's analysis of an interview of a black male that was conducted by a white male interviewer in order to investigate language use. Labov declares the black speaker to be incoherent because he "produces the 'turgid, redundant, bombastic and empty' English of the American middle class" and "fails" to speak using features of a black dialect, presumably because a white interviewer is asking him the questions (Pratt 56). Pratt berates Labov for assuming a coherency of response among speakers who are associated with a particular language community, saying that researchers have blinded themselves to the actual dynamic of contact between users of one supposed language community and another. On the same grounds, she attacks monolithic descriptions of language use that linguists categorize as "marginal," simply because such use differs from an assumed norm. She notes:

> The marginalization of speech forms associated with women and women's spheres is symptomatic not simply of androcentrism in linguistics, but of an extraordinary, really pathologically narrow conception of what "the normal system" or "straightforward communication" is. (Pratt 55)

A study of language communities in contact would allow linguists to better see "the dominated and dominant *in their relations with each other*" (Pratt 56), an eventuality that is likely to reveal more about how different groups make meaning with each other than an approach that assumes consistent and regular communication within a coherent language community. At their point of contact, language groups in conflict struggle to be recognized by one another; this is the place at which differences are fully addressed.

Our current tradition of teaching rhetorical conventions that are assumed to be accepted by all within a language community generally omits discussion of rhetorical practices "at the margin," except perhaps to regard them as generally unacceptable or in error. If authors naively assume that everyone in a given audience—even one narrowly defined as homogeneous by culture and circumstance—reads and interprets conventional forms uniformly and consistently, they are likely to misread or to miss altogether the responsive behavior of those persons whose language use does not include these conventions or whose attitudes toward their ideological content interfere with their reception of them. And furthermore, our current rhetorical pedagogy suggests that authors need feel no obligation to explore the point of contact between a particular audience's variant use of language and the conventions they have been taught to consider acceptable. In short, they are taught that to follow acceptable conventions is to communicate most effectively, period. The consequence of this behavior may be, at a very basic level, to blind authors from acknowledging that there are those in their audience who lead lives that are different from theirs, with different concerns and expectations as valid for them as the author's are for him or her. If we were to continue this argument along Nagel's lines, we might go so far as to say that for authors to behave as if another person's ways of speaking need not be acknowledged is to ignore reason and behave "un-prudentially," as it were. How can an author fail to acknowledge that the concerns of another are equally important without hearing their words or speaking to them on their own terms? Does not such action also fail to acknowledge the intrinsic worth of all persons who are my audience as others who are related to me by virtue of the person-to-person relationship that exists among all human beings (as Kellenberger describes it)?

Of course, we cannot dismiss the importance of convention in establishing the common ground through which speakers relate to an audience. Richard M. Coe reminds us that "conventional forms, as they function in both creative and communicative processes, are a major part of what makes these processes social" (19). But he also tells us that conventional forms can constrain "against the discovery of information that does not fit the form" and can carry "implicit moral/political values," such as when conventions either thwart or complement "the interests of some power elite" (Coe 20). Earlier, in chapter 2, I discussed the pragmatic value of conventional epistemological and rhetorical approaches to the advancement of knowledge in scientific and technical communication, and noted there as well the limitations on discovery that rhetorical and methodological conventions may impose. Given that we must take into account the pragmatic value of conventional forms, just what kinds of adjustments need we make in our use of them in order to acknowledge that others have concerns and interests that are different from but as valuable as ours, that is, to respect their intrinsic worth?

One adjustment we might make to our rhetoric is to consider, prior to strategizing and prior to settling on form, how our communications might contribute to some general good. In two publications that explore the aims of scientific and technical rhetoric, James P. Zappen draws a link between the ideal of acting for the public good espoused in ancient rhetoric and knowledge development in the sciences and technical professions, concluding that instrumental goals to advance scientific knowledge or to solve technical problems are indeed best addressed by rhetoric that serves the public good. Taking a historical view, Zappen notes how renowned scientists have used their rhetoric to encourage community participation, both professional and public, so that their methods of retrieving and analyzing data might be continually improved. Francis Bacon and Thomas Sprat, for instance, articulated "a public rhetoric designed to further the cause of the new science," a rhetoric that was intended both "to persuade others to join in the scientific enterprise and to inform other participants of observations and discoveries" (Zappen, "Historical Perspectives" 16). Darwin developed a "polemical" style that challenged "the prevailing scientific opinion on the immutability of species" (Zappen, "Historical Perspectives" 20); and Einstein perfected a style that acknowledged the influence of power politics, a style that hinted "at a kind of rhetoric suited to a time in which science has become both difficult and dangerous" (Zappen, "Historical Perspectives" 24). All of these scientists adjusted their language to what they believed to be others' conceptions of the world not only to persuade, but also to encourage further and better development of scientific ideas within the context of their societal consequences. The need to acknowledge difference in perspective is important not only to assure that scientific researchers effectively interpret information so that it adds productively to a knowledge base, but also to assure that their research is directed to an end that leads to our mutual benefit.

The path Zappen suggests for scientific rhetoric is to subject scientific research to the ground rule of acknowledging the needs of others and to do so through interpreting the results of research in terms of how they contribute to public debate about the public good. Implied in this approach is an interrogation of our notion of public good. Along with advances in science and industry since the nineteenth century, Zappen remarks, we have equated public good with "organizational good." If an idea promotes the health of an industry—adding to its productivity and profits—it is assumed to promote the public good as well. As we know now in the late twentieth century, by virtue of such public scandals as the exploding Pinto gas tanks and the fatally flawed Challenger, such an assumption reduces sensitivity to diversity, an outcome that puts scientific and technical communication at risk of disaffecting or disappropriating the public from concerns that are rightly theirs. Pluralism in rhetorical approach, Zappen argues, a melding of strategies that accommodate the "broad range of interests and points of view that characterize a complex, pluralistic society" and that incorporate, where appropriate, "the traditional forms suited to internal organizational decision making" would acknowledge both the greater good of society as well as the good of the organizational communities that contribute to our welfare (Zappen, "Rhetoric and Technical Communication" 39). Writers who behave sensitively toward both can respond best to the intrinsic worth of the persons whose interests are served by these collectives.

Acknowledgment as a rhetorical practice transforms how we profess the meaning of our experiences through finding the experiences of others to have a value that we attribute to our own. This acknowledgment allows us to view others as persons relating to us as persons, as having lives that we ourselves could live, but do not, lives that are every bit as significant as our own. To act upon that realization in our rhetorical practice involves sensitivity to the communication practices of others, both as realized individually and as enacted by groups at a particular point in time under particular circumstances or within a particular cultural or organizational society. But such response can be rote or a mere accommodation to the practices of others. In other words, I may respond to others on their terms with the ultimate goal of simply moving these individuals to meet my terms. Of course, the goal to move others to accept my own terms is not necessarily a selfish desire: My goals may indeed be goals that are good for the community that I address. But how do I know that? How do I appropriately address my response to a situation as an authentic response, one that is recognizable within the community as having value that contributes to a mutual good? It is this problem that we shall address next.

Authenticity

Were we simply to acknowledge that others have intrinsic worth as persons and likewise have goals that have every bit the significance of our own, this would not be enough to assure the authenticity of our response to others, that is, to guarantee that our communications with others are not directed by selfish and potentially irresponsible desires. After all, the hegemonic maneuvers of the business tycoon or the political autocrat are grounded in their knowledge that others have needs and desires very like their own. They, at times, employ this knowledge to thwart or to subdue the desires of others and thus assure their own success. In order for our acknowledgment of others to direct us to act for their and our mutual good, we must see our own self-worth to be dependent upon the well-being of others.

As I noted in the previous section, Nagel argues that mere recognition that the status of other human beings is similar to our own should direct us to behave altruistically toward them, given that we recognize that their lives have value as do our own. And similarly, Kellenberger argues that the intrinsic worth of human beings guides us—or ought to guide us—to behave as if our common interests were more important than our individual desires. But outside of these rational and moral reasons, in the face of pleasure and pain, what pure motivation do we have to behave in the interests of others; what inspiration can we cite that would urge us as human agents to pursue goals that are not entirely self-directed? And in particular, what reason can we give to behave responsibly toward others when we see ourselves—as I have argued that our current and most influential theories of self-agency present us—as beings who must resist the influence of others in order to maintain both self-integrity and the distance that is required to make objective and fair judgments?

I have proposed that the phenomenological approach to meaning both demonstrates the futility of viewing ourselves as separated from others in any way and suggests how we might actuate our integral relationship with others to increase knowledge. However, I have not demonstrated why both our individual desires and our knowledge of the world would be better served if we acted in the interests of others: The essential reason that we should so act is that our entire knowledge-making enterprise is dependent on it. In short, we cannot be sure that we have valid knowledge of the world unless we consider the interests of others. But there is more to the authenticity of our interpretive judgments than even this: We cannot make valid claims about the world without first considering our very function and purpose as human beings within it, a function and purpose shared by every creature like us. The authenticity of our expression is not dictated by either culture or personal will, but rather by its contribution to our essential function as human beings, that is, as individually conscious living entities with a temporal existence who develop singular histories that have meaning only within the extended history of our species across generations. With this statement I have made a grand claim about knowledge relative to the meaning of human existence and so am obligated to defend it, and I shall through referring in the main to the work of two contemporary philosophers, Alasdair MacIntyre and Charles Taylor.

In addressing the moral implications of knowledge development, both MacIntyre and Taylor discuss how personal expression preserves the integrity of the individual, adds to knowledge, and contributes to the social good. They define authentic expression in these terms, establishing a necessary relationship between regard for ourselves and others and speaking the truth. Authentic expression, they conclude, reflects our dependency upon others and responds to the very function or telos of what it is to be a human being. And they reveal, furthermore, that our modern conception that individuals are autonomous has stood in the way of our encouraging and achieving such authenticity.

MacIntyre develops his theory of how human beings came to be defined as autonomous and lacking in essential purpose in *After Virtue: A Study in Moral Theory*. In this work he explains how the Enlightenment project obliterated concern with the function of human existence espoused by ancient philosophers, and he calls for a restoration of this view. In *Three Rival Versions of Moral Inquiry*, MacIntyre extends this argument to claim that belief in a human telos or essential function is, in fact, necessary not only to inspire moral behavior but also to increase and validate knowledge. This is a very important claim for the phenomenological approach to communication that I endorse. In effect, MacIntyre conflates the concerns of epistemology and moral theory much in the way that phenomenology conflates objectivity and subjectivity. In short, to establish a valid knowledge claim is to attend ethically to our essential function in the way that to establish an objective fact is to acknowledge its subjective roots. MacIntyre gives us reason to believe—as I hope to show by presenting in quite some detail his arguments here—that the success of our truth seeking is contingent upon our developing a communal sense of purpose. And he explains the method through which we might achieve this sense, a method derived from the Thomist tradition of intellectual inquiry.

To begin, in *After Virtue,* an analysis of the state of moral theory and behavior in current society, MacIntyre demonstrates that the goals of the Enlightenment project to value the stance of the skeptical, impersonal observer obliterated classical and theological views of "man" as a functional concept, displacing them with the impersonal study of "man" as a natural object. Hence, since the Enlightenment, we have replaced ideas of what "man" *ought to be* with empirical descriptions of what "man" *is* (MacIntyre, *After Virtue* 59). In applying this logic to matters about humanity, we have lost a vision of ourselves as beings who are striving for some kind of ideal state, who not only "are" but "ought to be" some way or another. Hence, the function of the human being to perfect himself or herself or to emulate God's goodness has been supplanted as a moral goal by the desire for individual autonomy and self-actualization. Transgressions against persons now are described not in terms of how they are incongruent with a human being's moral function to act in certain ways, but rather in terms of how someone's "*rights* [are invaded] in the name of someone else's *utility*" (MacIntyre, *After Virtue* 71). Likewise a person's activities in a professional or "character" role, such as administrative management, are not evaluated in terms of their contribution to the essential function of a human being enacting a societal role, but rather in terms of how they "put skills and knowledge to work in the service of achieving certain ends" (MacIntyre, *After Virtue* 75).

Enlightenment rationality, claims MacIntyre, encouraged the development of emotivist theories of human progress in which we attend to the means by which we do something as opposed to the end achieved. If rationality rules the validity of an outcome, then the method is more important than the result, a position that MacIntyre finds morally untenable when applied to social issues. In obliterating concerns about ends, emotivist theories fail to acknowledge the "practical imperative" that Kant cited as necessary for all ethical behavior, and that is: "Act in such a way that you always treat humanity, whether in your own person or in the person of any other, never simply as a means, but always at the same time as an end" (Kellenberger 44; Kant 429). Particularly at fault for institutionalizing the primacy of "means" over "ends" in addressing social questions is Weberian management theory. The Weberian bureaucratic manager considers ends only when they match means that are judged to be economical and efficient (MacIntyre, *After Virtue* 25); the ultimate value of the end is not questioned by the bureaucrat, nor can it be settled rationally. Instead, the manager's job is thought of in terms of needing "to influence the motives of his subordinates" and "to ensure that those subordinates argue from premises which will produce agreement with his own prior conclusions" (MacIntyre, *After Virtue* 27), that is, choose means that will result in his own preestablished ends. The Weberian bureaucrat or manager is one who applies a method, rather than one who applies reasoned judgment. He or she is but a character whose legislative role "morally legitimates a mode of social existence" (MacIntyre, *After Virtue* 29).

For MacIntyre, a "character," such as the bureaucratic manager, is a modern invention, a social role that carries moral cachet within a culture. Characters rely upon an impartial, scientific epistemology to regulate their interactions with others. The bureaucratic moral authority of the "character," as well as the autonomy of the individual in modern society, MacIntyre claims, go hand in hand. We are in constant debate over the rights and authority of each, a situation that has created "the cultural climate of this bureaucratic individualism" (MacIntyre, *After Virtue* 35) in which we now live. What the roles of both characters and individuals share is the position they take toward the world they observe, and that is to stand back from a situation, "to pass judgment on it from a purely universal and abstract point of view that is totally detached from all social particularity" (MacIntyre, *After Virtue* 32). Because the authority of the individual and of certain characters, such as the manager, is thought to be objectively derived, persons adopting these roles can think of themselves and their actions as "morally neutral" (MacIntyre, *After Virtue* 74). What the manager decides to do on the basis of the facts of a situation in order to promote Weberian efficiency and effectiveness represents a moral commitment to methods, rather than results, and a conception of "fact" that is separated from any sense of "value" (MacIntyre, *After Virtue* 77). Change is advocated because it is scientifically sound. The bureaucrat's appeal is his or her "ability to deploy a body of scientific and above all social scientific knowledge, organized in terms of and understood as comprising a set of universal law-like generalizations" (MacIntyre, *After Virtue* 86).

In short, MacIntyre argues that within the technocratic management systems of modern society—whether they be economic, political, or cultural—individuals attain personal authority and authenticity through relying on technical systems to justify their actions, and such reliance places no obligation upon the individual to question the ends that are supported technically by the means of science, law, religion, or any other system of rules, laws, and regulations. For instance, a legal system that protects the right of individuals to free speech gives us little ground to question the continued expression of hateful and discriminating language by individuals belonging to the Ku Klux Klan, even though such language is personally hurtful to many other individuals. The consequence of abandoning consideration of the ends of our actions in favor of scrutinizing our conformance to regulatory systems to meet these ends poses a threat not only to individuals whose interests may be dismissed by such decision making, but also to our very ability to think together rationally about the meaning of the world we inhabit.

Classificatory and regulatory systems fix the world we inhabit so that we can identify, place, and categorize all that we find in it, and thus bring the world under our control and along with it the behavior of others in it. But individual interpretations of this world we share refuse to be bounded by such fixity of meaning. Although we may claim authenticity through deferring to scientific method, law, or even religion, the shifting grounds of individual and social influence affect meaning in every one of these domains. Both history and individual will stretch any interpretation to such an extent that even the methods we rely upon to validate it become multiply defined and thus groundless.

In his succeeding argument to *After Virtue,* MacIntyre wrestles with the problem of determining an authentic foundation for knowledge in the postmodern era, in which we acknowledge no foundation for belief. The legacy of the Enlightenment, which MacIntyre dubs the encyclopedist approach to inquiry, gives over human authority in matters of belief to a system of generalizations articulated by a language deemed to have fixed meaning. The opposing postmodernist approach, which MacIntyre identifies with Nietzsche's genealogist method of inquiry, finds all systematic "frameworks" to be the creation of cultures whose different systems of value are historically contingent and thus hopelessly irreconcilable. Yet the genealogist who studies the shifting ground of social influence upon thought must be encyclopedic in order to present his work to others: He must *fix* it in time so that others can understand it in time. And likewise, the reader of the genealogist's work must be able to fix himself or herself in time at the moment of reading. For the genealogist's project to make sense, there must be a commitment on the part of both writer and reader to agree upon meaning as they share in the interpretive enterprise. As MacIntyre puts it, there must be on both sides a "logical, ontological and evaluative commitment" to the knowledge-producing activity of interpretation so that each involved can critique the other, that is, potentially identify within the language of the other "inconsistency, falsity, and failure of reference" (*Three Versions* 46).

But what motivates writer and reader to commit to sharing a space in which they might come to some commonly held meaning, even in the midst of disagreement? And further, what might motivate them to struggle together to reach an understanding that accommodates their differences? MacIntyre suggests that the motivation to share meaning lies in a firm conception of our common function or telos as human beings, which is a predisposition or moral commitment to be transformed ourselves in the process of interpreting and attending to the interpretations of others as we move together both to understand more perfectly and to embody that understanding in our everyday life (MacIntyre, *Three Versions* 59–63). It is in realizing this mutual capacity that the authenticity of our expression resides. The fatal flaw, if one can be named, in Nietzsche's approach to explaining the validity of knowledge is that it may not leave room for the human agent, interpreting and being affected by other's interpretations. While pursuing historical research, the genealogist remains purposefully distant from the framework under question, so as not to be swayed by what he or she is attempting to uncover as masking our view of reality. The uncovering of "masking" contingencies leaves no room for the personal development of a willful agent who must always regard his or her own perspective as but another "masking" contingency.

The problem of agency in the genealogist's project, MacIntyre suggests, has been addressed partially by Michel Foucault, who shows the genealogist historian to be necessarily transformed through an engagement with the history of knowledge-making enterprises (*Three Versions* 49). The historian's place is to be changed or shift ground as he or she is exposed to the object of study. The transformation of those who construct academic genealogies occurs because history impacts on their projects in at least three ways: first, through increasing their understanding of "official academic history" through which significant intellectual figures become "masks of [themselves] as the producers of a charade," a realization that implicates as well the genealogist's own project to uncover the "charade"; second, through broadening their comprehension of both academics who study history and the subjects they study "as complex patterns of elements representative of their various differing cultures"; and third, through stimulating their conscious discovery of the "rancorous will to knowledge" that the history of knowledge production reveals in themselves and others (MacIntyre, *Three Versions* 50).

Foucault's depiction of the "historicized" academic, who wears many masks which represent the various transformations he or she has undergone while trying to understand the effects of context on knowledge production, implies an endless repetition of such role playing that could result in a dissolution of the whole project to uncover meaning. Foucault explores the need for agentive commitment to advance knowledge, but such commitment dissipates in an endless shifting of ground. Foucault himself, as MacIntyre notes, had resorted in his later years to the encyclopedist tradition, arriving "at the plain academic style of the *Histoire de la sexualité* and the even plainer explanations of his explanations" in "wearisome" responses to the academic community that longed for clarification, for a textbook contribution to a body of knowledge (*Three Versions* 53). Still, Foucault's declaration of the inseparability of text and author that literally disavows "any possibility of moving beyond and behind the text to authorized intention" (MacIntyre, *Three Versions* 51), ironically holds the key to an epistemological method that shuns the pitfalls of both the encyclopedic and genealogical approaches.

The very conception of developing knowledge through shifts in personal perspective and representation implicates personal transformation as a necessary component of knowledge formation. MacIntyre pushes this point even further to insist that our relationship to the past must transform us into understanding more perfectly our telos or moral function, so that we aim not so much to align our judgments to correspond with a historical reality outside us, but rather to transform ourselves to become more adequate to the circumstance and substance of what we are trying to understand. MacIntyre identifies this outlook with the development of Thomist philosophy in the thirteenth century. For the Thomist, the object of studying objects in order to discover their meaning, purposes, and ends is to help us determine our own meaning, purpose, and end because our knowledge making, truth seeking, and self-realization are, in fact, all one and the same thing. Rather than treating the world as something to be explained in terms of external, timeless principles, as might the encyclopedist, or as a reality constructed by cultures whose historical fictions are something to be struggled against, as might the genealogist, the Thomist

> treats the past neither as mere prologue nor as something to be struggled against, but as that from which we have to learn if we are to identify and move toward our telos more adequately and that which we have to put to the question if we are to know which questions we ourselves should next formulate and attempt to answer, both theoretically and practically. (MacIntyre, *Three Versions* 79)

The belief in a telos, an end, and in a source of intelligibility and purpose beyond oneself that is capable of being rediscovered within ourselves (since we are inevitably always connected to what is external to us that we seek to know) permeated the Thomist tradition, one that was born out of the necessity to reconcile Augustinian and Aristotelian conceptions of the nature of knowledge and reality. In practical terms, when Thomas Aquinas was faced with the dilemma of reconciling Aristotelian and Augustinian modes of dealing with evidence, textual and otherwise, he applied both deductive and dialectical reasoning to address both schemes in terms that could be understood, one within the other, and evaluated them in terms of a chosen end—to explain the world in terms of both causal and teleological functions. Aquinas began from this premise and moved backward through each theory to explain "the causal relationships in terms of which the present states and changes of all finite beings are made intelligible and the practical relationships through which and by means of which all finite beings move towards their perfected end" (MacIntyre, *Three Versions* 122–23). In projecting this telos that complemented the aims of both theories, Aquinas used, manipulated, and integrated the knowledge-making practices and traditions of both Aristotle and Augustine to account for various aspects of human consciousness, physical nature, spirit, and will and achieved this "in a way not merely concordant with but supporting and illuminating the specific Christian dogmas" (MacIntyre, *Three Versions* 124). MacIntyre suggests that what Aquinas did in practical terms to reconcile supposedly incommensurable schemes illustrates an approach to developing knowledge that has since been articulated more fully by contemporary theorists such as Donald Davidson and Paul Feyerabend. He cites three practical principles that guided Aquinas's masterful reconciliation. First, resources exist within a new framework for explaining reality (which succeeds a former framework) that can be used to explain the former framework. Second, a succeeding framework generally has the resources to explain the lapses or the inadequacies of a former framework in a way that cannot be addressed within the former framework. And finally, the superior adequacy of one framework as opposed to another can be determined "with a process of prospective reasoning to be justified retrospectively" (MacIntyre, *Three Versions* 120).

The Thomist approach to developing knowledge involves an openness or willingness to consider the framework in which one is thinking and acting to have some inadequacies in its capacity to fully explain worldly phenomena. This approach also reflects a selfless drive to serve not only one's own interests but also interests that are commonly shared. These inclinations come not from an autonomous and dispassionate decision to choose the most practical and effective method of assessing the world or behaving toward others, but rather from a deep commitment to be fully with and of the world we are trying to understand in order to perfect our knowledge of it. They come from believing ourselves to be designed to change and be changed through living in a world that precedes and succeeds us, the significance of which is rooted in our simply *being* in it. In short, with this approach we regard the historicity of our being and involvement with others not as an impediment to authentic knowledge but rather as requisite for it. We try to explain things by accounting for all the ways in which others are, reconciling the way we are with these different ways.

Authentic knowledge developed through investment in and involvement with others is simply unavailable to a culture that finds the skeptical perspective of the distanced and autonomous observer to be sacrosanct. It eludes a society that finds the validity of individual judgment to be contingent upon its congruence with a system of laws and regulations that hold dispassionate authority over other interpretations. In *The Ethics of Authenticity,* Charles Taylor points out that a lack of concern to forward common goals and to see the perspectives of others as having some value that we can possibly share is the result of our society's overriding commitment to individual autonomy—a value that has led us to end disputes through adjudication rather than to seek mutual resolution. Taylor argues that we have broadly, if not covertly, accepted individual rights as our primary moral standard. What has happened to us, he claims, is that in privileging individualism over community goals, we have, by default, committed ourselves to "soft relativism," a position that does not allow us to "talk in reason" about ideals as they may have communal significance (Taylor 31). Hence, our reasoning, although it may be technically flawless, is fundamentally inauthentic. True authenticity recognizes individuals as they stand in relation to one another, and involves rejecting technical quick fixes, that is, technical means of relating to one another that encourage instrumental behavior rather than that based upon true interaction (dialogism) with others (Taylor 61). To become truly authentic, that is, to properly address our traditional concern for the recognition of individual merit and also to consider fairly the interests of all, we need first to examine how our public institutions have favored instrumental reason to protect the rights of the individual at the expense of communal good. Modern societies champion individual causes and defend public policy on the basis of rights defended by law, in other words, on the basis of the mere congruence of decisions with a legal standard; this "penchant to settle things judicially, further polarized by rival special-interest campaigns, effectively cuts down the possibility of compromise" (Taylor 116). In effect, to defend the rights of an individual as protected by law is to pit persons against persons by way of a positioning that is personally disengaged; hence, standoffs occur, for instance, in arguments waged by the left to protect the environment or the rights of a mother to abort a fetus against those waged by the right for unrestrained capital development or the right to life of the unborn (Taylor 110–16). What is missing in these confrontations is any necessity for the persons who are pursuing these positions to debate as if they had a mutual obligation to form a communal solution.

Both MacIntyre and Taylor suggest that a mutual obligation to form a communal solution stems from our very quest to discover the right and truthful answer to a question. Behind any such quest must be belief in our common telos or function. Authentic expression, then, reflects commitment to that belief. Our current tradition of resolving debate over individual rights by relying on rules and regulations discounts the premise that true and right interpretations both account for the causal relationships we perceive in the world around us and acknowledge our collective telos or purpose. This point has been made most poignantly of recent by Carol McMillan, who defends the notion of a common human telos in the face of sexual difference.

In *Women, Reason and Nature,* a study of differences in reasoning attributed to gender, McMillan suggests how different our debates about what is true and right would be were we to begin discussion with a clear conception of our function as human beings and, in particular, our function as biological and spiritual creatures. To step outside ourselves as natural beings with creative and procreative functions when deciding issues of life and death is in McMillan's view patently absurd. Although I do not entirely accept McMillan's take on human nature, I think she is right that we must begin and end debates about what is true and right with some discussion of how contested actions relate to our nature and function. In her words, to ignore "the limited and conditioned aspect of human life" in our quest to understand it and sustain it is, in effect, to destroy "life itself" (McMillan 156). She employs this perspective in giving a sympathetic reading to the Catholic position on abortion so roundly dismissed by some feminists. McMillan argues that feminists have adopted a notion of agency that does not account for the constraint of women's biological function, for instance, in suggesting that only a woman's active efforts to reject through technological assistance the pain of childbirth give her power as an active agent in the birthing process. She asserts that a woman's "choice" to accept the pain of childbirth is also active; she deems this act to be an "intentional passivity" (McMillan 150) that allows a woman to fully experience a maternal experience without submitting to technical control. She similarly regards women's decisions against abortion and birth control as an intentional passivity, a refusal to interfere with a natural act, sexual union, whose purpose is creative. Such interference is for McMillan a denial of humanity and its special privilege to understand the role of sexuality; it gives human beings no elevated status above the animal kingdom whose creatures cannot reflect upon their purpose in this way (122–51). Putting McMillan's particular perspective on human nature aside, I endorse her choice to foreground one's commitment to the common function of humanity and to background one's right to choose without regard for the nature and function of choice within human life. For McMillan—and for me as well—authentic choice is not only a matter of exercising one's individual freedom to choose, but also of choosing to act in a way that complements our given nature and purpose.

How might we apply the principles I have discussed to authenticate our rhetoric, that is, our everyday efforts to speak and write? A number of rhetoricians and literary critics have suggested practical ways, although without grounding them in a phenomenological understanding of the relationship between human nature and truth seeking. I would like to think that my perspective reanimates our classical conception of authorial representation. I am asking that we think of creating authorial credibility as an intentional effort to experience the world so that we may better know it and to be transformed in the process, coming closer both to realizing our personal reason for being and to substantiating our place in this very same process as it is carried out in the lives of others. This conception of authorial representation unites language and action in ways that our current description of rhetorical strategies such as developing a "persona" or expressing "ethos" do not. Yet a commitment to personally addressing our larger collective purpose is indeed implied in the tension created in the author's attempt to express ethos and persona, as we currently think of these terms.

Using the terms with which I have been speaking of authorial representation and authenticity, persona parallels the agent's quest to be recognized as an individual within the terms of the culture to which he or she is presenting himself or herself, and ethos parallels the agent's quest to employ authoritative strategies for giving reasons and providing evidence to a community for the validity of his or her point of view. Roger D. Cherry has offered a helpful distinction between our conceptions of persona and ethos in current rhetorical practice. "Persona," Cherry tells us, is the "narrative voice" within a text "that presents characters and events to the reader" (261). The persona represents an active role that "authors create for themselves in written discourse given their representation of audience, subject matter, and other elements of context" (Cherry 268–69). Persona, on the one hand, represents authors' attempts to define for themselves "a certain role (or roles) in the discourse community in which they are operating" (Cherry 265), whereas ethos, on the other hand, represents authors' attempts to "garner credibility by identifying themselves as holding a certain position or having particular kinds of knowledge or experience, as well as by demonstrating their 'practical wisdom' and showing a concern for the audience" (Cherry 265).

The author's agency lies somewhere in the space between the effort to create a persona and to develop ethos, and can be identified in the text's expression of the "implied author," as Cherry explains, adopting Booth's designation of the man or woman "behind the text," as it were. But I see this space as more than a place holder for the "implied author," that is, a representation of the man or woman who creates a text that comes about as a subproduct of reading or writing. The tension created between persona and ethos forms the space in which an author authenticates his or her expression through intense attention to the function of his or her work in our collective lives; the author's technical task is to craft language so that his or her expression of persona and ethos truly communicates this commitment. In other words, authors/rhetors must communicate their roles as teachers, scientists, or politicians to be part of their lived experience within a community that understands both the function of these roles in our lives and the tasks performed by those who enact them to assure our common good; and likewise authors must communicate the depth of their personal understanding of the issues they raise, treating their implications for themselves and others with equal respect. In this act, they will secure their own authenticity as well as validate their expression. Here is also where a phenomenological approach to interpreting experience comes into play.

The phenomenological approach does not separate one's lived experience from one's expression of it, it rather asks the author to think of his or her rhetoric as an enactment of that ongoing experience. As such, the phenomenological approach invites the author to "live through" a communal role, as it were, rather than to create a persona, and likewise to "live through" the process of validating his or her interpretation of experience, rather than to demonstrate its validity. In short, the phenomenological approach asks the author to embrace his or her fundamental connection to others as like beings with a common telos.

Richard L. Lanigan offers a partial operational description of how authors might use rhetoric to link their experiences to our common telos in his text, *Phenomenology of Communication*. Through reinterpreting Merleau-Ponty's notion of embodied consciousness in rhetorical terms, Lanigan situates meaning in personal intention which, embodied in consciousness, is the focal point at which author and reader meet in the interpretive act. Our language does not exist "out there," separated from us, but rather it is interpersonal interaction, drawing our consciousnesses together in a transformative way. When an author or reader approaches a "phenomenological interpretation" of experience, that is, an interpretation that reflects our consciousness, or rather, our "informed connection among self, others and the world" (31), he or she performs a "hermeneutic judgment or specification of existential meaning—that is, the meaning of the phenomenon as the person lived it in the *flesh*" (32). This sense of experience as lived "in the flesh" involves an oscillation between what Lanigan identifies as "immanent" and "transcendent" (or existential) meaning. The former refers to language as it is conventionally meant or "sedimented" into just a few "possible significations-for-signs," the "level of empirical speech and meaning," whereas the latter refers to "language that creates personal lived experience" (Lanigan 53). Transcendent meaning is "existential," it is lived in our experience in the acts of speaking and interpretation. As an illustration, Lanigan likens transcendent meaning to the effect created by an optical illusion in which the "content" of the drawing revealed in its structure suggests a new meaning to the viewer not implied by the established or "sedimented" meaning of any of its parts (53).

Our meaningful connections to others are established through a juxtaposition of immanent and transcendent meaning: That which we express as immanent, or established meaning for us, may appear as transcendent, or new meaning for others. Our ability to participate effectively in this process of experiencing the interplay of immanent and transcendent meaning, that is, to treat communication as a means of conveying lived experience, requires us to adopt a specific attitude toward intentionality, one that views language as an effort to express transcendent meaning, which speaks not to an established, sedimented purpose, but rather anticipates a new relation to our common function.

Lanigan notes that attention to intentionality, instead of purpose, asks us to rethink conventional, public communication situations as interpersonal events. For instance, instead of thinking of the situation of a newscaster communicating to a television audience as one of enacting a "mass media" event, we might think of it as one of participating in an "interpersonal" situation, one in which "one viewer [is] listening (or expressing?) to one newscaster" (Lanigan 24). Such a perception obligates us to think of our communication in terms of its potential to transform individual lives, our own as well as the lives of others. Rhetoric thus becomes the responsible act of one person participating in the communicative transformation of another, and the authenticity of that act is confirmed by the potential of each to have understood the lived experience of the other. The measure of authors'/rhetors' authenticity in performing this act is their empathetic rendering of their chosen role within a community, expressed through the persona of their communication, a rendering that transcends the immanent or conventional understanding of the role of teacher, scientist, or politician, for instance, making it a personally interpreted commitment to add in some way to the communal good. Likewise, authenticity is achieved through authors' commitment to the concerns of their audience shown in their efforts to present their case so that it brings about a mutual transformation in the understanding of both.

The effort to bring about transformation, both in my own thinking and the thinking of others, is not necessarily pacific. It may require a kind of linguistic violence. Dawne McCance describes such rhetoric in her depiction of the almost heretical writing style of Michel Foucault that preceded his fairly conventional presentation of a "straight" history of sexuality toward the end of his life, a "linguistic turn," that, as I have noted earlier, MacIntyre also remarks upon. McCance defines Foucault's style as "catachretic," a style by which one works "down" through the layers of an idea (127): "Catachresis, so understood, is what 'the French' call *ethical writing,* a style of historical analysis that looks for lines of fragility and knots of resistance that are spread over the great surface network of words and things" (129). Catachretic writing allows one to think differently than one is; it forces a confrontation and engagement with ideas that is transformational. One interpreter of Foucault's suggests that his "straight" history of sexuality, in effect, pointed ironically to his own homoerotic and unconventional sexual history. Hence, the plain style ethically foregrounded Foucault's arguments for sexual freedom in a society "increasingly dominated by the concept of 'normality' " (McCance 128) to the point at which it is ineffective in dealing either compassionately or practically with such public health threats as AIDS (McCance 125–29).

Foucault's catachretic writing calls for a reciprocity of understanding: I learn more about my condition as I invite you to open yourself along with me to a deeper, more complex engagement with our common nature. Catachretic writing both agitates and heals, provokes and connects. While risking confrontation, at a deeper level, it asks for reconciliation through reciprocal engagement in a common difficulty, aspiration, or desire. It is this stimulating, binding attempt at reciprocity of understanding that I advocate as the measure of rhetorical authenticity.

Reciprocal understanding is certainly not an exotic concept, nor is it platitudinous. The essentialness of reciprocity, if you will, is acknowledged by literary critics and rhetoricians at large, not only for effective communication but also for effective development of self, both personally and socially. Louise M. Rosenblatt, of course, has emphasized the significance of reciprocity in coming to meaning in her now famous interactional interpretation of the reading process. She tells us:

> We have to think of [the text and the reader] not as separate entities, but as aspects or phases of a dynamic process, in which all elements take on their character as part of the organically-interrelated situation. Instead of thinking of reading as a linear process, we have to think rather of a complex network or circuit of interrelationships, with reciprocal interplay. (100–01)

Rosenblatt approaches the reading process as a kind of catachresis, a working down through ideas in the distinct methods through which we perform the reading act. She contrasts two styles of reading, efferent and aesthetic, that bring to mind Lanigan's discrimination of immanent and transcendent meaning:

> The predominantly efferent reader focuses attention on public meaning, abstracting what is to be retained after the reading—to be recalled, paraphrased, acted on, analyzed. In aesthetic reading, the reader's selective attention is lived through, cognitively and affectively *during* the reading

event. The range of ideas, feelings, associations activated in the reservoir of symbolizations is drawn upon. (Rosenblatt 101–02)

In short, for Rosenblatt, an aesthetic reading is a creative act wherein the reader lives through an experience and transcends his or her conventional understanding of it to reformulate ideas about its meaning. In this creative act, reading *is* lived experience, not the reporting of it. Language becomes inseparable from the meaning of human action. Paul Hernadi similarly speaks to the inseparability of language from lived experience and likewise of lived experience from language, claiming that our language all at once defines the self, establishes social relationships, and occupies a natural reality. For Hernadi, the relationship between language and our existence is ontological: "Writing and reading occur, therefore something is" (753). Authentic expression, as I have been saying, is achieved through drawing inclusive relationships among our individual conceptions of ourselves, our intersubjective meanings developed with others, and our experience of the objective world about us. Hernadi expresses the significance of this attempt at relational coherence most eloquently:

> To remain viable as selves, as members of a society, and as members of a species, we require subjective coherence within our increasingly complex individual experience, intersubjective consensus among the growing numbers with whom we coexist in mutual dependence, and objective correspondence between our continually enhanced technical and biological efficacy and the constraints imposed by the environment on human production and reproduction. At least one aspect of the future thus seems certain as the first generation born in a space-faring, postliterate age prepares to enter the next century. As long as our children and their descendants continue to exist as self-conscious social organisms, they will not leave behind the subjective, intersubjective, and objective dimensions of human existence that verbal meaning, doing, and making both reflect and help constitute. (755–56)

Hernadi describes human viability as dependent upon our maintaining individual integrity while communicating intersubjective consensus about the objective world, effectively arguing that authentic expression is grounded in our relationship to others. We must see ourselves as both transformed and transforming, attending to the history of our involvement in the history of knowledge developed and shared among many. We must, like MacIntyre, Taylor, and McMillan, see in our common purpose a way of thinking forward to envision a framework that accounts for our common way of being and looks back to incorporate our histories as part of that way to be. The implications of approaching communications with such broad expectations for reciprocity—being changed and changing others, looking forward and back, realizing both immanent and transcendent meaning—are far-reaching indeed.

Imagine, if you will, how scientific experimentation and its reporting would change if, prior to conducting each exploratory investigation and writing each conclusive report, scientists/authors considered precisely how both these acts, experiment and report, speak to our function as conscious beings who relate to one another person to person, work together for the common good, and reflect upon our own personal commitments to that enterprise. How would this consideration change individual and communal efforts toward developing a synthetic fuel, harnessing nuclear power, finding a cure for AIDS? In legal matters, how would a concern for authenticity change how we deal with drunk driving as a civil offense, abortion as a medical procedure, marriage as a union between same sex partners? What frameworks would we employ or question when evaluating judgments about any of these social activities? But, my readers might argue, these questions have no direct implications for developing new knowledge and communicating it. These are questions about differences in values. And, of course, this is precisely my point. Questions about developing and communicating knowledge are questions about values—human values. Our motivation to observe, interpret, and act upon our interpretations is entirely wrapped up in what we perceive to be our essential function on this earth, our value to ourselves and others. In fact, as I shall pursue next, an internal state of expectancy, of the potential for the fulfillment of value, is required in order for us to conduct projects with any hope of learning more about the world and our proper relation to it. That expectancy comes from attending to the ways in which we differ uniquely from others, and it is transformed by the phenomenological outlook into pure enthusiasm or ardor for knowledge of the other, the process we shall explore next.

Ardor

At the beginning of this chapter, the reader will recall, I invoked Pierre Teilhard de Chardin's observations about the ubiquity of love. Let us return to his words now and interpret them within a phenomenological approach to rhetoric. Teilhard de Chardin claims broadly that love, "huge, ubiquitous, and always unsubdued," runs "everywhere beneath our civilization." It accounts for all activity, from the practical affairs of business, to the tender matters of child rearing, to the lofty aspirations of science. Love, I submit, must underlie our efforts to communicate with one another if we are to have any chance of achieving common understanding and a common good. Love, expressed by the rhetor as *ardor*, as a passion for knowing, understanding, and valuing what is other, is essential for knowledge making and the rhetoric that supports it.

Love has never been absent from the attention of literary critics, either in their critique of its representation in literary art or in their exploration of its intrusion in the interpretive act. Frank Kermode speaks of the relationship between love and literary value when evaluating the impact of historical circumstances on our perception of aesthetic value. In *History and Value,* he discusses, in particular, the work of novelists and poets of the 1930s who sought to express their enthusiasm for Marxist ideals in literary art. In wrestling with the problem of discerning whether many of these works, which typically combined political zeal with creative storytelling, are of mere historical interest or of enduring aesthetic value, Kermode notes that the true value of these pieces may have little to do with their artistic merit. It may lie, rather, in their "enforced engagement with the almost unthinkable Other" (81), with the disenfranchised classes, the oppressed poor, the politically ardent. Acknowledging the difficulty of articulating this "enforced engagement" as an aesthetic value in the familiar rhetoric of contemporary criticism, Kermode concludes:

> What I have been trying to tell is, in its way, a love-story, almost a story of forbidden love. If asked to define that huge word I will not repeat my reference to the Eros of Freud, or to Caudwell's amorous economics, but simply repeat a definition of love Auden himself once gave: 'intensity of attention.' (qtd. in Kermode 51)

That total, enraptured obsession with every aspect of the other that we experience as love is certainly captured by Auden's description. Yet such "intensity of attention" is not peculiar to love; it marks as well the persistent effort to get to know something well enough to understand it thoroughly. To push beyond mere "attention" to enforced engagement with my subject is required for both loving well and knowing well. In loving someone else, I allow their contact with me not only to capture my attention, but also to direct my day-to-day actions so that they accommodate the act of attending more fully to them, of changing myself to be more receptive to their desires, needs, and ways of living in the world that we both share. This is the engagement we call love. But to understand—to truly know—the world I live in requires of me no less. I must relate to the world with the same intensity with which I relate to those whom I love, and it is in intensely relating to the world through directly engaging with it and with others' constitutions of it that I make of it a true part of my conscious existence.

In being fundamentally an act of relating, "knowing" is a moral act. Kermode, I believe, intimates this very claim in reflecting upon the emotional intensity of the politically motivated novels of the thirties that he studied. The authors of these works sought to convince us that to truly know the place of those persons in the world whose lives and dreams their pages depicted, we must invest ourselves in their plight, relate to them so that our own lives and actions are invariably changed for having known them. The moral act of knowing can be evaluated as it reflects the knower's care for the subject, a care that is essential to understanding. I make this claim now, drawing on the work of a number of philosophers who have struggled to define the ontology of truth, knowledge, and value within the phenomenological construct of intersubjectivity. Among those whose work is relevant to my purpose here are: Martin Buber, John D. Caputo, Wendy Farley, Christine M. Korsgaard, Emmanuel Levinas, and David Weissman. These scholars' depictions of the relational act of knowing support my thesis that ardor, a loving passion for knowing and valuing what is "other," both motivates and validates knowledge making and its rhetoric. In presenting their work, I shall argue here that the desire to relate, the "zest" for relation, as Teilhard de Chardin puts it, is the natural imperative at the very core of our experience of Being. Furthermore, our understanding of Being in all its earthly manifestation is contingent upon our relating to particular beings, a relating that is realized completely only when it is founded upon selfless care. Hence, I suggest, contrary to Heidegger, that the essence of Being is not a negativity, an unfathomable infiniteness that continuously escapes living, finite beings, but rather a positivity to be found in actual beings—the others on earth with whom we continually and lovingly relate. This perspective on the knowing of Being has powerful implications for our communicative practices. In short, if our understanding of Being is contingent upon our loving care for beings, a successful quest to express the truth about Being must be founded in altruism.

Let me begin by defending the distinction I am making between the Heideggerian concept of understanding Being and the one I propose, an understanding rooted in the particularity of beings. It amounts to a difference in ontological assumption about the nature of Being, one explained most eloquently by Caputo in his analysis of both Aquinas's and Heidegger's metaphysics. Caputo argues that although it is immanently evident that Aquinas never understood language to have ontological significance, that is, to be anything other than a human tool, this limitation does not suggest that he misunderstood the ineffability of Being. Aquinas surely did not acknowledge, as did Heidegger, that linguistic interstices reveal the nature of presencing or what we experience as presencing (Caputo 158–64). He never saw the distinction between the seamless continuity of Being and the temporal, moment by moment, finite experience of being as "a bestowal of language" (Caputo 158), that is, an effect created by the technology of language itself. At the same time, Aquinas did acknowledge Being as something we participate in but cannot fully capture in our finitude. The essential difference between Heidegger's and Aquinas's view of Being, Caputo claims, is that Heidegger proposes a secular perspective on ontology in which "the hiddenness of Being, the withdrawn depths from which beings emerge into presence, is something final" (280), whereas for St. Thomas, and the religious mystics in general, the ontology of Being may very well be concealed from us, but it is not concealed from the Being who gives Being, the "Godhead itself." In short, as Caputo puts it, "the concealed depths of the Godhead are not concealed from God; they *are* God" (280). In relating to God, we are granted the possibility of participating in Being, and we experience this, in part, by relating to all who participate in His Being: "The *esse* [or Being] of creatures is their com-ing-to-presence in the world; the *esse* of God is the mystery of presence which is intimately present in everything which is present" (283). The belief in our mutual participation in Being suggests to Aquinas and the mystics that our knowledge of Being in the world comes about not through "causal reckon-ing" (Caputo 283), but rather through learning "to see in the reflected light of creatures the light of Being itself" (Caputo 284). This embodiment of Being, its groundedness in a Godhead and His creatures, suggests an approach to truth seeking that is guided by the relating of beings to beings.

My intent in depicting the difference between Heideggerian secularism and Thomist theology is not to defend specifically a belief in God, but rather to suggest that the Thomist perspective gives us more reason for believing that knowledge is validated by our relationship to other beings than to believe it is validated by the logic and antilogic of language. Let me press this point further. To suggest that a true knowledge of Being is found somehow in the everyday existence of ordinary beings is, in effect, to authenticate the particu-lar experiences, cares, and aspirations of real, living beings. Wendy Farley ar-ticulates this point quite tellingly in *Eros for the Other*. She suggests here that it is the "reality" of beings, their palpable substance, their actual pain and suffering, which is not reducible to an abstraction or a quality, that discloses to us the truth of our existence. To suggest that some concept about the ineffability of Being holds primacy over the experience of particular beings is to presuppose that the uniqueness of each life is captured by a "*kind* of being living things have" (11). Farley accuses Heidegger of this very reduction, not-ing that for Heidegger, "everyday existence is inauthentic" (55).

Relying in the main upon arguments formulated by Levinas and Arendt, Farley notes that the "concrete acts and desires of everyday life are attempts by particular existents to wrest reality and meaning from anonymous power" (55). In the prison camps of Nazi Germany, the threat to human existence was the evocation of "an anonymous totality that systematically denudes one of personhood" (55). The truth of a person's existence is inextricably linked to a recognition of his or her particularity, and can be realized only if that par-ticularity is regarded as something irreducible and care is taken not to dissolve its significance. Like MacIntyre and Taylor, Farley finds the totalizing tech-nologies of law and science and the categories of existence defined by various ideologies to miss the significance of our common telos to exist together as a plurality, each person participating in the construction of existence. To acknowledge the experience of particular persons as authentic is not to dismiss the quest for a larger, all-compassing truth, but rather to admit to its moral ground: "Recognition of the constructed and pluralistic character of human experience does not obviate the struggle for truth, but reveals more dramatically its fundamentally ethical significance" (Farley 38). To recognize the "constructed and pluralistic character of human experience," we must recognize others as constructing along with us, as participating in our Being. This involves a care and desire for relating to them, a care that cannot be derived from conceiving of others as mere things that occupy another space in the world. Persons are not "parts" that can be assimilated as a totality or, in the reverse, be dismissed as not belonging to some totalizing whole. The "non-quiddity" of persons, their particularity, cannot be accounted for by a view that aims to recognize some persons and dismiss others (Farley 56–57). Because persons are not thinglike but rather, dynamic, irreducible entities capable of continuous relating, we must think of truths—a human conception—also as not thinglike. The essence of truth, like the essence of persons, is relation. Farley concludes that if we are to get at truth, then we must perfect the task of relation so that it captures the nonthinglike character of persons which is their reality. She defines and proposes eros as the perfect form of relation through which we come to know about others and our world.

Eros unmasks any illusion we have that the world is reducible to a conception that excludes experience as it is felt and lived by some and not others. Eros is the antidote to totalitarian visions promoted by exclusionary ideologies, such as Nazism, misogyny, or racial hatred. Eros treats others in the world not as things either to be dismissed or possessed, but rather as the source of our continuous experience of reality; Farley concludes:

> Eros reorients consciousness through a detachment from the ego and a passion for the other, which in turn bring into view the beauty, and ultimately, the suffering of others. This awareness of the uniqueness, beauty, and suffering of others is the prerequisite for a turn from illusion to reality. Knowledge of the kind of being others have makes possible the daily practices by which truth is discerned. (109)

Eros, the desire for relation, must underlie a quest to understand what is not thinglike. We must let go of the idea that truth about reality can be approached as a thing; rather, it must be approached as the transcending condition of relating. In short, as Farley says, "knowledge or truth concerning reality will not have the one-dimensionality, finality, or completeness possible only with things" (74). Truth is "erotic," moving with the sense of relation because "reality is not thinglike" (Farley 74). Along with Farley, MacIntyre, Taylor, and more distantly Teilhard de Chardin and Aquinas, I am making the case here that telling the truth is contingent upon our effort to maintain

relationships to others, to instill within ourselves and others an ardor for relation. But what is the exact character of this relating to others? How does it
play out in our hearts and in our rhetorical practice?

Perhaps the most engaging description of truth telling as relation has
been offered by Martin Buber in *I and Thou*. Here Buber describes human
conscience as relational in all aspects of its development, suggesting that our
most thorough, reliable, and moral way of relating to the world about us is
to understand ourselves not as an "I" who relates to the world as an "It," but
rather as beings who are always in the thick of relationship, always in a reciprocal state of I relating to You. Buber does not deny that there is a place for
acknowledging the world by distancing or detaching ourselves from it, by
studying the things of the world as an academic or scientist would who is
trying to ascertain what things mean without tainting their study with subjective input. But he claims that this is not how we need to get to know people
and things so that we might understand our place with them in the world
and lead productive and satisfying lives. It is within the I-You relation that
we realize this freedom, that is, our potential to make something of our lives,
to give them meaning on earth.

The freedom Buber speaks of is one in which we have the potential to
affect one another, to change, grow and develop based upon our continuous
and reciprocal relating: "Relation is reciprocity. My You acts on me as I act
on it. Our students teach us, our works form us. The 'wicked' become a revelation when they are touched by the sacred basic word. How are we educated
by children, by animals!" (Buber 67). This phenomenon of regarding what is
"other"—person, animal, institution, text—as meaningful to us within the
dynamic of our relating, of changing ourselves to keep in constant *touch*,
stands in bold contrast to the stultifying and constrained process of treating
persons and things as objects to which we respond in terms of causes and
effects. The former implies freedom to create together new selves in a new
world; the latter the restriction of bowing to conventions, rules, limits. Buber
strikes a contrast between the freedom implied in the I-You relation and the
oppressiveness of the I-It relation of causality in the following passage:

> In the It-world causality holds unlimited sway. . . .
> The unlimited sway of causality in the It-world, which is of fundamental
> importance for the scientific ordering of nature, is not felt to be oppressive
> by the man who is not confined to the It-world but free to step out of it
> again and again into the world of relation. Here I and You confront each
> other freely in a reciprocity that is not involved in or tainted by any causality;
> here man finds guaranteed the freedom of his being and of being. (100)

The I-You relation permeates our very being and is, in a sense, our reason for
being. Although physical and cultural realities may press us to submit to the
order of things around us, we have the freedom to relate to others and what

they say about the world reciprocally, with each making an impression on the other in their shared circumstance. Emmanuel Levinas, an interpreter of Buber who has elaborated many of Buber's themes to describe what he calls the essential "sociality" of human existence, claims that the I-You relation is central to all meaningful meaning, that is, all meaning that has some impact on the value of our lives. The "meaning of the meaningful," as he says, resides in our very "sociality":

> [The] meaning of the meaningful . . . shows no lack in relation to an ideal of adequation borrowed from the domain of knowledge nor from the full-ness of an intuitively revealed presence. [It is] the one-for-the-other of fra-ternity, which does not mean a privation of coincidence or of some sort of fusion, nor a finality failing to reach its goal. It is a semantics of proximity, of sociality that does not lead back to ontology, that is not based on the experience of being and in which meaning is not defined formally, but from an ethical relation to the other person in the guise of responsibility for him or her. (Levinas, "Meaning" 93)

If meaningful meaning, that which has value in our personal lives, is grounded in our ethical relation to others, our capacity to engage in meaningful mean-ing must be centered in the depth of our relation to others, in the regard for or value placed on our life together, which is manifested in our "responsibil-ity" for others. Let me trace the reasoning behind this claim, showing how "responsible" regard or value for human life provokes all our quests for knowl-edge.

In his recent discussion of the relationship of truth to value entitled *Truth's Debt to Value,* David Weissman, like Buber, argues that there are some truths in the material world that are dependent upon our separating ourselves from it and admitting that it has a substance and perpetuity that is beyond our control. These are salient truths that, given our material circumstances, we must accept about the world outside us if we are to survive within it. These salient truths range from observations about the natural world to the realities of human institutions: If we drive a car off a cliff, for instance, we know that we can be killed, and if we do not pay our taxes, we know that we can be prosecuted, and so forth. But given these truths that "correspond," if you will, to an objective reality, the motivation behind our drive to discover these and other truths and to deal with them in some coherent way is dependent upon the value system behind the whole dynamic of epistemological inquiry. Our acceptance that there are salient truths corresponding to a reality is the best answer, Weissman suggests, to the question of what metaphysics we might propose

> if the value directing [our] inquiry has this complex objective: proximately, of discovering where we stand in the world the better to secure and satisfy

ourselves there; more remotely, of knowing where we stand so as to achieve a certain closure as regards our self-understanding. (199)

Weissman intimates that "truth's debt to value," if you will, is that all we accept as true is in the service of our mutual continuance and survival as human beings. And this survival, of course, is equally dependent upon our realizing our proper end, to ensure our own and everyone else's prosperity. Weissman's conclusion is echoed in Levinas' claim that the meaningfulness of meaning derives from an ethical relation between one and another that implies the responsibility of each for the other.

If, as Weissman has argued, our epistemological enterprises are driven by a need to survive in the world and this is indeed a human value, then our established ways of knowing are by necessity intersubjective and as such are implicitly moral endeavors. Arguments leading to this conclusion are made convincingly by Christine M. Korsgaard in a discussion of the nature of ethical reasoning, which she extends to apply to all reasoning. The whole process of striving to know and to derive reasons and explanations for how and why things are is dependent, as Korsgaard tells us, "on the structure of personal relations" (25). Even personal epistemological ambitions to explore new territory or master a new skill are dependent upon the structure of relations. Using the example of desiring to climb a mountain, Korsgaard shows us how such an ambition may be cast by an agent as an objective desire, a goal that is a good in itself. But such a desire cannot be assessed in entirely objective terms because it represents one person's attempt "to stand in a special relationship to something which [he or she thinks] is good objectively" (38). It is on this basis that individuals invest themselves in interpersonal contact and engagement with objects or tasks that they seek to understand. The ambition to stand in a special relationship to the things of the world, which we desire to know, and the people within it, whom we respect and love, makes us human, inspires us to help "others pursue their ambitions" as well, "not because we recognize the value of those *ends*, but rather out of respect for the humanity of those who have them" (Korsgaard 40).

And so, Korsgaard argues, we do not seek anything for ourselves or others because that something has some objective value apart from ourselves, but rather because we wish to stand in relation to it in some way; likewise, the reasons we give for pursuing any earthly activity at all are relational and as such are normative claims. Korsgaard explains:

> [A reason] is not just a consideration on which you in fact act, but one on which you are supposed to act; it is not just a motive, but rather a normative claim, exerting authority over other people [at some times] and yourself at other times. To say that you have a reason is to say something *relational*, something which implies the existence of another, at least another self. (51)

And so to cite salient objective facts about the world, as Weissman calls the conditions under which we recognize natural cause and effect, as reasons for doing or not doing something is to say something about our relationship to certain things of the world and certain people within it. And such relational reasons, whether articulated publicly or not, always motivate our actions. The utilitarian perspective that suggests that we are motivated to act on the basis of agent-neutral values, ones that do not change relative to the character of individuals who respond to them, does not take into account, claims Korsgaard, that our individual character, as defined by our relation to things and people about us, may indeed drive our projects. Our values are developed on the basis of "the special relations in which [we] stand to [our] own ambitions or loved ones" (Korsgaard 44). This is why we can't make an objective judgment, or one divorced from particular concern for persons, for instance, in the case of whether we should allow harm to come to one person if it will save twenty others. Twenty persons' lives are not worth more accumulatively than the life of one: What is of value is our relationship to each one. A relational value of some sort stands behind everything we do and say; this circumstance leads Korsgaard to conclude that "the only reasons that are possible are the reasons we can share" (51), that is, ones that recognize the commonality of our relational existence, or our "sociality," as Levinas has put it. And more than this, behind everything we do and say is the intense desire we continuously feel for relation.

Even before language, claims Levinas, echoing the sentiments of Martin Buber, our way of being in the world is about relating, in both a bodily and a spiritual sense. We continually seek the experience of one hand touching the other, a communication that is both prior to and goes beyond all language, a desire that is fulfilled in separate moments and is endless, enveloped in peace and pierced with ardor. The handshake, Levinas tells us, in explaining the connections among perception, sense, and meaning that Merleau-Ponty described as the essence of our being, is the symbol of "mutual knowledge" that comes about through contact with others. This *touch* is what phenomenology attempts to understand. Levinas asks:

> Does not the essential, going beyond knowledge, reside in confidence, devotion and peace (and with an element of the gift, going from myself to the others, and a certain indifference toward compensations in reciprocity and thus with ethical gratuitousness), which the handshake initiates and means, instead of being a simple code transmitting information about it? Nor is the caress that bespeaks love the mere message and symbol of love, but rather, prior to that language, already that love itself. ("On Intersubjectivity" 101)

Peace is what is sought and desired in the attempt to relate, but the activity itself is shot through and through with anticipation, ardor, and desire. Relating is a perpetual state of tension, of awareness of the split between me and the things and persons I seek to know and love. Buber claims:

> The longing for relation is primary, the cupped hand into which the being that confronts us nestles; and the relation to that, which is a wordless anticipation of saying You, comes second. But the genesis of the thing is a late product that develops out of the split of the primal encounters, . . . out of the separation of the associated partners—as does the genesis of the I. In the beginning is the relation—as the category of being, as readiness, as a form that reaches out to be filled, as a model of the soul; the *a priori* of relation; *the innate You.* (78)

Buber points out that our longing for relation is reflected in the language of " 'primitive peoples' " (69) whose languages "designate the wholeness of a relation" (69) rather than recognize the split between people and things that occurs when I regard what is outside of me to be "it" in relationship to me. For instance, to designate a very distant place, Buber notes, we say " 'far away' " whereas "the Zulu has a sentence-word instead that means: 'where one cries, "mother, I am lost." ' " (69–70). Buber cites this and other linguistic examples as evidence that "what counts" for these peoples is not the "products of analysis and reflection . . . but the genuine original unity, the lived relationship" (70). Both knowledge of the world about us and love for others in it, as it would appear from Buber's perspective, spring from the anticipation or longing for relation, "a wordless anticipation of saying You," which comes second. The things we create upon relating, the knowledge we communicate in writing, the bonds we form between friends and loved ones, obligating ourselves to them, are but a "late product," as Buber describes them.

Similarly, Teilhard de Chardin finds knowledge, scientific progress, the stuff of our civilized existence, to be the product of a dynamic and zealous quest to relate, to bring ourselves closer together. Human beings are possessed by a "zest for unity," as he says, "in order to preserve the universal zest for action" through which we do not succumb to "individual needs and hopes, or . . . national or social pressures" (*Toward the Future* 50), but rather develop steadily toward a unification of our consciousnesses. Although we are free, humankind as a species cannot fail to move forward. The world and ourselves together, according to Teilhard de Chardin, are progressing toward "constantly increasing unification, centration, and spiritualization—the whole system rising unmistakably towards a critical point of final convergence" (*Toward the Future* 181–82). Teilhard de Chardin's theory of convergence is motivated by what he believes to be our telos, perfect unity at the Omega Point, the final cause of humankind, God Himself, "a supremely personal, supremely personalizing, being" (*Toward the Future* 188). His vision is that we will grow progressively to incorporate our differences into an ever more complexified and dynamic unity, feeding off of the input of one another that stimulates our zest, or ardor, if you will, to relate. Together, humankind will progress as a "social body . . . going through a process of organic differentiation," which is manifested in the products of our interactions with one another, which in turn, generate further interaction, further relation. These products include our

> collective heredity (or memory) for example, which is transmitted by education or stored in books; mechanization, gradually released from the hand which initiated it, and now extended to planetary dimensions; and, most important of all, progressive cerebralization which is ever more closely and more rapidly bringing together and co-ordinating an ever-increasing number of individual insights, and directing them towards ever more clearly defined targets. (*Toward the Future* 179–80)

Teilhard de Chardin projects a kind of dizzying perpetual motion machine in describing how our insights will collectively work off one another, inspiring each of us to greater enthusiasm for the quest for unification as our efforts complement the evolving sensitivity of our consciousnesses. The process of attending together to difference "leads ultimately to an ultra-personalizing, ultra-determining, and ultra-differentiating UNIFICATION of the elements within a *common focus;* the specific effect of LOVE" (*Toward the Future* 210). The telos of true loving is not a satiated and restful peace; it is not a stable unity, but rather a rapturous dynamic, one in which we come to know all through intensely relating. Harmony, accord, and consensus are not achieved at the cost of flattening edges, smoothing out disturbances, fusing and blending disparate parts into one. Perfect relation may feel like unification, but what we really experience is the all-embracing tension of our differences. Even what we regard as the most intimate, the most all-absorbing human bond results not in static union, but rather in dynamic relationship. Buber tells us that lovers in the ecstatic moments of erotic embrace "feel" a unification, but actually live the dynamic of relation felt to be more powerful than their separate beings:

> What the ecstatic calls unification is the rapturous dynamics of the relationship; not a unity that has come into being at this moment in world time, fusing I and You, but the dynamics of the relationship itself which can stand before the two carriers of this relationship, although they confront each other immovably, and cover the eyes of the enraptured. . . . What we find here is a marginal . . . exorbitance of the act of relation: the relationship itself in its vital unity is felt so vehemently that its members pale in the process; its life predominates so much that the I and the You between whom it is established are forgotten. (135)

The ardor for relation, I would argue, drives rhetoric that can move author and reader together to incorporate the richness of perspective captured in the dynamic of their difference. This rich perspective develops when neither party, author or reader, loses enthusiasm, ardor for realizing a mutual end; it comes, as Teilhard de Chardin has said, from having a "common focus," which he distinguishes carefully from the effort to establish a common ground. The latter is characterized by dissolving difference, reducing our commonality to "a sort of common stuff which *underlies* the variety of concrete beings" (209). Our individual identity then becomes subject to this common identity. In effect, this is what we experience in modern society when we cede our judgment to the impersonal rule of science or law, a rubric which defines our common ground. We must rather seek a unity that goes beyond what we can state in common, that does not relax the tension created by difference, and that does not obliterate, in our quest to know, our enthusiasm, our ardor for the vitality of continuous relation.

We have not, in fact, gone far afield from the concerns of rhetoric in speaking of the primacy of relation here. The emotional drive to relate that both Buber and Teilhard de Chardin describe surfaces as an underlying motivation for both rhetoric and literary art in contemporary criticism and rhetoric. I shall explore here but a few examples of rhetorical strategies through which the ardor for relation takes hold and communication conveys knowledge that secures for us mutually a better place in the world.

Jean-François Lyotard explains the hunger for relation, to understand fully the meaningfulness of meaning, as Levinas has put it, as the distinguishing mark of the postmodern condition. To be postmodern is to live in that terrible and yet vitalizing state of recognizing our difference from others and wishing to represent what is, in fact, unpresentable, the dynamic that is our desire to represent what we are. Postmodernism prefigures, in effect, the birth of the modern or, as Lyotard calls it, the presentable. So, ironically, Lyotard notes, "postmodernism is not modernism at its end, but in a nascent state, and this state is recurrent" ("An Answer" 13). To be postmodern is to seek the dynamic of connection; it is to long for the event that is continuous human relation, the event that allows us "not to take pleasure in [new presentations], but to better produce the feeling that there is something presentable" ("An Answer" 15) or, in my terms, the feeling of relating to what might be presented. Lyotard feels an enthusiasm, an ardor for this process, and advocates the postmodern perspective on art and its interpretation as a kind of moral imperative, an attitude toward doing that realizes—in its resistance of the stable and familiar—the tension between the presentable and the unpresentable. To give up the struggle and strive to make of our representations something more concrete, says Lyotard, is like making "the promise and its keeping amount to the same thing" ("Gloss" 90). Our effort must always be to maintain the struggle to relate, to both make the promise to do so and strive to keep it. The postmodern perspective advocates experimentation; it is forward looking, anticipatory, prerelational, as Buber depicts "the cupped hand" in anticipation of what may be placed in it. The postmodern celebrates a "*différend* [a difference of opinion] within which the fate of thought has, for a long time, been played out, and will continue to be played out" between "the presentable" and "the conceivable" ("An Answer" 13), between that to which I have related and have attempted to record and that to which I might yet relate and yet attempt to depict. Lyotard "likes" the postmodern condition, if we can say that, and zealously refuses the peaceful pursuit of a unity that dissolves differences; he encourages the struggle of relating those disparate differences in view that he calls the "differend":

> We have paid dearly for our nostalgia for the all and the one, for a reconciliation of the concept and the sensible, for a transparent and communicable experience. Beneath the general demand for relaxation and appeasement, we hear murmurings of the desire to reinstitute terror and fulfill the phantasm of taking possession of reality. The answer is this: war on totality. Let us attest to the unpresentable; let us activate the differends and save the honor of the name. ("An Answer" 16)

The kind of playful enthusiasm for encountering the discomfort of difference is not simply a fancy, a selfish desire to experience the tantalizing effects of surprise and discovery. Rather, it is fundamental to the process of shaping meanings with others. This process is one of bridging and building, of finding the keystone that supports the impending and opposing weight of the arch, of juxtaposing the slip of silk with the solidity of stone, of moving from dialectic that puts difference in relief to dialogue that puts difference to work.

To build relations with others, to experience the ardor of relation which puts difference to work, we must not only celebrate difference, we must also realize our indebtedness to others for that difference. We must sense, too, our "responsibility" for others, as Levinas has put it, as they have been and continue to be responsible for us. To put difference in relief in such a way that its display conveys the meaning of difference as lived by those beings who embody it, the ardor for relation we must feel cannot in its course merely absorb, acquire, and transform difference to accommodate ourselves. Our ardor to experience the "differend" rather must honor its essential contribution to others' histories and to the very possibility of our present existence. This "responsible" ardor for the differing of others means far more than to give oneself up to what is "other"; such giving, as Jeffrey T. Nealon has recently suggested, can have the quite selfish aim of enhancing one's own character without thought or care for the needs of others we seek to know.

The joyful interplay assumed to be directed openly toward others in postmodern depictions of dialectic and dialogic communication, Nealon tells us, is not a guarantor of "responsible" interaction in the way Levinas has characterized it. There is a difference, he claims, between the other-directedness of Mikhail Bakhtin's dialogics, for instance, which focus on our "answerability," or our "responsiveness" to others, and the indebtedness to others implied by Levinian "responsibility," a distinction, I should note, that proponents of Bakhtinian dialogics have generally not chosen to make. Katerina Clark and Michael Holquist, for instance, emphasize only the charitable "building" effort of dialogic practices as envisioned by Bakhtin. The problem of authoring for Bakhtin, they say, is one of "bringing differences into a tensile complex rather than into a static unity"; this activity is one of "building," the love labor of constructing a world that accommodates both our own and others' place within it. The object of authoring is to engage in a project, one that envelops ourselves and others and for which we never disavow responsibility. As Clark and Holquist conclude: "By shaping answers in the constant activity of our dialogue with the world [in authoring], we enact the architectonics of our own responsibility" (10). This building focuses on an end, a telos, without reducing difference to common ground. We work not to shape and mold the things we see to fit our preconceptions of their meaning, but rather we strive to see how differences help us see new ways in which we can continue our work together. The idea is not to make differences to fit together so much as to see each distinguishing element as it might occupy the place of another, to put ourselves in another's shoes, to use an old saw. And putting ourselves in the place of others is interpreted generally as a selfless act.

Yet Nealon reads into Bakhtinian "answerability" a notion of response that is ultimately self-directed rather than selflessly other-directed. Both Bakhtin and Levinas, he admits, incorporate "the ability to respond," which is the "first and foremost" component of "responsibility" (Nealon 131), and both see communication as open-ended and dynamic and not predirected "toward some philosophical end or conclusion" (Nealon 133). But it is here that similarities end. Bakhtinian dialogics ultimately center on the need for the self to develop his or her character, to become a more admirable self-conscious being. The self is open to others because the self "*needs* otherness" (Nealon 140). Nealon interprets Bakhtin's endorsement of a dialogic engagement in the act of reading through which the reader takes on the character of a novel's hero as an act of appropriation, rather than responsiveness. The reader continually substitutes others for himself or herself, acquiring them, as it were. As he puts it: "I generously open myself to the others in order to overcome them, to conquer and consummate their external opinions of me" (Nealon 142). In this depiction of interpretive acts, the reader not only substitutes what is other for himself or herself, but also assumes that the self is in control of that act of substitution. In Levinas's characterization of the relation of self to other, it is the self that is continually replaceable, subject to the other; and the other remains irreducible and unique (Nealon 136).

Levinian responsibility, by contrast, then, depicts the self's openness to others not as a function of self-control and development, but rather as a necessary condition of our social existence and our very freedom to act. As Nealon explains, for Levinas, the subject finds itself from the "get go" indebted to others whose histories require the subject to respond; he notes: "I first am marked, interpellated, subject to something other than myself before I respond and a trace of that marking inhabits all of my responses" (145). It is with a sense of humble indebtedness to the being and actions of others who have made our very existence and sociality possible that we exercise our freedom to act.

From my perspective, Levinas, Buber, Farley, Kellenberger, MacIntyre, and Teilhard de Chardin together offer a perspective on the nature of individual investment in dialogic practices that can lead to true and mutual understanding of the nature of human existence in the material world. We need not condemn dialogics, dialectics, or any other scheme for rhetorical practice on the ground that it may lead back, in the end, to the hegemonic desires of individuals or groups to assume and assimilate what is other in order to satisfy themselves. These techniques are but techniques, and part of a long tradition of developing techniques to stimulate the occasion for our communicative interaction with others. Attention to the differend, for instance, which is thought to be characteristic of the postmodern perspective on artistic and rhetorical communication, is fundamentally a very old idea. It is how we incorporate this familiar strategy in our dealing with others that can make its rhetorical focus phenomenological, to use my term.

Kathleen Welch reminds us that Plato defended dialectic because of its capacity to keep difference alive through stimulating the participation of many in our mutual knowledge building, a point Jasper Neel makes as well, as I have noted in chapter 1. Her endorsement of this technique reflects the altruistic attitude of responsible care that I am promoting here. Dialectic, she suggests, is a counter to the passivity that characterizes so much of writing pedagogy; she says:

> At the center of dialectic lies activity between two fully participating sides. Dialectic denies passivity, the attribute that most characterizes education and that depends completely on a denial of the capacity of students' *ethos*, traps them in triviality, and therefore stifles their power. (17)

Dialectic, when transformed by Bakhtin into the practice of dialogism, allows us to cede to others still greater power, because dialogism, as Clark and Holquist put it, celebrates alterity, embraces with enthusiasm the perspectives of others because they make my meaning more meaningful: "As the world needs my alterity to give it meaning, I need the authority of others to define, or author, my self. The other is in the deepest sense my friend, because it is only from the other that I can get my self" (66). It is in this deepest sense of friendship that the ardor of authoring must take place. What Levinas reminds us, as Nealon has so tellingly revealed, is that our extension of friendship is indeed essential to a stimulating and productive engagement with the other, but this engagement is not in my control, not within my power to define. Because the other is "always there already," Nealon concludes, "any act I perform is necessarily conditioned by—as Levinas would say *owed to*—the other" (135). Responsibility for and to others, then, is "the groundless ground of human subjectivity, inexorably open to the approach of the other" (Nealon 145). It is the overt recognition of this responsibility, I suggest, that must inspire our use of rhetorical technique within a phenomenological rhetoric.

The ardor for relation to others, then, which I claim must drive communicative acts, is an ultimate commitment to our functional telos of mutual responsibility, to the realization that I *am* but as I give myself to relate to others, as others *are* but as they give to me. And so, as a speaker or writer, what I really do when I reflect upon my experience and acknowledge the world in its relation to me, when I reason with open receptivity and consciously attend to our authentic function as self-conscious creatures with a spiritual life, when I regenerate concepts into new formulations that express my ardor to continuously relate, to seek to know—what I do in approaching my speech and my writing in this way is this: I interpret all that it is I claim to know as it reflects my indebtedness to and responsibility for others. Nealon has suggested that it is this attitude toward the essential necessity of other-relatedness, if you will, that permeates Levinas's approach to our subjectivity, an attitude that "begins to perform a gesture that we could call an ethics or politics of the other" (146). In the context of my effort to define a phenomenological rhetoric, I would conclude that it is this attitude that grounds the rhetorical practice of professing altruism.

Altruism: Authoring an Embrace

The complex process of professing altruism in rhetorical practice resists—if I can risk using this word that I have sought to abandon—reduction to a final set of axioms and procedures for rhetorical practice. As I have tried to suggest, the process is developmental, progressing from the perspective of the author with an intention to communicate to the object of that intention, another human being: Profession culminates in altruism. My reflection upon experience results in an acknowledgment of my personhood, of the sense that my own experience makes sense in the terms that others' make sense for them.

My receptivity to various criteria for valid evidence is focused by my quest for authenticity, for expression that perfects my understanding as it transforms others'. And finally, my regeneration of ideas positions my experience within the histories of others and my own, and it is motivated by my ardor for continuous relation, to state what I know without closing off the possibility of yet more knowing and of realizing my indebtedness to others for that knowledge.

Phenomenological rhetoric as a practice is perhaps more poetic than methodical, yet its application is apt and timely in matters ranging from the mundane to the sublime. Imagine a world where all in it understood knowledge and truth itself to be contingent upon our relating to each other with absolute selflessness, with an ultimate and unwavering commitment to a shared good. Even slight reflection upon everyday situations that are common to most of my readers who are teaching in colleges and universities and who are sharing homes with families will illustrate the importance of this approach for assuring mutual prosperity.

Consider with me, if you will, how a commitment to profession and altruism must change my own everyday activity as a professor who teaches writing, as a scholar in the field of rhetoric, and even as a wife of twenty-some years to my husband. In marking my students' papers, for instance, in placing my comments in the margins, constructing epistles at their efforts' ends, how must this behavior differ when I consider that ours—my students' and mine— is a common quest to know, to live out together our destiny to relate as beings who need to know? How must this consideration alter my ideas about what it is to be a teacher, about how I should relate to those in my classes, about what fault or triumph in their written expression I should choose to recognize? When faced with the task of embarking upon my next scholarly project, how must I consider my perspectives on an important problem in my field in relation to those of my colleagues? How must I deal with my desire to distinguish myself, to debate and win a point, to mark out a territory, to stake a claim in the domain of knowledge? And how must I reckon these desires with our mutual quest to know, to communicate what we have discovered to each other and to the public—often oblivious to our effort, yet whose concerns we also address? When I want to tell my husband, for perhaps the one-hundredth time, that I do not want to stay overnight with his relatives, to bring a "passing dish" to his office party, or to go shopping while he entertains his friends, how should I regard the problem of dealing with these little differences between us? Should I consider it one of marshaling arguments so that I can forward my position so successfully that I end our quibbling about these things once and for all? Or should I wonder instead about what his family means to him, to us, about how my need to establish a place for myself in the world at large jibes with scurrying up some deviled eggs for a potluck dinner, about how we both need to relate to family and friends on our own terms, for our own purposes, while yet together?

I am talking here about transforming our whole notion of rhetoric as driven by the narrow task of persuasion to consider rhetoric's larger function of relating me to you, to the world, and to the words of others. As such, rhetoric has no singular end, but rather a continuous task: to keep us together, relating purposefully so that we might know better what we are all about together. This is all to the good, my readers might justifiably respond, but how, in practical terms, can we do this? Where are the brass tacks? The meat on the bones? What are the criteria for practicing a phenomenological rhetoric? What do we *do* to speak and write in this way? And what are the real consequences of doing so? Can we survive them, literally, in a world where we cannot trust others to behave as charitably as we might pledge to behave? How do we practice a rhetoric that not only keeps the conversation going, as Burke might say, but that also makes our relating to one another primary, as Buber has enjoined us? And how might such a rhetoric concretely address our everyday, practical desire to nail down, define, articulate—once and for all— what it is that we know? It is with this task, that of guiding rhetoric so that it continually progresses toward mutual understanding through relating, that I will both close this book and hope with my readers to begin.

6

Practicing a Phenomenological Rhetoric

L ET US BEGIN by recapitulating the major themes that I have developed in
proposing a phenomenological rhetoric of writing. I began, in chapter 1,
by taking on relativism in critical theory and rhetoric as defended by Jasper
Neel and Barbara Herrnstein Smith. These theorists deny that the classical
quest to seek truth is a viable goal for rhetoric and dismiss the idea that truth
is attainable, concluding that each proposed version of truth is doomed to be
replaced by a more widely accepted or favored alternative. I suggested here
that the relativist interpretations of truth and writing that these theorists
propose reflect a rather narrow belief that truth is an immutable interpretation
that corresponds to a static reality. A more positive relationship between truth
and writing can be construed if we conceive of them both as processes rather
than static declarations, processes in constant motion, growth, and development. But having said this about truth and writing, and having expounded
upon this claim as I have attempted to do, we have said nothing about the
originating end of these processes, the speaker or writer, the human being
who tries to write about truth.

As I have argued in chapter 2, contemporary rhetoric and criticism have
not helped us with the other end of the truth equation, the truth speaker's
end, if you will, presenting us with the undesirable alternatives of, on the
one hand, a radically free and autonomous speaking subject who must resist
staunchly the influence of social input in order to derive a true conception of
the world, and on the other hand, a totally socially constructed cipher, unable
to make any choice, derive any thought, or propose any action that is not
predetermined by the circumstance of one's culture and environment. The
influential sway of these conceptions of the self as a rhetorical agent is reflected in a system of literary value which promotes narcissistic and fetishistic
rhetoric. The former puts a premium on developing a distinct, individual voice
and on distancing one's own views from those of others; the latter cedes one's
authority for personal expression to a sacred rubric, such as the dictates of
science, law, or religion, which becomes the true object of one's allegiance

rather than truth, which may lie outside these standards and which remains in "second place" behind them.

The alternative I propose to the limited conceptions of truth and subjectivity that I outline in my first two chapters is to entertain a phenomenological perspective on the relationship between truth and consciousness, one that I have derived in the main from the work of Edmund Husserl and Maurice Merleau-Ponty presented in chapter 3. Phenomenology defines truth as a concept that is developed in consciousness and that attains significance through the expression of our daily lives. Truth is, in other words, an essentially human phenomenon and not a divine creation or a perfect, inanimate abstraction. It is essentially human because our conception of truth can only be so; it has no meaning divorced from our physical, mental, and living selves. Phenomenology develops three important criteria for truth, each of which shapes analogous criteria for rhetorical practice. The first criterion is that all truths are located in subjective experience, that is, within one's own consciousness; the second is that truth is an outcome of intersubjective understanding, that is, of the interplay of one's conscious reckonings against another's; and the third is that intersubjective understanding progresses toward truth through expression, that is, speaking or writing. Our verbal expression of coherent, reliable, and socially viable truth depends upon our individual engagement in the process of truth seeking, an engagement that I have described as the rhetorical process of profession in chapter 4. Through inclusive reflection upon our lived experience of the world, attending to particulars as they have some general meaning that includes our own sense and that of others; through reasoning receptively by which we let go of the idea that conclusions from direct observation can be separated from subjective belief and thus acknowledge that reasoning is motivated human action; and through regenerating concepts, that is, animating and elaborating what appears to exist for ourselves and others, willfully committing to ideas as they have implications for our very being—through practicing all of these conscious activities, we have within our power the potential to speak and write in truth. But that potential must be developed further if it is to result in beliefs that are shared and acted upon by others with the same commitment we give them ourselves.

In chapter 5, I have proposed that truth seeking assumes a commitment to altruism, that is, to conceiving of truth as a shared value with a good end for others as well as oneself. For intersubjective contact to succeed in helping us to build truth, to construct truth through pairing our conscious responses to the world with those of others, we must be willing to alter our current view of the world in order to consider fairly views that are favored and valued by others. Through selflessly interpreting the world in ways that protect the interests of others as well as our own, we can act prudentially and respect our common telos to shape together, through personal choice, shared knowledge of our common world.

Altruism must direct the relationships we establish with others through rhetoric if we are to come to a shared understanding. In practicing altruism, we acknowledge that our reflections upon reality must square with those of others whose life experiences are as valuable as our own. Altruism authenticates our communication within a community of persons, assuring its contribution to the betterment of our communal life. And altruism animates an ardor to create meaning that relates us to others, meaning that expands our personal understanding of ourselves and our world as it changes others' understanding of the same. My argument for the primacy of altruism recognizes truth's debt to value, as David Weissman has put it. Truth is a shared value, related inextricably to our welfare and our survival: We strive to know the truth so that we can improve our lives and those of our progeny. And my argument relies, too, on the fact of our irrevocable indebtedness to others, of our responsibility to and for others, as Levinas has defined it. If we accept these claims about truth and our selfhood—ones to which I will return at the end of this chapter—we also must accept that we come to truth only through maintaining ongoing, sustainable, and loving relationships with others.

But how do we direct our rhetorical practice to maintain such loving connections to others? Especially, how do we maintain the will to do so in a world where love is talked about largely in terms of its presence in erotic excess or its absence in hateful abuse? Or in a world where rhetoric is thought to be at its best a strategic tool that we employ to promote the perspectives we favor and at its worst a ruthless weapon that we engage to manipulate others? In this chapter, I present the work of a few contemporary scholars whose approaches to rhetorical theory address in part the phenomenological perspective, focusing in the main on theories proposed by Jürgen Habermas, Charles Altieri, and Thomas Kent. This work addresses practical standards for evaluating discourse as it forwards intersubjective understanding, three of which I shall refer to as *congruence, consensus,* and *commensurability.* My object is to suggest how a phenomenological outlook toward these standards might push rhetorical theory an important step further, that is, toward defining communicative practice as intersubjective truth seeking. To accomplish this, theorists must address not only what writers and speakers do to maintain knowing relationships between themselves and others, the condition from which all intersubjective understanding must arise, but they must also account for the values that motivate and perpetuate this behavior. A practical intersubjective rhetoric inscribes a way of living together, enabling speakers and listeners to reach a mutual truth, even within the context of irreconcilable difference.

The contemporary approaches to intersubjective rhetoric that I shall review strongly imply that the dialogic dynamism of language itself motivates and assures communication that leads to common understanding. Where dialogism fails to resolve differences in views, theorists have suggested impartial criteria for achieving alignment or agreement. Drawing upon the work of Richard Bernstein and Hilary Putnam, I propose that a successful intersubjective rhetoric not only adheres to practical standards for resolving differences, but also is founded upon goodwill, a personal commitment to compassionate listening, an attitude that does not emerge from communicative interaction, but rather must serve as the basis for it. This chapter concludes with a personal account of a communication situation that I faced recently as a university administrator. It is one that for me foregrounded the role of goodwill and compassion for others in reconciling our accounts of what the world means. Openness to change and acceptance of diversity are essential, I believe, to maintaining the knowing relationships among speakers and listeners that keep a quest for truth alive; they are the foundation of the practices of profession and altruism as I have described them.

Congruence, Consensus, and Commensurability: Standards for Intersubjective Interaction

Let me begin by giving brief definitions of three standards that contemporary rhetorics have forwarded for evaluating verbal concepts developed intersubjectively, standards that address how we regulate our discourse and our actions to assure their consistency and validity. Verbal knowledge claims are said to meet the standard of congruence when they are consistent with some prevailing and well-accepted method for effectively conducting a human activity, such as the activity of practicing citizenship, or law, or science. Such principles and actions, furthermore, are thought to be endorsable when all members of a group have reached consensus about their meaning and validity, following some democratic process through which all may voice their differences.

Congruence and consensus tend to work hand-in-hand: To obtain the consensus of several as to whether to accept a principle or to endorse an action, the statement or procedure at issue must be congruent with and explainable within prevailing methods for validating belief, whether the method be a fair articulation of all points of view, a demonstration of logical reasoning, or the application of field-specific epistemologies. Likewise, congruence of a decision with prevailing belief systems and sensitivities often presumes a prior consensus about the validity of those epistemological systems that are called into play. Although the interdependence of congruence and consensus is obvious in practical affairs, traditionally these standards are thought to govern different domains. To strive for congruence with an epistemological system is to strive for an outcome that is truthful, that is, consistent with findings about the world within an accepted theory or knowledge base; whereas to strive for consensus in forwarding a decision or action is to strive for an outcome that is morally right, in that it will be accepted as so by all who participate in it or are affected by it.

Commensurability, the third standard that I am offering up for judging the validity of our verbal claims, works a bit differently than the other two. Commensurability has to do with the way in which one concept can be explained within a framework that irrefutably supports an opposing concept. It supersedes the notions of congruence and consensus because it deals not with the correspondence of words and deeds with some culturally constructed epistemology or perception of reality, but rather with the coherence of words and deeds when assessed by different epistemological methods. How we deal with commensurability in our interactions with each other, I contend, holds the key to our practice of profession and altruism in rhetoric. But more about this later.

First, let us talk about the application of congruence and consensus as standards for determining the truth and rightness of our rhetoric. In *Moral Consciousness and Communicative Action,* Jürgen Habermas outlines a method for coming to social agreement about various matters, given that diverse social commitments and entitlements are embedded in language use and that, in any communicative interchange, participants must work to assure that each person's interests are acknowledged appropriately and accommodated fairly. As one of his interpreters states, Habermas "builds the moment of empathy *into* the procedures of coming to a reasoned agreement: each must put him- or herself into the place of everyone else in discussing whether a proposed norm is fair to all" (McCarthy viii–ix). In practical terms, Habermas codifies the conditions for rhetorical interaction that will assure that such proceedings are just, justice being a value that he is convinced holds sway across a variety of diverse cultures. He acknowledges that interpretation is hermeneutical and infinitely various, yet he wishes to put limits and boundaries on it, to systematize it so that it works the same for everyone. One of the more important interpretive distinctions Habermas makes is one between factual and moral systems; he suggests that each are governed by a different set of standards that, in turn, must guide argument about what is truthful in either domain. Factual and moral systems include different controls for keeping their domains intact. Acceptance of a statement as fact is dependent upon one's juxtaposition of experience with accepted theory about the statement's meaning, that is, upon testing a statement's congruence with rational or scientific reasoning; in Habermas's words, such "theoretical criticism of misleading everyday experience serves to correct beliefs" (*Moral Consciousness* 51). Acceptance of a statement as morally justified, in contrast, is associated with "the authority of generally accepted norms" and "the impersonality of their claims" (Habermas,

Moral Consciousness 49), that is, their application with "good reason" in a variety of situations.

As I noted earlier, Habermas concedes that we accrue knowledge about the world through hermeneutical interpretation, continually establishing and reestablishing interpretations as valid; at the same time, he suggests that hermeneutical interpretation should be constrained by procedures that would objectify it, that is, allow one to evaluate the success of an interpretation against some immutable criteria, not subject to idiosyncratic or cultural perspectives. He attempts to establish such criteria as guidelines for communicative action, a form of argumentation that leads to consensus. Communicative action involves two ground rules; first, it is subject to what Habermas identifies as a universal moral standard for any claim or norm that has the potential to affect others. A claim or norm is judged to be moral under the following universal condition:

> *All* affected can accept the consequences and the side effects its *general* observance can be anticipated to have for the satisfaction of *everyone's* interests (and these consequences are preferred to those of known alternative possibilities for regulation). (Habermas, *Moral Consciousness* 65)

The means by which such a claim or norm comes to be established in a society is through interactive discourse itself; this is the technology through which all claims and norms are derived. Hence, the second ground rule for discourse that results in communicative action is this:

> Only those norms can claim to be valid that meet (or could meet) with the approval of all affected in their capacity *as participants in a practical discourse.* (Habermas, *Moral Consciousness* 66)

The process of arguing communally and cooperatively to achieve a consensus is all that, in fact, guarantees it, and furthermore, only such argumentation, according to Habermas, "can give the participants the knowledge that they have collectively become convinced of something" (*Moral Consciousness* 67).

Communicative action, or cooperative argumentation, is the ideal method to achieve consensus, Habermas concludes, because impartiality "is rooted *in* the structures of argumentation *themselves* and does not need to be *brought in* from the outside as a supplementary normative content" (*Moral Consciousness* 75–76). It is argumentation, he insists, that forces us to be moral, that is, to behave as if the consequences of one's actions will fairly meet everyone's interests. As soon as we leave the field of argumentation, we can shake off the compulsion "to respect one another as equal partners, to assume one another's truthfulness, and to cooperate with one another" (Habermas, *Moral Consciousness* 86). In other words, without cooperative argumentation, we have no moral center and thus no need to seek consensus as a moral goal.

Similarly, without the empirical or scientific method of evaluating experience, we have no basis for validating our claims about the world as it is, that is, no method to test the congruence of our experience with some established way of knowing about the world. Science and reasoning distinguish truths from our mere perceptions of experience; argumentation distinguishes moral universals from idiosyncratic desires to justify our actions. In short, it would appear that for Habermas, congruence with logical principles of deductive or inductive proof following the principles of scientific reasoning forms a rational standard for the validity of a stated idea, and consensus forms a moral standard for reconciling the views of individuals whose views differ in attempts to reach an agreement.

Additional support for congruence and consensus as standards for the validity and appropriateness of statements, decisions, and actions lies in our modern tradition of accepting the scientific method as a standard for verifying fact and scientific debate as the standard for validating ideas by consensus. Such acceptance may lead us to believe that these standards *on their own* guarantee decisions and statements that are both true and right. Yet this belief can be justified only if we can prove congruence and consensus not to have some prior value attached to them, that is, an underlying cultural belief that gives them authority.

As I explained in some detail in chapter 5, to find an idea or concept to be congruent with an accepted epistemology or method of reasoning, such as that proposed by science or law, is no guarantee that the method itself is value-free. Furthermore, to try to resolve disputes about what is right and true on such grounds is to ignore the significance of real differences between individuals when they stand in relation to one another, a situation that results in resorting to technical quick fixes to resolve disputes, the conclusion reached by Charles Taylor. On the one hand, Habermas's guidelines for communicative action account for the social basis of normative claims, designating how they might be resolved through debate. But on the other hand, the guidelines imply that individuals can impartially assess in all cases whether a cultural norm is fair for every individual in a comparable situation; individuals' participation in communal argument over such issues is presumed to regulate decision making and result in procedures that are fair and, consequently, conclusions that are just.

But argument can take place within the context of testing whether statements are congruent with a validity standard and whether they can be supported by consensus and *still* result in patently unjust conclusions. Steven B. Katz has illustrated, for instance, the callous effects of accepting congruence with accepted methodologies as an impartial criterion to judge the truth and rightness of an action in his chilly analysis of communications by Nazi military officials enacting the horrors of the Holocaust. Katz cites a memorandum written by a Nazi officer to his superior during World War II. The officer argues "for technical improvements to the vans being used in the early Nazi program of exterminating the Jews [and others] just months before the Final Solution of gas chambers and death camps was fully operationalized" (Katz 256). The memo is structured perfectly as a technical document, opening, for instance, with a statement of the problem, "ninety-seven thousand have been processed . . . with no major incidents" (255) thus far, and then presenting the need for technical changes to the vans to reduce the possibility of future problems. As Katz points out, it meets criteria for effective document design, being "divided into three numbered sections that are clearly demarcated by white space for easy reading" (257); and furthermore, its logic is congruent with preferred Aristotelian strategies for presenting an effective enthymatic argument. For instance, in describing the technical deficiencies of the van that warrant correction, the author effectively articulates a "cause/effect" argument for a "reduction in the load space" rather than supporting a reduction in the number of " 'pieces' " loaded to decrease operational time, as well as to secure vehicle stability. Of course, in making this perfect argument, that is, in methodically presenting evidence and following conventions for effective argumentation, the author "shows no concern," as Katz notes, "that the purpose of his memo is the modification of vehicles not only to improve efficiency, but also to exterminate people" (257). In short, Katz intimates that single-minded attention to the process of providing scientifically sound evidence and to presenting an effective argument completely outweighs concern with the end of the communication as it has implications for human lives. But Katz goes further than this to suggest that concern with the technical perfection of a process as opposed to its ends not only privileges what I have called the congruence of an action or statement with predetermined systems of knowledge or belief, but also hegemonically instantiates consensus among those inscribed by the process. This is not because adherence to processes in itself produces a consensus, but rather because processes that guarantee utility and expediency as their result reflect consensual values in Western culture.

The ethic of expedience reflected in scientific procedures and utilitarian rhetoric together create a " 'moral' warrant for Nazi action" (Katz 263), that is, that political expediency is necessary to achieve an ideal state and hence is the "basis of virtue itself" (Katz 263). When technology drives action, there is no argument about ends, but rather only a concern about the means. Hence, the need to achieve consensus is superseded by the mere demonstration that an action is procedurally effective. Alasdair MacIntyre has also made this point, noting that in a culture in which the notion of right and utility dominate in order to preserve individuality prior to any other human aspiration, managerial expertise will necessarily dominate; its claims to value neutrality and systematic attention to process allow individuals to effectively avoid confrontation with one another over differences in values, in other words, to avoid the scene that has potential to lead to dialogically derived consensus, the ideal of Habermas's process of communicative action. Rather than interrogating the need for social change as it has implications for humanity's progress toward some ideal state, MacIntyre has told us, individuals avoid participation in such debate and cede authority to experts who "justify themselves and their claims to authority, power, and money by invoking their own competence as scientific managers of social change" (*After Virtue* 86).

In other words, personal authority and integrity are invested in a technology that is assumed to guarantee action that is both true and right, in this case, congruent with scientific methodology and, by dint of this, meriting consensual endorsement. Furthermore, congruence and consensus here are treated as ways of relating people and things that operate for good or ill in themselves, rather than as practices that have implications for a person's commitment to certain values.

In critiquing consensus as a rhetorical goal, Greg Myers has noted its potential to disenfranchise individual commitment to a dissenting view. Myers strongly objects to Kenneth Bruffee's pedagogy of collaborative learning, defining consensus as hegemonic social control that diminishes the significance of individual differences. In teaching rhetorical conventions, such as those of business writing, he claims, we make the prior assumption that consensus is a social good. Conflating the principles of consensus and congruence here, Myers finds rhetorical conventions, that is, standards for linguistically representing acceptable evidence for belief, to be consensually derived. He warns us that calling writing a socially constructed process should not lead us, as well, to accept the "social construction of knowledge as something good in itself" (171).

Commenting upon Habermas's theory of communicative action, Susan Wells also notes the limitations of rational procedures for assuring the validity of discourse. She concedes that Habermas's hopes for communicative action may amount to a utopian dream. At one point, he predicted that discourse governed by the principles of communicative action would foster a kind of "social evolution" (Wells 116), claiming that we could compare less developed societies with more developed ones based upon their ability to develop rational truths and moral principles through the ubiquitous practice of communicative action. Wells agrees with Habermas that "movements for social change can be normatively secured," perhaps even through consistent application of the principles of communicative action, "but this possibility does not guarantee any such security for any social movement, no matter how benign" (117). At the same time, however, Wells does endorse Habermas's externalist view of the relationship between language and rational thought, regarding rationality as an "implicit assumption of communication" and not "an attribute of consciousness"; hence, she concludes that "it is not necessary to ground our preference for reason" in some ontological description of the workings of consciousness, but that "it is urgently necessary to specify—and argue about—particular understandings of what is rational" (115). Like Habermas, Wells optimistically posits a kind of regulatory role for discourse in our disputes about rationality, describing discourse as an organizing form of human action: "Discourse secures assent, organizing rational agreement, and discourse manages the energies that inhabit subjects and the texts they produce" (113). Communicative action forms a common ground that allows us to negotiate claims to validity that, according to Habermas, are "organized in differentiated discourses, mediated by prior understandings and rules" (Wells 113). To view rationality and validity claims as a mere matter of difference in discoursing habits is a fairly liberating gesture, freeing us from the metaphysical claims to truth to which various epistemological methods aspire. As Wells interprets Habermas, no metaphysical claims back incommensurable discourses; all such discourses are on the same footing within the arena of communicative action. Differentiation in our discourses externalizes our differences, puts them out there where we can deal with them, that is, where we can come together "to work out forms of talk within which very serious disagreements can be contained and resolved" (Wells 118).

An equally optimistic view of the capacity of discourse to mediate differences is posed by Charles Altieri. In *Act and Quality: A Theory of Literary Meaning and Humanistic Understanding*, Altieri asserts that textual strategies for validating belief capture the essence of a culture and hold the clues to our understanding of it. Texts reveal, in effect, a "complex cultural grammar":

> Texts afford knowledge not because they describe particulars but because they embody ways of experiencing facts. Their truth is one of possible labels, not of accurate propositions. So instead of grasping texts as ideas, we come to possess them as features of a complex cultural grammar, which extends the power to make discriminations that we learn when we learn a language. (Altieri, *Act* 12)

Altieri sees a text's embeddedness in the values of a culture not as a drawback to determining its truth, but rather as the means by which we more fully experience that culture's particular ways of engaging with the world. All knowledge has meaning within the everyday activities of a culture, even scientific knowledge. It may be true that scientific knowledge cannot always be articulated adequately in everyday terms, but, as Altieri notes, the scientist "cannot easily contradict the basic terms in which the phenomenon itself is commonly understood" (*Act* 15). In short, the ordinary experience of persons both validates scientific knowledge and is constituent of its truth.

Of course, ordinary experience is never closed; and it is the open-ended-ness of experience that poses the problem of how to relate "the structures of a written textuality and the realm of experience it continually displaces as it *names*" (Altieri, *Act* 35). The text is fixed, experience is not, and hence, a text's interpretation of experience cannot be fixed. If this is so, asks Altieri, how can we develop a mode of interpreting and evaluating texts that is not relativistic, moving and shifting as the grounds of experiential knowledge shift? And furthermore, how can we hope to produce coherent and consistent meaning through producing texts? We can relate these questions more specifically to our concerns at hand. How can we apply impartial standards, such as congruence and consensus, and declare that a given discourse is "valid," when our experience and knowledge of the world is continuously shifting and changing?

Altieri approaches this problem phenomenologically, developing a conception of discourse validity derived from Ludwig Wittgenstein's, J. L. Austin's, and Nelson Goodman's approach to the nature of philosophical analysis, which, as he notes, is "concerned more with the conditions of rightness or fit than with traditional criteria of truth" (*Act* 13). In short, he attempts a philosophical description of discourse that reconciles the rhetorical aim of analytic philosophy to provide a coherent argument with the "endless questioning which is 'serious' philosophy" (*Act* 29). A truly responsible philosophy of language as it represents truth telling, he concludes, "must give a coherent picture of the grounds and implications of the multiplicity and duplicity that characterize human language" (*Act* 39).

To show how language works to project our changing experience of the world, Altieri explores ways in which texts overtly convey the dynamic nature of person-to-object and person-to-person relationships. Continuing in the tradition of Wittgenstein, Altieri attempts to describe how we arrive at public meaning by suggesting a grammar of human actions that neither makes suppositions about a direct relationship between reality and language nor admits that our actions and our expressions are all random free play (*Act* 53–60). A coherent textual grammar must show how our "grammatical competence enables us to understand and to assess the full performance of a speech act" (Altieri, *Act* 81), that is, to assess the agency or intention behind the text. Altieri tries to capture how represented actions fit with specific "motives, plans, judgments, etc." attributable to an agent or an actor trying to solve a problem or deal with a situation in order to understand it. He refers to this methodological perspective as *"dramatism"* (*Act* 103).

Altieri defines three kinds of terms that locate a ground upon which speakers and listeners attribute the relation between human motivation and action. The complexity of assessing the fit between action and motivation depends on the linguistic terms in question. *"Brute facts,"* a term he takes from John Searle, are those linguistic expressions "which we take as features of the physical world (including immediate sensations) and can be described by the physical sciences" (Altieri, *Act* 58). *"Institutional facts"* are those that depend on what Searle calls *"constitutive rules"* that "create the conditions determining what will count as relevant facts" (Altieri, *Act* 58; Searle 31–42). Our most complex terms for describing motivated action are those he calls "dimension terms," the meaning of which are developed through long-standing experience within a culture as well as an assessment of our personal experience against what is felt to be the experience of others. "Being in love" is such a dimension term. We don't understand "being in love" to bear a one-to-one relationship with a discrete experience; rather, we allow ourselves to grow in understanding of this term through personal and literary experience. As Altieri explains: "Our passage into a fully adult understanding [of a term like "being in love"] depends in large part on our effort to meet the demands on our grammar imposed by the complex perspicuous examples which poets and philosophers create" (*Act* 68). We learn the meaning of dimension terms through relating to one another, through continuously seeking a state of mutual understanding within the cultural grammars and texts we share, a condition that does not come easily, but rather is cultivated.

Altieri's dramatistic approach to language and meaning draws connections between intentions and external manifestations of them without making claims for the primacy of either in expressing "the truth." I cannot provide in this brief introduction to his method an adequate description of his grammar, but I hope to leave my readers with a sense of how dramatistic analysis might address the question of how we reach mutual understanding of a text and determine the validity of its meaning. Altieri attempts to link the fixity of a text with the malleability of human interactions within a cultural grammar that grounds the basis upon which we reach mutual understanding; he notes:

> Mutual understanding is not an easy social ideal but a condition gained by careful and concerned performance of the self. A poem can achieve so much by so little explicit content just because its author recognizes how fully performance relies upon and elicits the implicit grounds of grammatical competence which serve as the foundation for achievable and achieved meanings. (*Act* 175)

We rely on our cultural grammars to enhance our interpretation of a text, to more firmly link it to an authorial intention. A choice to produce and receive texts as literary, for instance, as opposed to rhetorical, is a choice to treat verbal expression as a kind of life performance, to read a text, as Altieri says, so as "to understand the dramatic situation as a particular experience, and to reflect upon the implicit activity of the author as he imposes his formal and thematic argument on the situation" (*Act* 210). In other words, it is to project a "dramatistic" relationship to others and, in particular, to the author as an intending agent within that relationship, as the primary basis upon which we interpret meaning. In effect, for Altieri, a test of a statement's validity, that is, its ability to effect a mutual understanding, rests on the place of that statement in establishing relationships among these who share it. His dramatistic grammar is an attempt to describe the parameters upon which these relationships are established.

In a more recent work, entitled *Subjective Agency,* Altieri explores in greater detail how authors establish an identity and how their identity both impacts upon knowledge claims and secures their power as an expressive agent among others. In this work, Altieri concludes that the motivation to express a truth and the dynamic of truth building within a community are related to the agent's intention to project himself or herself as a particular kind of person in relation to others. Furthermore, this intentional desire is, in fact, congruent, if you will, across cultures; Altieri believes that "we can locate a single, shareable understanding of subjective agency in all cultures that have related concepts of intentionality and responsibility if we are elemental enough in our description and if we realize that there will be many different ways of putting the concept into practice" (*Subjective Agency* 7).

The universal, elemental description of agency that Altieri suggests goes something like this: Agents become substantive by pursuing identities within cultural grammars that they care about, that allow them to become a person who is regarded as worthy among others. Altieri pursues in great detail the ways in which aspects of linguistic expression, such as style, allow agents to map their intentionality onto the real world: "At one pole, style is expressive and individuating, with the other it seems as given as it does chosen because it so intimately binds the psyche to material properties and binds individuals to historical situations and trends." Style, claims Altieri, "can display one important model for what we mean when we use predicates like 'genuine' and 'truthful' in relation to persons" (*Subjective Agency* 60). What style does is to materialize our commitment to a specific identity among others, an act that Altieri suggests, cannot "be subordinated to a will to truth" (*Subjective Agency* 73), that is, to its reliance on some third-order authority, such as a god, for its validity.

We judge the validity and truthfulness of others' expressions by how well they project an identity that signals certain mutually understood and respected commitments. In short, we apply standards of congruence and coherence—as I have called them—to personal expression, Altieri suggests, when judging whether expression consistently conveys an identity that is articulated within a cultural grammar. To make valid judgments, then, "becomes a process of exploring the range of identifications or processes of reciprocity we can develop through our modeling of cultural grammars" (Altieri, *Subjective Agency*

215) If this is what we mean by validity and truth telling, then we cannot think of either congruence or consensus as impartial validity standards. Underlying their very application are assumptions about relationships that hold between observer and observed, and between observer and observer, in specific communication situations in which persons express specific, mutually understood identities.

Altieri proposes a method for defining rhetorical agency as it emerges within human relationships, examining simultaneously the nature of both linguistic phenomena and being, and he rejects the urge to set up a distinction between the two. It is such a distinction that Habermas categorically maintains in separating the domains of factual and moral knowledge, the former supposedly dealing with the world out there as it is and the latter with our normative construction of it. Altieri focuses rather on the relationship between human values and our conception of the world as a real presence, and between individuals as willful agents and our negotiation of this agency within our cultural practices. His perspective on language and consciousness brings to mind Martin Buber's view that in order to know the world, we should relate to it as a "You" with which we are engaged perpetually, as opposed to an "It" from which we are separated and removed. Such a perspective closes the gaps between thought and language, language and action, and self and other that are presumed by epistemologies that separate reality from consciousness, and fact from moral action, finding these domains to be distinct and our ways of speaking about them to be incommensurable.

In fact, it is the very notion of incommensurability that Altieri attempts to dispel. In his view, philosophy must be flexible enough to account for disparate beliefs about who we are and how we do things. To create an enfolding view of how we interact with others to reach common ground, we must be able to identify provisionally with the positions of others, to be willing to not set rigid borders around our thinking, and to seek rather those areas, however small, in which mutual understanding can result "by breaking large, apparently incommensurable assumptions into units small enough that we can talk about degrees of sharing or can come to recognize how contrasting paths intersect and diverge" (Altieri, *Subjective Agency* 14). We must deconstruct, if you will, the wholesale belief that judgments can be incommensurable before we can assess how our rhetoric contributes to mutual understanding. We find ways of speaking about the world to be incommensurable because we believe the conscious world and the real world, the factual world and the moral world, to be separate domains across which the best that we can hope for is a one-to-one correspondence. We believe in incommensurability because we also believe that some of our conceptions correspond with reality and standard belief and others simply do not. We believe, too, that many ways of speaking about the world are categorically incompatible with one another, presenting different and incongruous versions of experience. If we refuse to separate reality from our conscious interpretation of it, and fact from belief, then we can find no interpretation to be divorced from reality, and all ways of speaking to be commensurable with our own.

As we have shown, congruence and consensus have pragmatic value as standards for the conceptual validity of rhetorical interaction; if we acknowledge, in turn, commensurability across systems of meaning, we have, then, the potential to apply these standards when judging whether our rhetoric is leading us to a shared truth that respects the needs of all. To attend to commensurability is simply to consider that a proposed idea has been derived from a system of understandings that is commensurable with one we ourselves understand and believe and, in the reverse, to propose ideas such that they are comprehensible within a system of understandings and belief that may not be the same as our own. Commensurability addresses the way we relate to others to establish the possibility of mutual understanding. In short, commensurability speaks to the problem of dealing with interpretive differences as they are embedded in our ways of discoursing, the problem that Habermas asserts with such confidence we can resolve through various regulatory rhetorical strategies. But regulatory strategies, as I have pointed out, can be manipulated to disguise or dismiss differences. And although the externalist approach of locating epistemological differences in discourses, rather than somewhere in our heads, creates a space in which we can confront them openly, what difference does this make if we believe our differing discourses to be incommensurable? How can we ever hope to talk about—let alone value—the same things if we can never hope to mean the same thing? How can we, as Altieri might ask, cultivate the practice of seeking mutual understanding?

In *Paralogic Rhetoric: A Theory of Communicative Interaction,* Thomas Kent challenges the possibility of discourse incommensurability head-on, claiming that differences in discoursing methods are not categorically distinct, and hence, the very idea of finding discourses to be incommensurable is irrelevant. Bringing together the philosophical arguments of Donald Davidson and Jacques Derrida, Kent claims that our persistent attempt to view linguistic behavior in terms of distinct conventions that mean something is misguided, and consequently, our whole conception of thinking of ways of speaking and knowing in terms of conventional systems that may or may not be compatible or congruent with one another is wrongheaded. Our various ways of making and interpreting meaning are not lacking in "intertranslatability," to use Davidson's term, but rather they are quite commensurable. A recognition of certain conventions or patterns of seeing and knowing may guide the way one person interprets the words of another or structures his or her own discourse, but these conventions do not predict infallibly how a person will choose to interpret or to compose a future discourse, nor do they prohibit that person's ability to understand and interpret the discourses of others that may be guided by different conventions. We are mistaken, Kent believes, in regarding either "discourse production" or "discourse analysis" as tasks for which the outcome can be predicted or interpretation be dictated by some conventional ways of speaking. Furthermore, interpretation is not constrained by some necessary correspondence between language and reality or between language and some metaphysical set of concepts that govern the way the world is. For Kent, the "hermeneutic act intrinsic to discourse production and discourse analysis is paralogic and unsystemic in nature"; hence, "both discourse production and discourse analysis may be described as open-ended dialogic activities" (36).

"Paralogic rhetoric," Kent's term for the strategies we use to engage with one another in "open-ended dialogic activities," is adapted from Jean-François Lyotard's conception of "paralogy," which refers to "the moves we make when we employ a language game" (Kent 4); more concretely, paralogy has to do with "the unpredictable, elusive, and tenuous decisions or strategies we employ when we actually put language to use" (Kent 3). What paralogy describes is not a logical system of conventions or marks that serve as placeholders for referring to the world that we employ in order to ground or establish a meaning; but rather it moves "beyond logic" to name "the unpredictable moves we make when we employ a logical construct—a system of marks or noises, for example—in order to generate utterances" (Kent 5).

While acknowledging that the exact "moves" we will make in producing discourse and interpreting it are unpredictable and endlessly various, Kent finds the process of doing so to be straightforward and simple. Again drawing on the work of Donald Davidson, Kent suggests that we enter each new communication situation having developed a "prior theory" (86) about what strategy to employ to understand and talk to someone else. In the midst of our interactions with another speaker, whether these be in conversing face-to-face or in composing or reading a written text, we develop a "passing theory" (86) about what we together, speaker and listener, are meaning. Kent concludes that

> once communication takes place—[that is,] once a listener becomes satisfied that her interpretation is close enough to the message the speaker intends— the passing theory, in a sense, disappears to become part of a prior theory that may or may not be used in future communicative situations. (87)

Our success in articulating prior theories and developing successful passing theories depends on "know-how" and "background knowledge" (Kent 47), which cannot be taught, like the rules of grammar or the conventional patterns of the rhetorical modes, for instance, but rather must be experienced. While indeed we may pay attention to and even heed conventions in structuring and interpreting our discourse, the whole process of creating and deriving meaning is one of matching what we are saying and meaning with what we believe someone else to be saying and meaning, making a tentative guess that resolves a connection between the two, and then going on to repeat the process all over again.

Instead of regarding rhetoric as a system of strategies and techniques to be learned and mastered, Kent proposes that rhetoric is rather the process of making good guesses and deriving tentative conclusions about meaning as it is triggered by language. Hence, he holds that in the writing classroom, no teaching of rhetorical forms or composing processes will equip a student to do the job of hermeneutic guessing; students must simply get into the thick of this experience themselves, thus "entering into specific dialogic and therefore hermeneutic interactions with others' interpretive strategies" (Kent 48).

Kent's paralogic rhetoric is quite compatible with my phenomenological approach. Paralogy, like phenomenology, refers to a strategy for developing meaning intersubjectively with others. Both are developmental, referring to integral conscious processes, rather than to discrete textual features or linguistic moves. Kent notes that to acknowledge that rhetoric is paralogic is not to demand that writing teachers should abandon teaching students about specific rhetorical conventions; but rather, it is to suggest that they let go of the belief that knowing about conventions will make writers of their students. Becoming a writer is a lifelong project of developing background knowledge, becoming better at opening oneself to the possibilities that make us better "guessers" of intended meaning, and of becoming more adept at "shifting ground" in order to understand ways of meaning that do not connect with our "prior theories," as Kent would say. Writing teachers subscribing to this scenario of language production and reception behave more like coaches than teachers, assisting students in conducting more successful linguistic interactions through helping them analyze their choices, showing them by example what it is to acquire and make use of background knowledge and to develop a passing theory. Teachers become not adjudicators of their students' successes and failures, but rather collaborators and helpmates in a project in which they are engaging and will continue to engage for the rest of their own lives. Teachers, in short, "assume the pragmatic responsibility for helping students adapt their discourses to the discourses of others" (Kent 52), just as they themselves must do.

If we let go of the idea that conventions predictably prescribe meaning, we must also abandon the more insidious belief that meaning can correspond perfectly to some external reality. Knowledge is indeed a social construction, and the truth, in turn, is a story that is developing as each of us continues to speak about it. To look at both knowledge and truth this way is to bring both within human reach. Knowledge is no longer something "alien, foreign, or radically other that must be dominated, appropriated, and consumed" (Kent

67); but rather, it is to be developed in what Kent advocates as the "thoroughly public activity" (68) of speaking, listening, reading, and writing together. Likewise, truth is not something that must correspond perfectly to an objective and separate reality; but rather, it is a belief that coheres with what most of us already believe. The implications of abandoning the belief that language corresponds to reality or some ideal system for articulating the relationship between language and truth are clear. Kent tells us:

> Within a coherence theory of truth, the truthfulness of sentences cannot be judged according to the degree to which they faithfully represent objective reality. Instead, sentences can only be evaluated according to the degree to which the claims they make cohere to the beliefs most of us already share about the world. (69)

Two concerns come to mind if we are to apply Kent's interpretation of how rhetoric works to the practice and teaching of writing. The first concern is about evaluating writing on the basis of how it comes to terms with what we already believe. If this is indeed our major criterion for validating our rhetoric, what do we do with the beliefs that many of us share about the world that are dead wrong? If we declare effective rhetoric to be about what we commonly believe, we could fall susceptible to endorsing the program of the Nazis, for instance, one that surely was built on the back of a common belief. But, to be fair, paralogic rhetoric, if it is taking place on all sides, should not lead to this result. The fact that we are continually "shifting ground," accommodating different perspectives, and refusing to regard truth as immutable should, in the long run, protect us from fanatical devotion to a well-articulated but wrongheaded idea. In addition, according to Kent, what we commonly believe to be truth is always changing. Our knowledge of the world is not fixed, but develops as our ways of describing the world change; we are continuously redescribing our state of affairs, inventing "a new vocabulary replacing one that is worn out" (Kent 67). We naturally engage ourselves in the continuous activity of triangulating, a term Kent borrows from Bakhtin, that is, of developing beliefs that we determine to be valid by checking to see if they are believed by another and mean the same in our shared world (a process quite similar to "apperception" as it is described in Husserl's phenomenology; see chapter 5). The way we do this is to "match at least partially our utterances with the utterances of another," in an attempt to define our shared world. Kent tells us that "if we cannot successfully match our language with the language of another, we can never be sure what our concepts are concepts of, and, therefore, we can never be sure our concepts are concepts" (91).

The process of triangulation incorporates the *attitude toward* and *attention to* the concerns of another person that I have advocated as the basis for a phenomenological rhetoric. Because the objective is for two language users to match their ways of looking at the world—their apperceptions—in a kind of reciprocal gesture to accommodate one another, the result is a truth or knowledge claim that is not merely relative. The whole process of triangulation assumes that there is no body of knowledge that exists separate from language users to which their knowledge of one another's minds is relative; there is no "private language" inside the heads of each language learner to which he or she is trying to match a "public shared language." There is no incommensurability in translating one kind of meaning into another; all ways of speaking are commensurable. A "public shared language" is *the* language we use to fulfill our common objective of developing a shared sense of the world about us (Kent 98).

Paralogy, in its elegant description as the process of shifting ground to accommodate meaning and to develop sense, appears to be a process that if left to its own devices would eventually lead us to some kind of perfect understanding of one another and the world about us, that is, if we don't institute the usual roadblocks of refusing to listen to one another, letting petty jealousies obstruct open communication, and suppressing the rights of some persons or groups to speak or listen at all. But the fact of the matter is that we *do* do things like this, and often. There is no "moral center" to our paralogical rhetoric as Kent describes it; nothing to guarantee that the shared truth we reach through paralogic interaction is not simply the product of the hegemonic domination of one group foisting its commonly held beliefs on another. Of course, this very reality is addressed by Habermas in his designating rules for communicative action as a guarantor of moral consciousness. But as I have argued earlier, the constraints of Habermas's guidelines for achieving congruence with accepted belief also do not assure truthful or moral resolution of our verbal differences. This concern brings me to a second reservation we may share about paralogic rhetoric and communicative action as theories of discourse behavior with implications for guiding practice: These depictions of rhetorical practice presume a great deal about our motivations to behave in certain ways toward others, that is, with openness and willingness to accommodate others' concerns.

Not all of us are naturally motivated to continuously match our discourse with that of others in order to understand them better, particularly when we don't see it to be in our direct interest to do so. Yet we must agree that in the very act of producing discourse, we commit an act of faith, a faith that others will attempt to take our version of truth seriously or at least regard it as something we ourselves believe and respect it as such. Kent rightly enough points out that "when we produce discourse, we presuppose that our interpreter will assume that we intend her to hold our sentences true, and in a reciprocal manner, we will attribute beliefs to the interpreter that agree with our own"

(107). To really engage in dialogic activity with another, Kent asserts, we must go further than this, applying in our dealings with one another what Davidson has identified as the principle of "charity," that is, a willingness to believe that others are indeed trying to make sense, a willingness to understand as much as we can about what others hold true, about the "other utterances" that make them believe that a given utterance is true (Kent 105). But what motivation do we have to behave in this way? If we are perfectly comfortable with our own beliefs—if they work for us—what reason do we have to extend the principle of charity toward another, to be willing to put aside our perspective on the world to entertain that of another? What compels us to listen?

There is one sense in which we might think that no internal motivation at all is required in order to urge us to respond with continual openness toward the expressions of others. The process of triangulation could be conceived as a kind of perpetual motion machine; the complex of utterances to which we refer when interpreting our own and others' discourse serving as grist for the mill with which we grind out new utterances. As Bakhtin conceives of dialogic interaction, the time- and space-bound character of the utterance of one speaker creates a gap that invites another to respond, and the generic nature of our discourse, having a compositional frame that gives each speaker a sense of a beginning and an ending and the sense of addressing and being addressed by another, perpetuates its continuity. Genre, in this Bakhtinian sense, as Kent interprets it, does not exist as a static totality, a linguistic frame that carries sense to which we refer, rather it is constituent of the process of discoursing. It is characterized not by form but rather by strategy; genres, in effect, "are hermeneutical strategies that propel the guessing games we employ in order to produce utterances and to understand the utterances of others" (Kent 145). But even if we are to accept that our strategic use of language in dialogic interaction naturally compels us to continue this behavior, what motivation do we have to do this in a manner that respects the knowledge and beliefs of others?

Kent surmises that there is a psychological hunger we all feel to know and understand one another, a consequence of our individual feelings of alienation and separation from the world outside of us. When we communicate, we naturally focus upon the "dialogic object," the point about which we wish to find ourselves to be of "common mind," (148) so that we might continue together the dialogic process. As Kent tells us, the "dialogic object" has a psychological correspondence with "the desire to possess the other, to have our views dominate the other, to posit our consciousness in place of the other" (149). Yet paradoxically, the "dialogic object" comes into being only "through our contacts with other minds"; its creation is dependent upon our open interchange with others. How a psychological desire "to possess" and "dominate the other" is somehow to be mitigated by a more social temperament of charity toward others and their views is not clear in Kent's depiction of paralogic rhetoric. Kent does admit that his and Davidson's externalist view of linguistic interchange as it develops knowledge and belief requires "us . . . to make quite congenial avowals about our historical being and about the interdependence of our beliefs with the beliefs of others" (126). But if it is to truly *work* all of the time—and by this I mean if it is to truly bring us unfailingly to mutual understanding—paralogic rhetoric requires much more of us than an acknowledgment of interdependence: It requires us, quite simply, to commit to behave toward one another with nothing less than perpetual goodwill.

In all the contemporary approaches to intersubjective rhetoric I have discussed here, goodwill is assumed to be either requisite to the success of intersubjective interaction or counted as some kind of subproduct of the interaction itself. In *Beyond Objectivism and Relativism: Science, Hermeneutics and Praxis,* Richard J. Bernstein argues that the assertion that dialogic techniques are the means to assure goodwill and productivity in rhetorical argument ignores the fact that goodwill must be present, in fact, for dialogism to take place at all. In short, Habermas's and others' views of the regulatory function of dialogic interaction within a community idealize the capacity of actual communities to achieve the meeting of minds to which dialogism aspires, a meeting of minds that results in praxis, or shared practical knowledge. Bernstein characterizes this presumptive oversight as symptomatic of

> what might be called the modern (or postmodern) paradox concerning the prospects of human praxis—that the type of solidarity, communicative interaction, dialogue, and judgment required for the concrete realization of praxis already presupposes incipient forms of the community life that such praxis seeks to foster. (175)

In other words, the kind of affinity among persons that binds a community, that condition in which the recognition of each person's worth is entailed by that person's recognition of another's worth, not only is fostered by dialogic interaction, but also is a necessary condition for it. If this is so, then establishing conversational ground rules to ensure rational and fair debate, or creating administrative procedures to guarantee inclusive and comprehensive decision-making processes, or even endorsing the charitable principle of regarding others' beliefs as potentially true merely because they believe them cannot and will not guarantee that decisions or communications ring either true or right. Rather, what is essential to that success is an a priori commitment to maintain goodwill among the participants in such interaction because we respect their intrinsic worth as persons; this belief drives and motivates participants to entertain all points of view, to listen to each other with charity, and to be open to change.

But what kind of understanding of the function and purpose of communication must we have in order to conduct ourselves with goodwill—one to-ward the other—in our rhetorical practice? We must, I would submit, believe that rhetoric fulfills our function as beings conducting the lifelong project of becoming more consciously aware of what it is to be human and sharing that understanding with others like us. This is a totalizing conception. It can be nothing less. Otherwise, we would live denying the telos of our biological and psychological nature, our destiny to grow and develop—physically, emo-tionally, cognitively—as singular, mortal, and morally self-conscious beings. It is this belief, I wish to suggest, that underlies the optimistic portrayals of dialogic interaction outlined by Habermas, Wells, Altieri, and Kent, but this circumstance is not acknowledged overtly in their work, perhaps for obvious reasons.

A theory of rhetoric, language, or even moral behavior becomes suspect when it appeals to totalizing conceptualizations of the function of the indi-vidual as a conscious being, to projections of human life that suggest that the moral nature of our species is fundamental, and even further, that we share a common destiny to improve our collective lot. Yet these kinds of concep-tualizations of our existence are remarkably pervasive. They are constitutive of the human experience; they are about who we believe we are. In acknow-ledging our proclivity to conceive of our existence in these totalizing ways, we need not accede to a particular philosophical or religious view; rather, we need simply acknowledge that a concern with a totalizing vision of our com-mon telos is fundamentally human, part and parcel of our lived experience from birth to death. And, as I have argued in the previous chapter, such a totalizing conception of our mortality and dependence upon others forms the rational ground for altruistic behavior toward one another.

The problem of how a totalizing conception of life affects the way we communally develop knowledge and conceive of truth has been discussed re-cently by Hilary Putnam in a series of essays derived from his Gifford Lec-tures, delivered in 1990 and anthologized in a volume entitled *Renewing Phi-losophy*. Putnam finds the arguments both of analytical philosophers, who attempt a correspondence theory of truth by demonstrating how language relates to reality in some causal way, and of postmodern externalists, who de-clare truthful meaning to be ephemeral since it shifts ground with each rein-terpretation of a text, to suffer from the same narrow conceptualization of the relation of language to existence. The arguments of analytic philosophers and postmodern theorists despair the lack of an exact match either between language and reality or between one interpretation and another (Putnam 125–28). In the process of living our daily lives, when we try to match our sense of the meaning of something with its reality or with someone else's interpre-tation, we do not worry about whether there is an exact correspondence be-tween what we say and the real world or an exact match between our meaning and that of another person. Rather, we try to conceive of how, within the projects of our separate lives, we can make sense of reality in a way that allows us to deal successfully with the physical world, developing the same sense of it as others, within reasonable bounds. In our attempt to perceive the same meaning, we make the judgment that, despite our differences, our efforts to come together for a particular project are on the same track, that we are, in effect, talking about and meaning the same thing. Putnam characterizes the judgment we make about sameness of meaning as a normative evaluation: "The kind of 'sameness of meaning' we seek in translation might be an interest-relative (but still quite real) relation, one which involves a normative judgment, a judgment as to what is *reasonable* in the particular case" (Putnam 127)

The primary objection that Putnam has to most analytic and postmodern externalist approaches to describing how language relates to truth are two. First, they are, in general, utopian theories, attempting to reduce language and reality to some elegant, all-encompassing scheme. In this regard, these theories—holding respectively that reality causes invariable linguistic meaning or that meaning is the variable result of perceived linguistic or semiotic difference—are equally hegemonic totalizations of the relations between language and experience. We neither expect a perfect one-to-one match between language and reality, nor do we regard linguistic meaning as unstable in the day-to-day workings of our lives. Second, they do not account for the way we actually conceive of truth in our everyday experience; and that is, as a normative conception that flexibly applies to a number of situations, ranging from those in which language has a quantifiable correspondence with reality (as with some scientific language) to those in which language merely gestures toward some relationship its users hold between themselves and the things they relate to, between one another, and between various interpretations of reality about which users have some "reasonable" agreement without concern about "exact" correspondence. The bottom line for Putnam—and for me—is that truth is a viable concept in our daily experience. We live and act as if it were a reasonable goal to look for truth, to aspire to some truthful interpretation of the value of our lives, of the way the world works, and of how the two intersect. Like Weissman and Korsgaard, whose work on the relation between truth and value I discussed in chapter 5, Putnam believes that "the idea of a sharp cut between 'facts' and 'values' is deeply wrong" (135). Declaring that we can make right and wrong normative judgments about truth, goodness, and a host of other moral and ontological matters, in Putnam's view, is not a metaphysical pronouncement; we can make such declarations because "that is the way that we . . . talk and think, and also the way that we are going to go on talking and thinking" (135). But if indeed this is the way that we talk and think, what then are the specific tasks of philosophy and rhetoric in explaining how we do so—perhaps in helping us to do it better with more satisfying results, both individually and within our communities?

The major job for philosophy, Putnam suggests, is to acknowledge from the start the way that we truly are: We are creatures who develop totalizing conceptions of who we are, why we are here, and why the world is the way it is, and doing so is what allows us to feel that we exist for a purpose. The job of philosophy as it describes our conceptions of being and moral value—and, I might add, rhetorical theory as it describes how we use language to do things—is to reflect upon what we do to make sense of the world as beings who are born, live, and die over a limited stretch of time. It is to explain what we do to identify a meaningful place for ourselves in the world, to make certain judgments about physical and other palpable realities, and to hold certain beliefs about matters for which we can offer no empirical proof, yet that have as great a significance in our lives as those matters for which we can.

Like Altieri, Putnam turns to Wittgenstein's philosophy as an example of the kind of serious study of the relationships among language, fact, belief, and truth as they are lived by us that is needed. He is particularly impressed with a notion Wittgenstein introduces about the relationship between language and reality in his three Lectures on Religious Belief (Putnam 141–42; Wittgenstein). Here Wittgenstein suggests that in assessing the meaning of some linguistic expressions, we are on the wrong track if we insist on judging their relationship to reality or, if finding no clear relationship, judging them merely to express an attitude. To make this kind of judgment, we must have a clear metaphysical notion of what is a fact as opposed to a value, and, of course, we do not. To get at how linguistic expression means, as Putman interprets Wittgenstein, we need to understand "the form of life to which it belongs" (154). By this he means the form of day-to-day human experience to which it belongs, with all its attendant assumptions, beliefs, expectations, hopes, and fears. This is the view we need to take toward religious language, for instance. To understand such language, we cannot turn to semantic theory; rather, we must understand what it means to lead a religious life, which amounts to "understanding a human being" (154).

The device that Putnam employs to get at the relationships between linguistic meaning and lived experience is "using a picture," an analogical tool that Wittgenstein employed to explain to a student what a friend might mean if saying to you before embarking on a long journey "we might see one another after death" (Putnam 152; Wittgenstein 70). We cannot substitute another phrase for this; rather, we can think of it only as a picture, a totality expressing the meaning of what it means to exist as this is experienced within someone's life. What we are doing when we try to argue "in reason" with a religious person, is "combatting"—a word Putnam discusses in some detail—the way they lead their lives. This being so, we should give considered thought as to where and when we engage in such battles. If we wish to "combat" another person's "language game," in Wittgenstein's terms, we must consider how we are regarding them as other persons with the right to lead fulfilling and meaningful lives. Putnam notes that Wittgenstein himself would "combat" a language game that involved testing the truth of conclusions through subjecting speakers to an "ordeal by fire" (Putnam 172), but those that involved validating conclusions by more benign means must be respected as they have value within the fabric of other persons' total lives. Putnam concludes that Wittgenstein's conception of the language game is that it "rests not on proof or on Reason but *trust*" (177). We must trust something and trust someone in order to use language fruitfully to build a conception of our relationship to persons and things that works usefully and productively in our everyday experience. And our success in dealing with one another as we try to negotiate a common understanding of our life on earth, Putnam suggests, rests upon our capacity for "compassion" for one another as persons who each have placed our trust in something, each of us being—all at once—a "wise, flawed, deeply individual human being" (Putnam 179, 178).

So in the end, while, technically speaking, it may help us to evaluate whether our rhetoric is congruent with prevailing epistemologies, whether it reflects the consensus of all upon whom it has impact, and whether it assists the matching process by which we come to find our meaning commensurable with others', our knowing these things is not sufficient guidance to ensure that we use rhetoric to bring us to a common understanding of our shared experience. For this we must understand ourselves as creatures who try to picture our lives as a totality, as coherent wholes with meaning for ourselves and, hopefully, for others. And we must deal with one another compassionately as creatures who do so. It is this understanding that grounds a phenomenological rhetoric and the separate interpretive tasks that I have described as profession and altruism in the last two chapters. Without a totalizing conception of who we are in relation to others, we cannot judge which standards of technical validity will both bring us to mutual understanding and lead us to maintain knowing relationships between ourselves and others. I shall close my argument for a phenomenological rhetoric with a discussion of a rhetorical event in my own experience that illustrates how attending to profession and altruism might so guide us.

Profession and Altruism in Rhetorical Practice

To illustrate how profession and altruism might guide the standards we apply when evaluating the validity of our rhetorical claims, I have chosen a rhetorical situation that I experienced as a university administrator, one in which my administrative role and rhetorical tasks were overtly intermixed. My account of this rhetorical situation, which involved the interests and participation of a great many people in the university community, is given from the only perspective I can rightfully claim, my own. Undoubtedly, the others involved would remember different details and interpret their significance in different ways. But my account is intended to describe the situation and my rhetorical choices as I perceived them in my role of facilitating an administrative process that resulted in a written document that forwarded specific recommendations. In short, my account stands as a description of how I reflected upon this communication situation, how I attempted to remain receptive to the various perspectives of others engaged in it, and how I regenerated a verbal interpretation of a communal understanding. It is an account of my rhetorical process of profession, as I saw and felt it.

Three years ago, I served as the chair of a search committee to select a chair for our English department. The administrative and rhetorical tasks defined within my responsibility as chair of the search committee were ostensibly clear. My administrative job was to manage the process so that we fairly and efficiently reviewed applications for the job, interviewed candidates, and made a recommendation to the dean; my job as a writer was to present a document to the dean that listed no less than three candidates from which a choice of chair might be made. The provision that the list contain at least three candidates is stipulated in our American Association of University Professors (AAUP) contract. But this picture of where the end document stood in relation to my administrative role and the roles of the committee and the dean was not the only picture that was to figure in this process. Several "pictures," in the Wittgensteinian sense, telling about the lives of all involved in the process, were also to come into play. There were the pictures inscribing the life projects of: a new black female dean with a retreat position in the English department; an all-white committee made up of male and female members of the department from several different areas, each perceived by someone to be in need of more faculty; a group of individual faculty members who communicated their concerns about the search procedure to the dean in separate memoranda and conversations, outside the framework of the committee's search process; a team of executive officers who, along with the dean, had deep concerns about strengthening minority hiring at a major urban university; and finally, a female chair of the search committee who was a university administrator with a retreat position as a professor in the composition program of the English department, an area in perpetual contest with more traditional venues there.

During the search process, the dean monitored the proceedings of the committee fairly closely, asking to see a list of potential candidates to be interviewed prior to their being brought to campus. From a list of eight the committee wished to interview, the dean approved bringing five to campus and made suggestions to the committee as to which five. I was charged with negotiating this decision with the committee. The dean also stipulated that if we were to bring five candidates, we must list all five candidates in the memorandum that would carry our final recommendation to her, along with a detailed description of our opinion of each. The committee as a whole agreed to this procedure, although some members were quite vocally reluctant to do so. From their perspective, the request to submit a list without removing any names effectively diminished the role of the committee in making a selection. From the dean's perspective, the committee, if allowed to remove names of candidates that she and they had interviewed, would be able to do so without justifying such a decision to her, a decision that she had reason to believe would discount what may be strong minority preferences held by some individuals within the department and, additionally, her own preferences.

In reflecting upon the choices I made in managing the committee's activities and in drafting our recommendations to the dean, I can summarize categorically how the relational principles of congruence and consensus might validate my procedures; and I can do so without suggesting anything about my commitment to the practices of profession and altruism as I have developed them in previous chapters. In short, I can demonstrate that I applied procedures for validating the truth and rightness of my discourse without asserting that a totalizing vision of my life, in relation to others, directed my choices. For instance, in carrying out my responsibilities as an administrator, I can say that I worked to see that the committee's procedures were congruent with those outlined in the AAUP contract, with notions of university governance as declared in our Statutes of the Board of Governors and Executive Orders, and with the facts of the case as represented on candidates' vitae and in the written and otherwise recorded responses of faculty to the qualifications of each. As a writer, I designed the memorandum to present evidence in a manner that was congruent with expected rhetorical strategies for such documents, giving a clear statement of its function, a record of the procedures of the committee, and a statement indicating the significance of the order in which the candidates were discussed. Furthermore, as an administrator, I worked to see that the committee's discussions led to decision making by consensus, believing this would lead to a stronger recommendation than one that reflected a majority vote; hence, as a writer I recorded perspectives on the candidates' qualifications that reflected the consensual view of the whole committee, presenting neither extreme views that were held by some and not others, nor dismissing dissenting views.

My process to achieve this end involved holding a separate committee discussion about each candidate, in which all views were expressed and during which I took copious notes. At the end of each discussion, I read back my notes to the committee and summarized for them what I perceived to be the more salient points. Following discussion of my summaries, the committee voted on a ranking of the candidates and discussed the outcome until all agreed that the ranking reflected the views of the committee as a whole. After drafting the memorandum, which listed the candidates in ranking order along with several paragraphs articulating the committee's views of each, I read it to the committee, changed portions in response to their comments, and then distributed a copy, asking each committee member to sign off on this copy or suggest changes. When I found suggested changes to be substantive, I discussed these with all committee members before producing the final memorandum that I sent to the dean, under my signature with copies to all on the committee.

Certainly, the procedure as described here met an impersonal standard of congruence with accepted procedures for reaching and recording such decisions, and it attempted a consensual decision-making process that was documented in the final report. Yet in at least one sense, the selection process and memorandum were not at all congruent with what some faculty regarded as accepted procedures for these activities, despite their congruence with written policies and contracts. At several points in the process, the dean intervened, directing the committee to act in certain ways—for instance, promising that we might have funds to interview five candidates, but *only* following her review of the list of interviewees and *only* if the committee would send up a list with all five names as well as a detailed discussion of each. Many faculty members felt the procedures to be in violation of the AAUP contract, which, in fact, specifies that chair search procedures are determined by the administration, not the committee; and it is silent on the matter of executive intervention in committee matters, a silence that was interpreted differently by the dean and some members of the committee.

Furthermore, the memorandum could be perceived to not at all represent a consensus of the committee: Each committee member did indeed sign off on the text, but this simply indicated their willingness to have it sent forward as a representative document and said little about whether each individual felt that a decision had been reached consensually. In fact, it could be said that— taking into account the perspectives of every committee member; the dean; the provost, who also spoke her mind about the matter through the dean; the president, who made his views known through the provost; and myself as committee chair—each of us had a different perspective on the document as it represented a true and right decision of the committee. And this does not include, of course, the department faculty, whose views were interpreted by the committee but who did not view the document, the writing of which, as agreed to by the parties involved, was designated a confidential proceeding. Yet to evaluate the truth and rightness of the chair search document from each of these individual perspectives is to lapse into what Charles Taylor would call a kind of "soft relativism," a condition that leads us to defer to some technical procedure to stand as evidence of right actions, being unable to adjudicate our individual differences in the matter.

It became clear to me, in the process of managing the chair search, that no document that recorded the committee's assessment of the candidates could adequately express the truth of their convictions or reflect the complexity of the selection process. Nor would any document lead us together to a decision that was infallibly true and right according to logical or empirical standards. In the long run, it was simply one gesture in a series of dialogic moves involving the dean, the executive officers of the university, the chair search committee, and the members of the English department—a "paralogic" move, to use Kent's term, one that represented each party's attempt to match their ways of speaking with the other's, to find them wholly commensurable—or, at least, it was a move that represented my efforts to do so.

But the chair search document in its ephemeral life as a moment in dialogic interaction was also the concrete realization of the intention of its writer, the person responsible for its construction, diction, phrasing, inclusions, and omissions. In short, it reflected my efforts to manage the communicative process, which were far more pointed than to simply try to match up what these diverse parties were trying to say to each other. I was trying, in the face of deep differences in views about the efficacy of the process, to maintain a knowing relationship among these participants, to keep open the opportunity for them to deal with each other with trust and compassion, rather than with contentiousness. At the only point of control in the process I could rightfully claim, my own intentions, I strove overtly to enact the practices of profession and altruism as I had been thinking about them and recording them here in constructing the chair search document. And that enactment involved both a choice of presenting the committee's views in the form of a standard argument and shaping that argument through a process that maximized opportunities for participation and response. My intention was not in making the argument to avoid controversy, but rather to approach it, as Kellenberger has advocated, through a method that honored and respected the inherent worth of persons affected by that controversy.

In assessing the input of the dean, the faculty, and the chair search committee, for instance, I reflected upon their individual commitments to the chair search process, the areas of the department and university they represented, the positions of power they held or perceived themselves to hold. I tried to remain receptive to their divergent views about how the chair search would proceed, ranging from the inflexible interpretation of the AAUP contract to taking liberties with the procedures surely not covered by the contract and perhaps not anticipated by its creators. And I attempted to regenerate, in a record of the committee's discussion of candidates' merits, a constructed, pointed, consensual evaluation. Likewise, I strove to acknowledge the perspectives of all contributing to the decision-making process: the faculty committee's wish to maintain authority over its role in the selection process, the dean's wish to have full freedom to evaluate all candidates interviewed aside from the committee's assessment of them, the dean's and executive administration's concerns about efforts made toward minority hiring. I aimed for authentic expression, checking and rechecking at each point in the construction and review of the document whether my words respected the values of the people they represented. Finally, backing all of my choices, was my own ardent commitment to assure that the search process itself articulated my interest in maintaining a productive and knowing relationship between the committee and the dean, one that gestured toward the goodwill of both parties, and that respected the personal investment of all in reaching a decision that was both true and right.

The point I am making here is that I judged my rhetorical choices to be technically congruent with an acceptable epistemological method and respectful of consensual decision making on the basis of whether they reflected a totalizing vision of altruistic profession, that is, a commitment to maintain a productive and knowing relationship between the committee and the dean. This being my intention, only a document that listed all five candidates as the dean requested could represent to her the committee's "goodwill" attempt to address minority interests and respect her personal investment in this project. Likewise, only a document that summarized the divergent views of the committee and the department with respect to some candidates—so as to make clear that selecting some individuals, for instance, would be received with mixed reaction—could fairly address the dean's intent to act with goodwill toward the committee, as well as fairly reflect the personal investment of that group in their role of representing the department. In effect, my attempt was to represent the committee and the dean as intending a relationship of goodwill toward one another and to profess altruistically a commitment to maintaining that relationship. If neither the dean nor the committee in actuality were willing to grow together toward a decision that would make their relationship progress and be productive, the document I produced could not force them to do so. Nevertheless, in my view, it stood as a reflection of committed intent at the moment of its production to keep open this possibility. My object was to manage the procedure through managing the rhetoric, through actively directing it to keep the lines of communication open, rather than to resort to combativeness. I did so, not only because I believed that this approach would keep the process moving forward successfully (an offer was made eventually to the committee's top candidate, although this offer did not result in the appointment of a chair), but also because I believed that this approach respected the life projects of all those involved in the process.

Again, were I simply to apply impartial standards for judging the validity of my conclusions, I could have justified several alternative approaches. A number of the faculty, for instance, suggested to me that when the dean began to intervene in the process, asking that the committee list and comment upon all candidates interviewed, rejecting none, that we should follow the AAUP contract to the letter and submit a list of only three candidates, the minimum number contractually required, ignoring her request. They argued that procedurally this was right and just. However, in my estimation, to do so would have been a message to the dean that her project to fully determine whether all minority interests in the search had been satisfied and represented, something that is not always guaranteed by the technical application of democratic procedures, was unimportant. And perhaps more damaging, this rhetorical move would ignore the importance of this issue within the totality of the dean's professional and personal life. Likewise, to have omitted from the document the deeply divided perspectives faculty members had on some candidates would have been to ignore the importance of these views to these people's conceptions of themselves and their professional standards. Yet it was perfectly clear to me that others in my position would have made the choice to do either of these things and could have justified such a move as congruent with some stated procedure and as reflecting some consensual standard. And likewise, it was clear to me that I myself could have made such choices in order to satisfy my own needs rather than allowing myself to be changed by the experience of trying to reach mutual understanding.

My approach was neither to assume irreconcilable differences nor that continuous discoursing would lead us benignly to a common understanding. I actively worked toward commensurability, toward clearing a space where the differences could stand head to head, not in preparation for combat, but in preparation to live together in the same space. The specific strategies I chose to achieve this outcome were, of course, derived from numerous prior theories I had developed about communicative outcomes in similar circumstances, but the particular choices I made, while mitigated by an effort to match my communicative style to those involved with me in the process, that is, to change myself as the process of finding truth together required, were more importantly directed by my totalizing *vision* of the process as one in which we would and *could* come to a common understanding together. In short, I *believed* that our common effort to profess what we know is ultimately authenticated by our altruism, our care to attend responsibly, as Levinas might say, to the views and needs of others. This stance is more than a rhetorical strategy; it involves a choice of rhetorical strategies, to be sure, but it neither dictates nor is realized through a specific strategy.

The choice to forward a traditional argument, for instance, is not inherently more or less directed toward the goal of mutual understanding than the choice to communicate through a narrative, a dramatization, or some other, perhaps less familiar, form. As I noted earlier in chapter 2, conventional forms do have their limitations that must be properly acknowledged, but these limitations do not necessarily outweigh their pragmatic value in specific situations. What grounds and justifies a choice of strategy is not only how well it fits our rhetorical purpose, but also how well it expresses a philosophical commitment to the idea that truth is within our grasp so long as we behave always with compassion toward one another.

My readers might suggest that the scene I chose to illustrate the practice of altruistic profession, as I am calling it, is a tale of moral standards for social behavior, about how we should treat each other, and that, as such, it has no direct bearing on our struggle to discover empirical or metaphysical truths. It has no bearing on whether we shall indeed discover the means to generate boundless energy, to travel across the universe, or to determine the origin of life. Nor does it hold the key to resolving our society's intractable moral dilemmas, such as whether to sanction assisted suicides or fetal abortions. It may very well be true that altruistic profession will not lead us to understand one another perfectly or to articulate a comprehensive and nonreductive knowledge of our world. But it is also true that if we resist one another, remain combative in the face of our differences, and refuse to view communication as a process that requires change not only in the perspectives of others but also within ourselves, we will come no closer to the truth nor acquire any greater knowledge than what we can already claim to know.

We cannot predict, of course, our society's future success in unraveling the mysteries of our physical world, applying civil justice with ubiquity, or effectively distributing earthly goods. But we can claim that the commitment to reach common understanding is central to the success of all these endeavors. This commitment directs our quests for knowledge, our search for the truth; it is what ensures that such efforts will progress—as predicted by Husserl, Merleau-Ponty, Teilhard de Chardin, MacIntyre, Weissman, Korsgaard, and a host of others who still believe in the viability and power of the human spirit—toward meaning and action that not only answers our questions, but also bolsters our sense of worth and sustains our lives in this world, both as individuals and as members of the common family of humankind.

Toward a Phenomenological Rhetoric: Epilogue

It is a timely matter, perhaps, to suggest that we adopt a phenomenological approach toward seeking truth through our rhetoric, closing in, as we are, on the end of a century. The fin de siècle marks a time for historians, philosophers, scientists, and various other cognoscenti to wonder about whether we—the family of humankind—are getting anywhere, or indeed, are going anywhere in particular, in the first place. Are we moving forward as part of some grand design, through becoming more complex, both physically and spiritually, perhaps moving toward some common destiny, as some phenomenologists have surmised? Or are we expending our energies randomly, following as we must the prescribed course of the second law of thermodynamics, until we return to dust and the chaos that some scientists predict began and shall end our universe? This is also a time of both hope and nostalgia. We hope for a future in which we have learned from the past, one bright with the possibility of discovery and the opportunity for each of us to be more prosperous and happier. And we experience a nostalgic longing for a past that, in our sad inability to ever recapture it, may appear more glorious, more perfect, more bright than any conceivable feature.

In the closing pages of this proposal that we adopt a phenomenological outlook toward our future of speaking, listening, reading, and writing together, I wish to suggest what I believe is the most powerful argument for doing so: To approach our rhetoric as altruistic profession allows us to live with our past as it builds our future, to reject neither as out of reach, a perspective that neither hope for a future of absolute knowledge and perfect happiness nor nostalgia for the glories of an irretrievable past can sustain. We have been seduced into thinking that only a rhetoric of resistance and contention, a rhetoric that conquers and subdues, will lead us to knowledge, truth, and personal recognition. This is a legacy and a promise, I wish to assert, that should neither follow nor lead us. It is the outcome of a perspective that rightfully inscribes our lives as a continuous struggle, yet wrongfully finds the struggle a battle that must be won against what is other or unknown. Let me explain by referring to two visions of our existence as two popular accounts show it to have added up, here at the end of the twentieth century.

A few short years back, a former member of the United States State Department, Francis Fukuyama, proposed in *The End of History and the Last Man,* a reflection on international politics in the light of social theory, that history has ended. It gasped its last gasp, in effect, with the culminating events of the collapse of communism "throughout much of the world in the late 1980's" (Fukuyama, *The End* 12) and the simultaneous rise of liberal democracy. History, which Fukuyama interprets as the record of societies and their leaders continuously conquering one another to establish different systems of rule, may now be finished. With liberal democracy spreading like wildfire across the globe, societies will no longer produce individuals with the will to conquer, to rise above, to be considered and recognized as greater or better than others. What liberal democracy has and continues to gain for so many people is the right for more people to be recognized, to exercise their "spiritedness," or *thymos,* a value that Fukuyama elaborates in his interpretation of the writings of Plato and Socrates (*The End* 162–67). Without *thymos,* the thirst that compels us toward something, and without the hunger to be recognized for subduing the less powerful, for conquering the unknown, we cannot achieve.

The catch-22 dilemma for liberal democracy as Fukuyama sees it is this: Although liberal democracies establish a space in which all people can achieve individual recognition, they are also sustained by the notion that all should be given *equal* recognition. Turning to Nietzsche's critique of modern democracy, Fukuyama claims that the "typical citizen of a liberal democracy [is a 'last man'] who, schooled [by the founders of modern liberalism, gives up] prideful belief in his or her own superior worth in favor of comfortable self-preservation" (*The End* 300). Such systems quickly result in entire communities of men and women who are lacking *thymos*. Autocracies inspired the great struggles that created new, more democratic systems of government and provided the sponsorship for artistic pursuits, as well, clearing the space for the monumental achievements of architects, artists, and musical composers in past centuries. Each of these conquering pursuits in war and art was evidence not only of individual *thymos* but of individual or national *megalothymos*, the desire to be recognized as clearly superior to others, or in my terms, the desire to resist influence, to keep one's identity and choices pure, autonomous, and consequently superior.

Throughout his argument, Fukuyama intersperses the speculations of Alexander Kojève, who built upon Hegel's theories of history to suggest that with the rise of liberal democracy, sustained by "the principles of liberty and equality that emerged from the French Revolution," we had reached "the end point of human ideological evolution beyond which it was impossible to progress further" (*The End* 66). This end produced along with it many other ends, for instance, not only "the end . . . of large political struggles and conflicts, but [also] the end of philosophy" (*The End* 67). In short, we now have nothing else to learn about the meaning of humanity and its struggles; our battles in politics and metaphysics have been won. Our mission from here on in is to work out the details of running democratic bureaucracies and to pursue not truth, but our own self-interests, a pursuit that is reflected, Fukuyama claims, in our passion for personal physical fitness as opposed to our ancestors' devotion to religious or philosophical values (*The End* 306). We turn to ourselves because to address questions that implicate the behavior of others, moral questions that involve "a distinction between better and worse, good and bad, . . . seems to violate the democratic principle of tolerance" (Fukuyama, *The End* 306). Within a society of self-absorbed individuals, all believing themselves to be equally meritorious, it will "no longer be possible to create the great art that was meant to capture the highest aspirations of an era." In short, there will be "no particular distinction of the human spirit for artists to portray" (Fukuyama, *The End* 311).

We have few outlets for *megalothymia* within a liberal democracy, Fukuyama concludes, unless we resort to snobbish pursuits, such as those of the "tea ceremony" and "flower arrangement" in Japan, "with their own masters, novices, traditions, and canons of better and worse" (*The End* 320). But of course, we have not yet reached a perfect state of equilibrium, in which all nation-states have evolved perfect systems of liberal democracy. In the end, there will continue to be bumps along the road enough to sustain our interest; we will recognize the differing positions we hold as we all together pursue the same path, to perfect our implementation of the social system to which we all aspire. Fukuyama, at the end of his musings, proposes a rather weak hope for us when we reach the point at which all of our destinies have converged, when the world is one large, self-sustaining liberal democracy. He employs the metaphor of a "wagon train," viewing humankind not as a tree with "a thousand shoots blossoming into as many different flowering plants, [but more] like a wagon train strung out along a road." When men and women all in their separate "wagons eventually reach the same town," we cannot predict "whether their occupants, having looked around a bit at their new surroundings, will not find them inadequate and set their eyes on a new and more distant journey" (Fukuyama, *The End* 339). A belief in what is unknown, in the end, consoles Fukuyama, abating temporarily his fear that, having found a perfect societal system to sustain our needs and wants, we have left little reason to pursue anything else. Haunting Fukuyama as we close the century, having cast our fates in common with the promise of liberal democracy for individual and equal recognition, is a nostalgic attraction to distinction through conquering, through winning our battle with the other, as well as a belief that without the ambition to conquer, we have little reason to learn more about our world, our universe. Along with that loss of ambition will come a loss of beauty, truth, and all that we have traditionally held as values that sustain our humanity.

A similar theme is entertained by John Horgan, a staff writer for *Scientific American,* in his recent book, *The End of Science: Facing the Limits of Knowledge in the Twilight of the Scientific Age.* In this collection of short anecdotes, Horgan recalls several of his interviews with scientists who have made their mark by establishing or adding to theories in physics, cosmology, biology, social science, and neuroscience. Horgan also entertains the views of scholars who have theorized about ontological matters, who have proposed theories of genesis from chaos ("chaoplexity"), the evolutionary limits of human progress ("limitology"), and the development of superior intelligence ("scientific theology"). The great scholars who are Horgan's subjects are, in the main, shown to be motivated by the notion that truth is out there somewhere to be found, yet equally troubled by the notion that once it is found, we may have nothing left to do. Hence, in somewhat contradictory fashion, when quizzed about the nature of truth, they conclude that truth will never be found, that there are no limits to knowledge, to scientific investigation, to the insatiable curiosity of human beings and their natural quest—the pursuit of truth. They leave open the possibility that there may always be something left for us to do, some unknown realm to define, to describe, to conquer.

The progress of science, Horgan speculates, is marked by a search for "The Answer" (1–8), for a theory of everything, and at the same time by an anxious concern that with our finding The Answer will come the end of everything, the end of our reason for being. Horgan makes a general distinction between the practice of "ironic science," which addresses "unanswerable" questions that pose possibilities beyond our capability to render logical or empirical proof, and "empirical science," which relies upon the rules of logic and the scientific method and is constrained by the limits of our physiology and machinery to perform material investigations of the real world (30–31). Interestingly, he reports that those scientists who have concluded, as we close in on the end of the twentieth century, that all the great theories are now known—from Newton's theory of gravity; to Darwin's theory of evolution; to Einstein's theories of relativity and gravity; to modern theories of quantum mechanics, incompleteness, and chaos—also conclude that solving the physical problems we have yet remaining, such as conserving our natural resources, curing fatal diseases, and ameliorating the disabilities of aging, is but a matter of working out the details (Horgan 16–18, et passim). This goes for solving our socioeconomic problems as well, such as distribution of wealth, access to education, and ubiquity of social freedom. In other words, now that all the major theories have been discovered through the practice of ironic science, we shall merely play out their proofs in the practice of empirical science, an effort that may indeed lead to the cure of disease and the promise of interplanetary travel, but which is not very much fun, not worthy of our *thymos,* or spiritedness, as Fukuyama might say. The last vestige of human authority will remain in the creation of art, music, poetry, and the like, which Hans Moravec, a robotics engineer at Carnegie Mellon, in commenting on the situation to Horgan, has dismissed as "primarily ways of autostimulation" (Horgan 250).

Both Fukuyama and Horgan echo a refrain that has been given both casual speculation in populist literature and serious treatment in philosophy and science and, of course, that has stood as the impetus or goad for the arguments toward a phenomenological perspective that I have set forth in this book. They believe that we distinguish ourselves through resisting physical constraints and the influence of others and, above all, through holding suspect the comforts of a system that constructs us and determines our destiny. We thrive through retaining the will to conquer, to win a battle with the other. This belief, as I have shown, is reflected in our rhetorical practice. It plays itself out in the rhetorics of narcissism and fetishism, which I discussed in the early part of this book. We fear losing our identity, and so we resist others; we cannot absorb what is different or unknown, and so we acquire the authority to subdue or unmask it. And all this because we fear, at bottom, a lack of recognition, a sense of worthlessness, nothingness, death—the ultimate dissipation into nonbeing. We fear that we mean nothing because we are mortal; we will die before we discover The Answer, the knowledge of everything that lives forever. To keep ourselves going, to make our lives worthwhile, we spend our days acting in ways that assert our own worth and assure our pleasure and happiness. Psychologically, we carry the burden of this limited existence, fearing all the while we live that we will not learn or understand the meaning of our existence, or find the key to perfect happiness, or understand everything there is to know about this earth in which we live, and fearing, as much, that if we were to discover all these things, there would be nothing left for us to do—not just for us—but all other beings like us, whose recognition of our efforts and desires is central to our valuing ourselves, to our sense of worth as persons.

In the final chapters of *The End of Science*, Horgan speaks of this anxiety over death and nothingness as the Terror of God. He projects fears about our own mortality onto an omniscient being, whom he calls the Omega Point—the being who represents all that we and our universe are or can be—crediting this idea to Teilhard de Chardin (Horgan 256–60). Horgan muses that if there is indeed an Omega Point, a point at which all living creatures merge into an infinitely intelligent being, wouldn't this being be bored, fresh out of anything else to do? Wouldn't an infinitely intelligent being actually fear the possibility that nothing is responsible for its existence or continuance but itself, a fear that, Horgan muses, would "compel it to flee from itself, from its own awful aloneness and self-knowledge" (262)? Horgan concludes—interestingly, along with Teilhard de Chardin, although without having entertained the full implications of Teilhard de Chardin's work—that a "solution" to the ultimate problem that faces both God and us mortals, a fear of nothingness, is to think of the omniscient Omega Point as continuously awestruck with the wonder of being while simultaneously fully understanding it. We might think of the Omega Point, then, as a renewable resource, always already reinventing itself, growing, progressing, living.

We assuage both our fear that we will not distinguish ourselves by finding The Answer and our fear that we will find The Answer and summarily dissipate into nothingness by thinking of our quest for truth and knowledge as an endless process—dynamic, continuous, exciting, and like the Omega Point, promising the discovery of everything yet never lacking the enthusiasm for discovery. We each contribute to this endless truth-seeking dynamic, to this continuous willful effort of beings like us to discover the unknown, to understand the misunderstood. What sustains our efforts to do so is a belief in this idea, in this mutual destiny of truth seeking that continues beyond our mortal selves. And what bolsters our self-worth is being recognized as having contributed to the process, having been a link in the wagon train that ever continues down the road. Is it possible, really, we must ask ourselves, to retain commitment to that mutual destiny and at the same time resist one another, best one another, mistrust one another's potential ardor for this common goal? I am proposing, of course, that it is not.

A few years after writing *The End of History and the Last Man*, Francis Fukuyama published a sequel to his thesis that our history of achievement through resistance is at an end, predicting a future that progresses beyond our nostalgic attachment to recognition through conquering the other, a future in which hope springs from our compassion for others. In *Trust: The Social Virtues and the Creation of Prosperity*, a work clearly influenced by the life of his father, who was a sociologist of religion, Fukuyama reflects about how we will solve the socioeconomic problems remaining, now that the major ideological battles are ended and liberal democracy reigns supreme. He concludes that the solutions will not arise from resistance and revolution, but rather from a renewal of social affability, through an investment in trust, in the practice of what he has labeled *"spontaneous sociability"* (Fukuyama, *Trust* 27), a willingness to join together to solve problems and thus ensure our mutual prosperity. I will not go into the details here of how Fukuyama develops this idea, providing anecdotal and empirical evidence of the economic success of societies whose citizens display a high level of trust "between individuals who [are] not related to one another, and hence a solid basis for social capital" (*Trust* 57); his economic argument is not germane to my discussion. What is relevant, however, is Fukuyama's premise that trust is the foundation for our mutual progress and prosperity. The building of social capital creates safe places for us to work together on the problems that face us all; in the end, our care for and trust in one another will ensure our progressive success, will spark our continued capacity to discover new things.

We fend off our anxiety about alienation, dissolution, and inevitable death by investing in one another's fate. In the end, making a mark as an individual resisting the influence of others is not enough to sustain us, either physically or spiritually. In the midst of his speculations about the Omega Point and immortality, John Horgan notes that Woody Allen once said, "I don't want to live forever through my works. I want to live forever by not dying" (257). In reading this quip, I was reminded of my own grandmother, who lived into her nineties and who, when asked over and over again how she was feeling by those of us as anxious about our own mortality as the seeming imminence of hers, would always answer, "I keep walking." I keep walking, placing one foot in front of the other, responding to the ground beneath, balancing my body, moving to let others pass, holding on to them for support. Certainly, to "keep walking" is indeed the greatest protection against dying. Might to "keep writing" be as well? To keep placing one word after another, responding to the history that grounds us, balancing our views against those gone past, compassionately reconciling them with the beliefs of others, practicing the rhetoric of altruistic profession?

We are designed to think through attending to others, as I have tried to show. This is our phenomenological reality. We are neither autonomous agents nor socially constructed subjects. We are conscious because we are *conscious of*, always already directed toward what is other than us. Social systems, scientific methods, the vagaries of logic, and our sheer will to power alone will not lead us to The Answer we seek. They cannot because The Answer lies in the very process of our *answering* to others in a mutual quest to discover and realize who we truly are meant to be. In trying to understand all of who, what, and why we are, The Answer, I believe, is in our walking, writing, loving together.

Works Cited
Index

Works Cited

Altieri, Charles. *Act and Quality: A Theory of Literary Meaning and Humanistic Understanding.* Amherst: U of Massachusetts P, 1981.

——. *Subjective Agency: A Theory of First-person Expressivity and its Social Implications.* Cambridge: Blackwell, 1994.

Apprey, Maurice, and Howard F. Stein. "The Intersubjective Constitution of Anorexia Nervosa: A Descriptive Psychoanalytic Study." *Intersubjectivity, Projective Identification and Otherness.* Pittsburgh: Duquesne UP, 1993. 7–75.

Auden, W. H. "Review of V. Clifton, *The Book of Talbot.*" *The English Auden: Poems, Essays, and Dramatic Writings, 1927–1939.* Ed. Edward Mendelson. London: Faber, 1977.

Bacon, Francis. "Narcissus, or Philautia (Self-Love)." *The Wisdom of the Ancients, The Works of Francis Bacon.* Ed. James Spedding, Robert Leslie Ellis, and Douglas Denon Heath. Vol. 13. Boston: Taggard. 15 vols. 1860–64.

Bataille, Georges. "The Notion of Expenditure." *Visions of Excess: Selected Writings, 1927–1939.* Trans. Allan Stoekl, with Carl R. Lovitt and Donald M. Leslie Jr. Minneapolis: U of Minnesota P, 1985. Trans. of "La Notion de dépense." 1933.

Batchelor, Howard. "Humanism." *Academic American Encyclopedia.* Vol. 10. Danbury, CT: Grolier, 1982. 299.

Beauvais, Paul Jude. "Sartre's Plea and the Purposes of Writing." *PRE/TEXT* 10.1–2 (1989): 11–31.

Bernstein, Richard J. *Beyond Objectivism and Relativism: Science, Hermeneutics, and Praxis.* Philadelphia: U of Pennsylvania P, 1983.

Bersani, Leo. *The Culture of Redemption.* Cambridge: Harvard UP, 1990.

Berthoff, Ann E. "Rhetoric as Hermeneutic." *College Composition and Communication* 42 (1991): 279–87.

Booth, Wayne C. *The Rhetoric of Fiction.* Chicago: U of Chicago P, 1961.

Borgmann, Albert. *Technology and the Character of Contemporary Life: A Philosophical Inquiry.* Chicago: U of Chicago P, 1984.

Brand, Alice G. "Hot Cognition: Emotions and Writing Behavior." *Journal of Advanced Composition* 6 (1985–86): 5–15.

Buber, Martin. *I and Thou.* Trans. Walter Kaufmann. New York: Scribner's, 1970.

Caputo, John D. *Heidegger and Aquinas: An Essay on Overcoming Metaphysics.* New York: Fordham UP, 1982.

Cherry, Roger D. "Ethos Versus Persona: Self-Representation in Written Discourse." *Written Communication* 5 (1988): 251–76.

Clark, Katerina, and Michael Holquist. *Mikhail Bakhtin.* Cambridge: Belknap–Harvard UP, 1984.

Coe, Richard M. "An Apology for Form; or, Who Took the Form Out of the Process?" *College English* 49 (1987): 13–28.

Coney, Mary B. "The Implied Author in Technical Discourse." *Journal of Advanced Composition* 5 (1984): 163–72.

Crusius, Timothy W. *A Teacher's Introduction to Philosophical Hermeneutics.* Urbana: NCTE, 1991.

Dasenbrock, Reed Way. "Taking It Personally: Reading Derrida's Responses." *College English* 56 (1994): 261–79.

Derrida, Jacques. "Differance." *Speech and Phenomena and Other Essays on Husserl's Theory of Signs.* Trans. David B. Allison. Evanston, IL: Northwestern UP, 1973. 129–60.

———. *Of Grammatology.* 1974. Trans. Gayatri Chakravorty Spivak. Baltimore: Johns Hopkins UP, 1976.

———. "Speech and Phenomena: Introduction to the Problems of Signs in Husserl's Phenomenology." *Speech and Phenomena and Other Essays on Husserl's Theory of Signs.* 3–104.

Elbow, Peter. "Forward: About Personal Expressive Academic Writing." *PRE/TEXT* 11 (1990): 7–20.

———. "Toward a Phenomenology of Freewriting." *Journal of Basic Writing* 8.2 (1989): 42–71.

———. *Writing with Power: Techniques for Mastering the Writing Process.* New York: Oxford UP, 1981.

Fahnestock, Jeanne. "Accommodating Science: The Rhetorical Life of Scientific Facts." *Written Communication* 3 (1986): 275–96.

Faigley, Lester. *Fragments of Rationality: Postmodernity and the Subject of Composition.* Pittsburgh: U of Pittsburgh P, 1992.

Farber, Marvin. *Phenomenology and Existence: Toward a Philosophy Within Nature.* New York: Harper, 1967.

Farley, Wendy. *Eros for the Other: Retaining Truth in a Pluralistic World.* University Park: Penn State UP, 1996.

Fukuyama, Francis. *The End of History and the Last Man.* New York: Free-Macmillan, 1992.

———. *Trust: The Social Virtues and the Creation of Prosperity.* New York: Free-Simon, 1995.

Gadamer, Hans-Georg. *Philosophical Hermeneutics.* Trans. David E. Linge. Berkeley: U of California P, 1976.

Garver, Newton. Preface. *Speech and Phenomena and Other Essays on Husserl's Theory of Signs.* By Jacques Derrida. Trans. David B. Allison. Evanston, IL: Northwestern UP, 1973. ix–xxix.

Gergen, Kenneth J. "Warranting Voice and the Elaboration of the Self." *Texts of Identity.* Ed. John Shotter and Kenneth J. Gergen. London: Sage, 1989. 70–81.

Gibson, Walker. *Persona: A Style Study for Readers and Writers.* New York: Random, 1969.

Gould, Stephen Jay. *Time's Arrow, Time's Cycle: Myth and Metaphor in the Discovery of Geological Time.* Cambridge: Harvard UP, 1987.

Gregerson, Linda. "Narcissus Interrupted: Specularity and the Subject of the Tudor State." *Criticism* 35 (1993): 1–40.

Habermas, Jürgen. "An Alternative Way out of the Philosophy of the Subject: Communicative Versus Subject-Centered Reason." *The Philosophical Discourse of*

Modernity: Twelve Lectures. Trans. Frederick Lawrence. Cambridge: MIT P, 1991. 294–326.

———. *Moral Consciousness and Communicative Action.* Trans. Christian Lenhardt and Shierry Weber Nicholsen. Cambridge: MIT P, 1990.

———. "The Undermining of Western Rationalism Through the Critique of Metaphysics: Martin Heidegger." *The Philosophical Discourse of Modernity: Twelve Lectures.* 131–60.

Hamlyn, D. W. *Metaphysics.* Cambridge: Cambridge UP, 1984.

Haney, Kathleen M. *Intersubjectivity Revisited: Phenomenology and the Other.* Athens: Ohio UP, 1994.

Harré, Rom, and Grant Gillett. *The Discursive Mind.* Thousand Oaks, CA: Sage, 1994.

Hayward, F[rank] H. *Professionalism and Originality* [1917]. New York: Arno, 1974.

Heidegger, Martin. "Language." 1950. *Poetry, Language, Thought.* Trans. Albert Hofstadter. New York: Harper, 1971. 189–210.

———. *The Principle of Reason.* 1957. Trans. Reginald Lilly. Bloomington: Indiana UP, 1991.

Hernadi, Paul. "Doing, Making, Meaning: Toward a Theory of Verbal Practice." *PMLA* 103 (1988): 749–58.

Herrnstein Smith, Barbara. *Contingencies of Value: Alternative Perspectives for Critical Theory.* Cambridge: Harvard UP, 1988.

Horgan, John. *The End of Science: Facing the Limits of Knowledge in the Twilight of the Scientific Age.* Reading, MA: Addison, 1996.

Horkheimer, Max, and Theodor W. Adorno. *Dialectic of Enlightenment.* 1944. Trans. John Cumming. New York: Continuum, 1982.

Husserl, Edmund. *The Crisis of European Sciences and Transcendental Phenomenology.* Trans. David Carr. Evanston, IL: Northwestern UP, 1970.

———. *The Paris Lectures.* 1950. Trans. Peter Koestenbaum. The Hague: Nijhoff, 1967.

———. " 'Phenomenology,' Edmund Husserl's Article for the *Encyclopedia Britannica* (1927)." Rev. trans. Richard E. Palmer. *Journal of the British Society for Phenomenology* 2 (1971): 77–90. Rptd. in *Husserl: Shorter Works.* Ed. Peter McCormick and Frederick A. Elliston. Notre Dame: U of Notre Dame P; London: Harvester, 1981. 21–35.

———. "Philosophy and the Crisis of European Man." 1936 ms. *Phenomenology and the Crisis of Philosophy.* Trans. Quentin Lauer. New York: Harper, 1965. 149–92.

———. "Philosophy as a Rigorous Science." 1911. *Phenomenology and the Crisis of Philosophy.* 71–147.

Kant, Immanuel. *Groundwork of the Metaphysics of Morals. The Moral Law or Kant's Groundwork of the Metaphysic of Morals.* Ed. H. J. Paton. 3rd ed. New York: Barnes, 1956.

Kastely, James L. "In Defense of Plato's *Gorgias.*" *PMLA* 106 (1991): 96–109.

Katz, Steven B. "The Ethic of Expediency: Classical Rhetoric, Technology, and the Holocaust." *College English* 54 (1992): 255–75.

Kellenberger, J[ames]. *Relationship Morality.* University Park: Penn State UP, 1995.

Kent, Thomas. *Paralogic Rhetoric: A Theory of Communicative Interaction.* Lewisburg, PA: Bucknell UP, 1993.

Kermode, Frank. *History and Value.* Oxford: Clarendon P, 1988.

Kidd, Sunnie D., and James W. Kidd. *Person to Person Inspiration.* American University Studies 5: Philosophy, vol. 164. New York: Lang, 1994.

Korsgaard, Christine M. "The Reasons We Can Share: An Attack on the Distinction Between Agent-Relative and Agent-Neutral Values." *Altruism.* Eds. Ellen Frankel Paul, Fred. D. Miller Jr., and Jeffrey Paul. Cambridge: Cambridge UP, 1993. 24–51.

Kristeva, Julia. "Freud and Love: Treatment and Its Discontents." *The Kristeva Reader.* Ed. Toril Moi. New York: Columbia UP, 1986. 238–71.

———. "Motherhood According to Giovanni Bellini." *Desire in Language: A Semiotic Approach to Literature and Art.* Ed. Leon S. Roudiez. Trans. Thomas Gora, Alice Jardine, and Leon S. Roudiez. New York: Columbia UP, 1980. 237–70.

———. "The Novel as Polylogue." *Desire in Language: A Semiotic Approach to Literature and Art.* 89–136.

———. "Revolution in Poetic Language." *The Kristeva Reader.* 89–136.

Lacan, Jacques. "Ego-ideal and Ideal Ego." *The Seminar of Jacques Lacan.* Book I: Freud's Papers on Technique 1953–1954. Ed. Jacques-Alain Miller. Trans. John Forrester. Cambridge: Cambridge UP, 1988. 129–42.

Laib, Nevin K. "Territoriality in Rhetoric." *College English* 47 (1985): 579–93.

Langford, Thomas, and William Poteat. Introduction. *Intellect and Hope.* Durham, NC: Duke UP, 1967.

Lanigan, Richard L. *Phenomenology of Communication: Merleau-Ponty's Thematics in Communicology and Semiology.* Pittsburgh: Duquesne UP, 1988.

Latour, Bruno, and Steve Woolgar. *Laboratory Life: The Social Construction of Scientific Facts.* Beverly Hills: Sage, 1979.

Levinas, Emmanuel. "The Meaning of Meaning." *Outside the Subject.* Trans. Michael B. Smith. Stanford: Stanford UP, 1994. 90–95.

———. "On Intersubjectivity: Notes on Merleau-Ponty." *Outside the Subject.* 96–103.

———. "Outside the Subject." *Outside the Subject.* 151–58.

Llosa, Mario Vargas. "Updating Karl Popper." Trans. Jonathan Tittler. *PMLA* 105 (1990): 1018–25.

Lyotard, Jean-François. "An Answer to the Question, What Is the Postmodern?" *The Postmodern Explained: Correspondence 1982–85.* Trans. Don Barry et al. Trans. ed. Julian Pefanis and Morgan Thomas. Minneapolis: U of Minnesota P, 1992. 1–16.

———. "Gloss on Resistance." *The Postmodern Explained: Correspondence 1982–85.* 87–97.

———. *Phenomenology.* 1986. Trans. Brian Beakley. Albany: State U of New York P, 1991.

MacIntyre, Alasdair. *After Virtue: A Study in Moral Theory.* 2nd ed. Notre Dame: U of Notre Dame P, 1984.

———. *Three Rival Versions of Moral Enquiry: Encyclopedia, Genealogy, and Tradition.* Notre Dame: U of Notre Dame P, 1990.

Maclagan, W. G. "Respect for Persons as a Moral Principle—I." *Philosophy* 35 (1960): 193–217.

Macrorie, Ken. "To Be Read." *Rhetoric and Composition: A Sourcebook for Teachers and Writers.* 2nd ed. Ed. Richard L. Graves. Upper Montclair, NJ: Boynton, 1984. 81–88.

Marsh, James L. *Post-Cartesian Meditations: An Essay in Dialectical Phenomenology.* New York: Fordham UP, 1988.

Massey, Irving. "Introduction." *Criticism* 32 (1990): 275–93.

McCance, Dawne. *Posts: Re-Addressing the Ethical.* Albany: State U of New York P, 1996.

McCarthy, Thomas. "Introduction." *Moral Consciousness and Communicative Action.* Jürgen Habermas. Trans. Christian Lenhardt and Shierry Weber Nicholsen. Cambridge: MIT P, 1990. vii–xiii.

McCullough, Laurence B. "Particularism in Medicine." *Criticism* 32 (1990): 361–70.

McMillan, Carol. *Women, Reason and Nature: Some Philosophical Problems with Feminism.* Princeton: Princeton UP, 1982.

Merleau-Ponty, M[aurice]. "The Body as Expression, and Speech." *Phenomenology of Perception.* Trans. Colin Smith. London: Routledge; New York: Humanities, 1962. 174–99.

———. "Man and Adversity." 1951 lecture. *Signs.* 1960. Trans. Richard C. McLeary. Chicago: Northwestern UP, 1964. 224–43.

———. Preface. *Phenomenology of Perception.* vii–xxi.

Miller, J. Hillis. "Literature and Value: American and Soviet Views." *Profession 92* 1 (1992): 21–27.

Miller, Susan. *Rescuing the Subject: A Critical Introduction to Rhetoric and the Writer.* Carbondale: Southern Illinois UP, 1989.

Mulkay, Michael. *Science and the Sociology of Knowledge.* London: Allen, 1979.

Myers, Greg. "Reality, Consensus, and Reform in the Rhetoric of Composition Teaching." *College English* 48 (1986): 154–74.

Nagel, Thomas. *The Last Word.* New York: Oxford UP, 1997.

———. *The Possibility of Altruism.* Oxford: Clarendon, 1970.

Nakhnikian, George. Introduction. *The Idea of Phenomenology.* By Edmund Husserl. Trans. William P. Alston and George Nakhnikian. The Hague: Nijhoff, 1964.

Nealon, Jeffrey T. "The Ethics of Dialogue: Bakhtin and Levinas." *College English* 59 (1997): 129–48.

Neel, Jasper. *Plato, Derrida, and Writing.* Carbondale: Southern Illinois UP, 1988.

Olafson, Frederick A. *Principles and Persons: An Ethical Interpretation of Existentialism.* Baltimore: Johns Hopkins P, 1967.

Patai, Daphne. "Sick and Tired of Scholars' Nouveau Solipsism." *The Chronicle of Higher Education* 23 February 1994. A52.

Plato. *Phaedrus and the Seventh and Eighth Letters.* Trans. Walter Hamilton. New York: Penguin, 1973.

Popper, Karl R. *The Spell of Plato.* London: Routledge, 1945. Vol. 1 of *The Open Society and Its Enemies.* 2 vols. 1947.

Pratt, Mary Louise. "Linguistic Utopias." *The Linguistics of Writing: Arguments Between Language and Literature.* Ed. Nigel Fabb et al. New York: Methuen, 1987. 48–66.

Putnam, Hilary. *Renewing Philosophy.* Cambridge: Harvard UP, 1992.

Ray, William. *Literary Meaning: From Phenomenology to Deconstruction.* Oxford: Blackwell, 1984.

Reynolds, Nedra. "*Ethos* as Location: New Sites for Understanding Discursive Authority." *Rhetoric Review* 11 (1993): 325–38.

Ricoeur, Paul. *Husserl: An Analysis of his Phenomenology.* Trans. Edward G. Ballard and Lester E. Embree. Evanston, IL: Northwestern UP, 1967.

Rorty, Richard. "Inquiry as Recontextualization: An Anti-Dualist Account of Interpretation." *The Interpretive Turn: Philosophy, Science, Culture.* Ed. David R. Hiley, James F. Bohman, and Richard Shusterman. Ithaca: Cornell UP, 1991. 59–80.

———. "Science as Solidarity." *The Rhetoric of the Human Sciences: Language and Argument in Scholarship and Public Affairs.* Ed. John S. Nelson, Allan Megill, and Donald N. McCloskey. Madison: U of Wisconsin P, 1987. 38–52.

Rosenblatt, Louise M. "Viewpoints: Transaction Versus Interaction—A Terminological Rescue Operation." *Research in the Teaching of English* 20 (1986): 174–97.

Searle, John. *Speech Acts.* Cambridge: Cambridge UP, 1969.

Smith, Jeremy. "Religious Experience and Literary Form: The Interrelation of Perception, Commitment, and Interpretation." *Religion and Literature* 21.3 (1989): 61–83.

Smith, Paul. *Discerning the Subject.* Theory and History of Literature 55. Minneapolis: U of Minnesota P, 1988.

Stanley, Manfred. *The Technological Conscience: Survival and Dignity in an Age of Expertise.* Chicago: U of Chicago P, 1978.

Stewart, David, and Algis Mickunas. *Exploring Phenomenology: A Guide to the Field and its Literature.* 2nd ed. Athens: Ohio UP, 1990.

Taylor, Charles. *The Ethics of Authenticity.* Cambridge: Harvard UP, 1992.

Teilhard de Chardin, Pierre. *On Love and Happiness.* 1966, 1967. Trans. J. M. Cohen. San Francisco: Harper, 1984. 3–6.

———. *The Phenomenon of Man.* 1955. Trans. Bernard Wall. New York: Harper, 1959.

———. *Toward the Future.* 1973. Trans. René Hague. New York: Harcourt, 1975.

Thom, René. "Itinerary for a Science of the Detail." *Criticism* 32 (1990): 371–90.

Trimbur, John. "Articulation Theory and the Problem of Determination: A Reading of *Lives on the Boundary.*" *Journal of Advanced Composition* 13 (1993): 33–50.

Valdés, Mario J. *Phenomenological Hermeneutics and the Study of Literature.* Toronto: U of Toronto P, 1987.

van Peursen, Cornelis A. *Phenomenology and Reality.* Duquesne Studies Philosophical Series 30. Pittsburgh: Duquesne UP, 1972.

Volosinov, V[alentin] N. *Marxism and the Philosophy of Language.* Trans. Ladislav Matejka and I. R. Titunik. New York: Seminar, 1973.

Weissman, David. *Truth's Debt to Value.* New Haven: Yale UP, 1993.

Welch, Kathleen E. "The Platonic Paradox: Plato's Rhetoric in Contemporary Rhetoric and Composition Studies." *Written Communication* 5 (1988): 3–21.

Weller, Barry. "Pleasure and Self-Loss in Reading." *ADE Bulletin* 99 (Fall 1991): 8–12.

Wells, Susan. *Sweet Reason: Rhetoric and the Discourses of Modernity.* Chicago: U of Chicago P, 1996.

Wittgenstein, Ludwig. *Lectures and Conversations on Aesthetics, Psychology and Religious Belief.* Ed. Cyril Barrett. Berkeley: U of California P, 1966.

Zappen, James P. "Historical Perspectives on the Philosophy and the Rhetoric of Science: Sources for a Pluralistic Rhetoric." *PRE/TEXT* 6 (1985): 9–29.

———. "Rhetoric and Technical Communication: An Argument for Historical and Political Pluralism." *Iowa State Journal of Business and Technical Writing* 1.2 (1987): 29–44.

Ziman, John. *An Introduction to Science Studies: The Philosophical and Social Aspects of Science and Technology.* Cambridge: Cambridge UP, 1984.

Index

Abortion: moral function and, 159
Absence, 11
Acknowledgment, 136, 212; of reality of other, 139–41; as rhetorical practice, 137–38; of value of personhood, 142–50
Act and Quality: A Theory of Literary Meaning and Humanistic Understanding (Altieri), 192–95
Adorno, Theodor W., 53–54
After Virtue: A Study in Moral Theory (MacIntyre), 151–54
Agape, 146
Agency (*see also* Will), 3, 7, 40–42, 159; Altieri on, 195–97; in genealogical history, 155–56; humanist individualism and, 33–37; profession and, 131–34; regeneration and, 124–28; shared meaning and, 101–2; social determinism and, 37–40
Altieri, Charles, 5, 185, 204; on agency, 195–97; on texts and cultural value, 192–95
Altruism, 4–5, 99; and acknowledgment of other, 137–50; ardor and, 165–80; authenticity of, 150–65; in rhetorical practice, 135–37, 180–82, 207–14, 215; truth seeking and, 184–85
Answerability: in relation, 177, 178, 179, 180, 185, 213
Appresentation, 139
Apprey, Maurice, 103
Aquinas, Thomas, 156–58, 169; on Being, 106, 167–68
Ardor, 136–37, 185, 212; for knowing, 167, 168, 178–80; love as, 165–66; for relation, 170–77
Argument (*see also* Rhetoric), 110–11, 213; congruence and, 189–90; profession and, 132, 133–34
Art, 38, 129; fetishism and, 52–53
Auden, W. H., 166
Austin, J. L., 193
Austrag (Heidegger), 107
Authenticity, 108–9, 136, 185, 212; of expression, 150–51; MacIntyre on, 151–58; as rhetorical practice, 160–64; Taylor on, 158–59

Authentic moment, 108–9
Autonomy: human telos and, 151–58

Bacon, Francis, 149
Bakhtin, Mikhail, 200, 202; on relation, 178–79
Bataille, Georges, 19
Batchelor, Howard, 34
Beauvais, Paul Jude, 132
Being (*see also* Meaning; Reality): Derrida on, 69–70; essence of, 65–66, 84; existentialist concept of, 126; nature of, 106–8, 115–16, 117; reification of, 79–80; understanding, 167–68
Bernstein, Richard J., 186, 203
Bersani, Leo, 129
Berthoff, Ann E., 3, 28
Beyond Objectivism and Relativism: Science, Hermeneutics and Praxis (Bernstein), 203
Body, the: signification through, 127–28
Booth, Wayne C., 46, 160
Borgmann, Albert, 56
Bracketing, 67, 87
Brand, Alice G., 120–21
Brentano, Franz, 74
Bruffee, Kenneth, 191
Brute facts, 193–94
Buber, Martin, 5, 167, 176, 179, 196; on relation, 170–71, 173, 174
Butler, Judith, 70

Caputo, John D.: on dynamic difference, 106–8; on understanding Being, 167–68
Catachresis, 162–63
Change, 21–22, 23
Character, creation of, 153
Cherry, Roger D., 160
Choice (*see also* Agency; Will), 126, 127–28
Clark, Katarina, 178, 179–80
Coe, Richard M., 148
Commensurability, 5, 185, 187, 203–7, 211, 213; of discourses, 196, 197–203
Communal values, 185
Communication (*see also* Language; Speech), 128, 133, 146, 162; consciousness and, 80–82

Barbara Couture is a professor of English at Wayne State University. During her career there, she has directed the composition and technical writing programs of the English Department and has served as director of the Humanities Council and associate dean for the Colleges of Liberal Arts and Lifelong Learning. She is the editor of and a contributor to *Functional Approaches to Writing: Research Perspectives* and of *Professional Writing: Toward a College Curriculum*. She also is the coauthor, with Jone Rymer, of *Cases for Technical and Professional Writing*, winner of the NCTE Excellence in Technical and Scientific Communication Award for "Best Book"; and she is the author of several journal articles and book chapters on business/technical writing and linguistic approaches to analyzing written discourse. Couture serves on the editorial boards of *Technical Communication Quarterly*, the *Journal of Business Communication, Language and Learning Across the Disciplines*, and *Issues in Writing*. Of recent, she has been writing about relationships between philosophy and rhetorical theory.